Reading the Classed Child

MAGGIE E. MORRIS DAVIS

Reading the Classed Child

The Language of Depression-Era Children in Poverty

The University of Georgia Press Athens

Athens, Georgia 30602
www.ugapress.org

Set in Arno Pro by Westchester Publishing Services

Printed digitally

EU Authorized Representative
Easy Access System Europe—Mustamäe tee 50, 10621
Tallinn, Estonia, gpsr.requests@easproject.com

Library of Congress Cataloging-in-Publication Data
Names: Morris Davis, Maggie E. author
Title: Reading the classed child : the language of depression-era children in poverty / Maggie E. Morris Davis.
Description: Athens : The University of Georgia Press, 2026. | Includes bibliographical references and index.
Identifiers: LCCN 2026008341 | ISBN 9780820375601 hardback | ISBN 9780820375618 paperback | ISBN 9780820375625 epub | ISBN 9780820375632 pdf
Subjects: LCSH: Poor children—Language | Speech and social status—United States | Children—United States—Social conditions—History—20th century | Literacy—United States—History—20th century | Children in popular culture
Classification: LCC P40.5.S63 M67 2026
LC record available at https://lccn.loc.gov/2026008341

for Dad, who was always my first reader

Contents

Figures

Acknowledgments

I now realize that the questions that shape my research formed long before I had the entrances that disciplinary tools have provided. These questions first emerged from the economic precarity that shaped the rural town and school of my youth, generations of my family's history, and my own childhood. These questions have gained nuance through my time in classrooms where I've worked to hear and to learn from student voices that speak of and are shaped by growing up when hunger is the norm or when transience provides only a momentary reprieve from the burden of never having enough.

So much shapes a book. The work of librarians and archivists has made possible my access to so many of the texts central to this book: Rebecca Wingfield, Curator for American and British Literature, Stanford University Libraries; Jane Siegel, Rare Book Librarian, Rare Book and Manuscript Library, Columbia University; Chris Geherin, Archivist, Center for Southwest Research, University of New Mexico. Patient folks at the FDR Presidential Library and across research centers in the Library of Congress routinely pulled for me more files and boxes than daily limits allowed. My months across 2023–24 as a Kluge Fellow at the Library of Congress also gave protected time and resources for research, drafting, and significant revision.

Colleagues who have become beloved friends have sustained my work in our shared labors of writing or teaching alongside each other and with the gift of conversations that return me to the questions that guide my inquiry. I'm grateful, Danielle Lillge, for the purposeful ways you've journeyed in the margins of this project. To the indomitable FWP Writing Group—Wilson Chen, Michele Fazio, Maureen Curtain, and Anna Kaplan—thank you for the weekly time to pause, to laugh, to think aloud, and to make progress. Robbie Woolridge, Stacy Nicklow, and Tony Vinci, our atypical paths to and through graduate school were our shared strength in our years at Southern Illinois University, Carbondale. Oh, to again be gathered around a table together!

Edward Brunner and Jane Cogie, it was often your table we gathered around, and the conversations we built there continue to shape my scholarly work and teaching life. Ed, your meticulous feedback and willingness to read broadly in support of my learning was a gift. Your critical engagement with my emerging arguments made possible my growth as a scholar and writer.

I remain grateful for the intersections of your expertise and mentoring with others I was fortunate to learn from while in graduate school. Joe Shapiro, David Anthony, and Natasha Zaretsky, thank you for your feedback on this project in its early years as a dissertation.

I would also like to thank the Department of English and the Office of Research and Graduate Studies at Illinois State University for support in completing this work. I am grateful for the permission to include in *Reading the Classed Child* my scholarship that first appeared in the following publications: Part of chapter 1 appeared as "Tommie's Resurrection: The Role of the Impoverished Child in Stephen Crane's New York Sketches," *Steven Crane Studies* 22, no. 1–2 (2017): 22–23; a section of chapter 2 appeared as "'When He Saw the Pencil Put to Paper': The Meaning-Making of Children's Language in Depression-Era Harlem," in *Producing Children: Critical Studies in Childhood Creativity*, edited by Peter C. Kunze and Victoria Ford Smith (New Brunswick, N.J.: Rutgers University Press, 2025), 85–100; and sections of chapter 4 appeared as "'I Thought Maby You Might Help as You Other Little Children': Using Letters to Mrs. Roosevelt to Reread the Classed Other in Depression-Era Children's Literature," *Children's Literature* 52 (2024): 156–75, published by Johns Hopkins University Press, copyright © 2024 Children's Literature Association. The peer review processes of these publications have helped me rehearse and hone my thinking about the ethics of reading the language of children in poverty.

Significantly, the feedback of the anonymous readers of earlier drafts of this manuscript offered the kind of critical feedback that I crave, careful reading and layered questions that helped me return to the manuscript and see it anew. This feedback and the support of my editors—most notably Sarah Shermyen and Jon Davies—and the design and production staff at the University of Georgia Press have strengthened this book and helped ready it for multiple audiences, just as Mary M. Hill's meticulous copyediting and Ben Shaw's careful indexing work will support a readers' use of the text. While the errors that remain are my own, this book also importantly represents one moment in what will continue to be the ongoing evolution of my own thinking about language, reading, young people, class, and texts.

My thinking was first and profoundly shaped by my parents, Bill and Marilyn Morris, who modeled for us lives of service that meant our dinner table always needed more chairs. Central, too, was my Grannie, whose childhood and ways of listening to young people shaped how I read the texts within this project. My brother, Will, has read sentences and paragraphs along the way with the attentiveness of a reader who both knows me and can separate that knowledge from that which is on the page.

Lastly, I am most grateful for my partner, Jacob, whose quiet steadfastness sustains me and made possible the time to write, revise, and pause within the archive and my stacks of books. To live and learn alongside our children while reading and writing about children often unheard and dismissed calls me to listen carefully and consider continually my own responses across moments in our everyday life and within my reading. Clara and Willa, my fierce reminders of a world renewed, I love to watch you make meaning as you read texts and the world and listen as you write and speak in response. I find such joy in learning from you. When my copy of this book arrives, the first thing I will do is tuck inside the front cover my small envelope of scraps of paper you have left on my desk and the bits of your marginalia that I've cut from my drafts across the years I have been working on this project. Loved ones, this book is our shared work.

Reading the Classed Child

Prologue
Writing as the Classed Other

The most visible representations of young people in poverty in the Great Depression come from photographs from the Farm Security Administration (FSA), a non-revenue-generating program designed to "sell the nation on the severity of the hardship the New Deal intended to redress."[1] To this day, these photographs function in popular culture and media as representative of the horrors of the nation's widespread suffering and struggle. Books of FSA photographs of children are always in print and commonly in circulation in school libraries and classrooms. These volumes are frequently more sentimental than scholarly and are predicated on the notion that photographs of children "tell us something that words alone cannot express" and provide "an immediate emotional connection."[2] Some volumes work to provide a wider range of representations of children's lives in the Depression, from "unhappy" to "resilient," yet they also champion the child as the "embodiment of hope [and] humanity as yet undisappointed."[3] While some volumes include written material from or about children such as letters, diary entries, or oral histories, the photographs lead, framing for the reader the child as passive, temporarily immobile for the camera's lens.

Unsolicited letters young people wrote to First Lady Eleanor Roosevelt during President Franklin D. Roosevelt's nearly four terms in office present young people in need as decidedly *not* passive. The richest archival trove of the language of American children in need, the letters are archived within the Eleanor Roosevelt papers at the Franklin D. Roosevelt Presidential Library at Hyde Park, New York. The letters were carefully constructed for a named audience, Eleanor Roosevelt, and offer both expression and justification of need.[4] Young letter writers often explicitly stated that they were writing in secret, an intentional choice framed as preserving the pride of self-reliant families that did not need to ask for help. "I will have to stop riteing as my ma is comeing home and I dont want her to see this," an eleven-year-old wrote.[5] The rugged individualism of these letters is often paired with promises of repayment or "a sense that only the most dire emergency had led them to appeal for government aid."[6]

Some of the Roosevelt letters maintain a commitment to optimism. One child, for example, whose leg was torn off below the knee in a farming accident, promised "to get an education and make my life worthwhile to serve my home and my country."[7] Many children presented American ideals as literal truths, yet other letters held accountable faltering national promises, calling attention to language that no longer seemed authentic or believable. "I don't know exactly how to begin to write you or just why I should, but my pen keeps moving on," a child began. "Some where off I still hear a little of the words 'hope' and 'faith.'" Before the letter's closing salutation, she added a single word, without punctuation: "Tired." [8]

Collectively, these letters demonstrate a shared insistence on the now, of hunger, suffering, and the certainty of an uncertain future. The address written on each envelope makes plain that these letters were carefully constructed for a specific, named audience, Eleanor Roosevelt, and they offer one of the few examples of the language of the child in poverty from the Depression era not written by adults. Though, technically speaking, the letters reveal grammatical mistakes, awkward passages, and errors of many kinds, what is important is the child's forthright effort to make meaning through language. And in many ways, the letters are autobiographies in miniature, offering matter-of-fact, tight synopses of need. "My sister was operated on recently and it took all our money for Dr. bills," F.B. wrote in May 1934 from Winnsboro, Louisiana; from Daleville, Alabama, three months earlier, C.D. wrote, "[P]lease loan me fifty dollars to buy a mule with so we can raise us something to eat at home. seven of us have to live."[9]

In her chapter "In the Archives of Childhood," Karen Sánchez-Eppler unpacks common assumptions of both archival work and childhood studies as "grant[ing] access to the authentic and original." Similarly, she notes the difficulties of knowing with certainty claims of agency or rationales for decisions made both in the archive and in artifacts made by young people. Yet by tending to the processes of the construction of the archive or the artifact, Sánchez-Eppler suggests, we can gain insights from representative "moments of choice." Applying this dual frame to the Roosevelt letters offers several entry points. Letters from young people were filed alongside letters from adults. All letters were filed first by the purpose of the letter (e.g., "Material Assistance Requested") and then by the letter's date. This demonstrates the rarity of archives using age as a means of classification, a trend Sánchez-Eppler notes in archives more broadly.[10] This also makes finding the letters from young people tedious, as they often contain requests similar to those of adult letters, leaving the reader to look for evidence that the letter was, indeed, written by a young person.[11] The filing of all letters together, however, signified the value of these letters for Mrs. Roosevelt and her staff. An adult's letter and a child's letter often received a similar variation of the form letter aligned to the nature of the letter writer's request, thus honoring the child's request as worthy of response, just as the adult's letter was.

Reading the Classed Child takes up the question of what becomes possible, then, if we reread children in poverty as active producers of language instead of passive recipients of assistance, as commonly depicted in 1930s cultural media.[12] The language in the Roosevelt letters provides a standard by which to consider how the voices of poor children in fictional representations of the Depression era can provide nuanced entry points or, at times, misleading impressions of how children coped with poverty in their own words. I'm not interested in using the Roosevelt letters as a yardstick by which to measure fictional representations of poor children. Instead, I'm interested in thinking about the ways we read the language of children in poverty by turning to the cultural productions of Depression-era young people to prompt a return to representations of children in literature of the period. How did the devastation of the 1930s expand (or contract) literary representations of children in need? How might expanded definitions of modernism help us reread these representations? How did cultural narratives of childhood shift in the Depression era, and how were such shifts negotiated and represented in literature?

THE LETTERS CHILDREN WROTE to Eleanor Roosevelt offer the possibility of rereading the Depression-era child because they offer evidence of the ways children's language worked within and against Depression-era cultural scripts. Sociolinguistics considers this "anti-language," language that disrupts discourses of power and privilege and defines its own parameters in ways that, at first, may seem absurd. To study the language use of young people within a rigidly classed society, I build on the work of Roger Fowler, for whom anti-language is not just verbal play; instead, it "facilitate[s] an alternative social and conceptual reality for [its] speakers."[13]

This idea of anti-language was first developed by M. A. K. Halliday from real-life examples of languages formed by an "anti-society" that operates largely as metaphorical. These languages create an alternate reality that becomes a "*counter*-reality, set up *in opposition to* some established norm." Therefore, anti-languages are created and sustained by a hyperawareness of power structures within society.[14] The letters to Eleanor Roosevelt demonstrate this awareness even in their structure. The majority conform to an unwritten template: first, autobiographical explanations of need supplemented by proof of hard work and deservedness (Robert Cohen calls these "exercises in self-justification"); second, a clear understanding of class differences that suggests an awareness of both audience and class position; and third, a clear articulation of a specific need and, most often, a matter-of-fact way for Mrs. Roosevelt to meet this need.[15] Such homogeneity is a powerful reminder of the poor child's awareness of cultural scripts for how children must speak to be heard, as well as their commitment to offering up a practical solution to an adult who represents what is still tangible to the child about the American project in the Depression: hope. "Surely a woman like you can understand," one child wrote, and thousands of others used similar terms.

The raw and unprocessed nuances of these letters return us to Halliday's original discussion of anti-language as the intentional language of an underclass. "[S]peakers of anti-language," he argues, "are constantly striving to maintain a counter-reality that is under pressure from the established world. This is why the language is constantly renewing itself—to sustain the vitality that it needs if it is to function at all." These nonfiction letters display the anti-language of children intent on making Eleanor Roosevelt, whose high public visibility positioned her as a viable acting arm of the White House, aware of their counter-reality. Out of necessity, these children felt they had to find a way to position themselves as outsiders (to justify need) while still communicating within an accepted discourse of politeness and deference (to prompt a response). In the words of Halliday, these letters demonstrate anti-language "used for contest and display."[16]

Such letters are perhaps the most compelling example of how young people in poverty intentionally used anti-language to create a public sphere in which the "norm society and the deviant group confront and negotiate."[17] The child, by choosing to write, was convinced of their right to speak, to articulate their position, and to negotiate through language something better. One 1936 letter, for example, is without punctuation beyond three inconsistently used ellipses. It reads as a patchwork of broken clauses, slips of phrases overheard, and fragments of concern quickly interrupted by something more pressing:

> Dear sir I am riting you about my Little Brother who sick see if could get you help send him to some hospital i see in paper where help other Little children i dont see how could Be any worse of then my Little Brother is my Little Brother be 5 years old June he cant walk are talk are he cant feed his self he suck a Bottle only when mother feed him he just sit propt in chair that is all the country Dr said is just had him took where Be

operated he thought get all rite some says he got Pralizes of Bone some say it from his spine he had Ricket when he Little never grew very much he had very Big now.[18]

Significant to T.L.'s grammar is the capitalization of words—highly visible in the surface structure of the letter—that we can assume the child felt would be persuasive: Little Brother, Bottle, Dr, Pralizes of Bone (see figure 1). Yet imbedded within the deep structure of the letter's fragments and run-on sentences is a complex set of grammatical relationships that the child carefully scaffolded to demonstrate the way others, including himself, witnessed his brother's suffering. For example, the repetition of the verb "to see" signifies the child's understanding of his brother's illness in relationship to other children who are ill. In what would grammatically be the third clause of the letter, T.L. identified his purpose in writing: "*[to] see* if i could get you [to] help send him to some hospital" (emphasis added). The next clause gives the child's awareness of the relationship of his brother's medical need and his family's inability to pay for such care: "*i see* in paper where help other Little children *i don't see* how could Be any worse of then my Little Brother is" (emphasis added). Though he can contextualize his brother's suffering, he is powerless to alleviate it. His only act is to "rite ask you," an offering of language designed to witness. While the child only sees, the doctors have the authority to speak: "some says he got Pralizes of Bone some say it from his spine he had Ricket when he Little." This contrast makes plain the purpose of his letter.

Another set of verbs reinforces this binary of helplessness (that of both the paralyzed brother and the letter writer) and the adults who attempt to help. The child wrote: "he *cant walk are talk* are he *cant feed* his self he suck a Bottle only," which is the opposite of his mother's efforts: "when *mother feed him* he just sit propt in chair" (emphasis added). Ultimately, however, the adults in T.L.'s family are powerless, too, for in their class position they do not have the money to send him to the hospital for further treatment. Therefore, the final paragraph of the letter begged for a response, an acknowledgment of suffering. "tell me what think about him as do hate see him go through Life way he is," T.L. wrote. Especially in such a broken state, the anti-language of letters such as this one is an expression of a commitment to language, to articulating suffering and offering a solution, even if the situation seems irremediable, such as T.L.'s little brother, or the solution is a temporary patch, as many other letter writers requested.

These letters' unedited presentations of suffering and need present a view of poverty that reveals the ingenious anti-language of children who refuse to

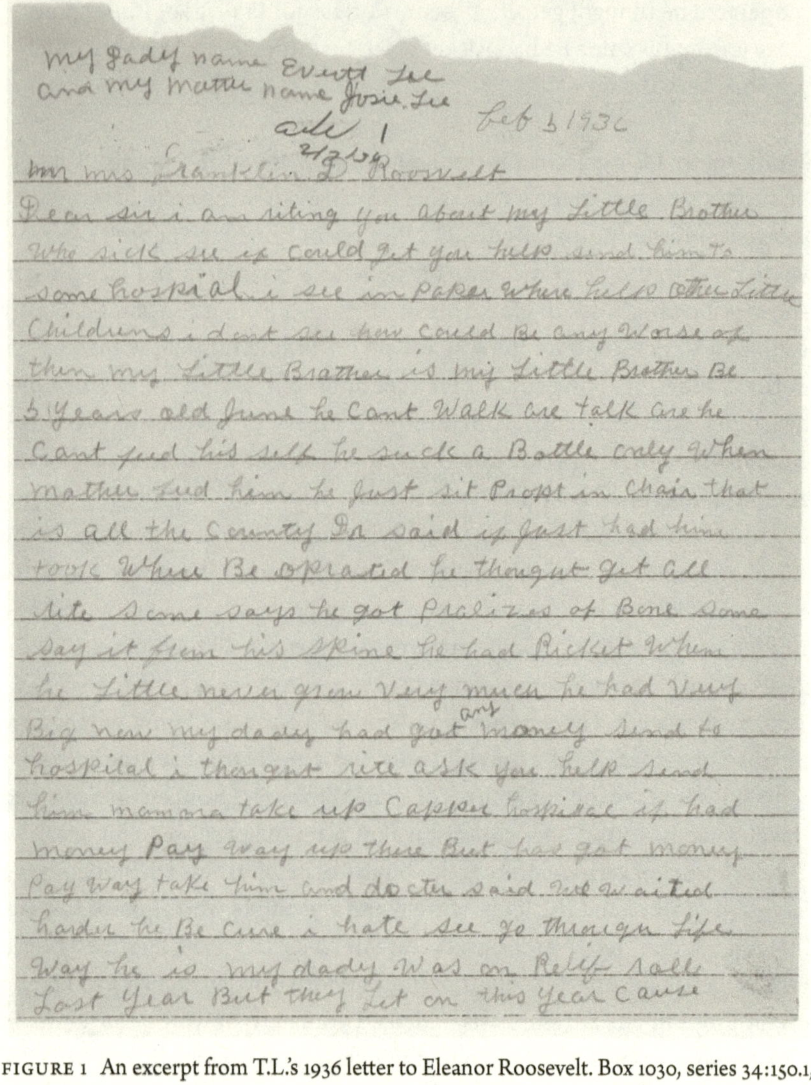

my dady name Evertt Lee
and my matter name Josie Lee
ack 1
2/3/36
feb 3 1936
mr mrs Franklin D. Roosevelt
Dear sir i am riting you about my Little Brother
who sick see if could get you help send him to
some hospital i see in paper where help other Little
Childrens i dont see how could Be any worse of
then my Little Brather is my Little Brother Be
5 years old June he Cant walk are talk are he
Cant feed his self he suck a Bottle only when
mather feed him he just sit Propt in Chair that
is all the County Dr said if just had him
took where Be operated he thougut get all
rite some says he got Pralizes of Bone some
say it from his spine he had Ricket when
he Little never grew very much he had very
Big now my dady had got any money send to
hospital i thougut rite ask you help send
him mama take up Capper hospital if had
money Pay way up there But has got money
Pay way take him and docter said we waited
harder he Be cure i hate see go thrugu Life
way he is my dady was on Relif rolls
Last year But they Let on this year Cause

FIGURE 1 An excerpt from T.L.'s 1936 letter to Eleanor Roosevelt. Box 1030, series 34:150.1, Anna Eleanor Roosevelt Papers, Part I, 1884–1964, Franklin Delano Roosevelt Archive, Franklin D. Roosevelt Presidential Library and Museum, Hyde Park, N.Y.

break beneath privation's weight.[19] T.L., whose family did not have the resources to transport his little brother to an in-state hospital, received a response that suggested he reach out to a hospital in Detroit for help. What follows is a similar, commonly used form letter from Mrs. Roosevelt's staff:

> Mrs. Roosevelt asks me to acknowledge your letter and to express her regret that because of the great number of similar requests she

> received, she has found it impossible to comply with them, much as she would like to assist all those who appeal to her. Assuring you of Mrs. Roosevelt's sympathy, I am
>
> Very sincerely yours,
> Secretary to Mrs. Roosevelt

It is thus not the "*distance* between the two realities," as Halliday writes, "but the *tension* between them that is significant."[20] Mrs. Roosevelt's form letters—modified, at times, to respond to the specifics within the child's letter—demonstrate a distance with language that reads as particularly passive, especially when reading example after example in the archive.

These letters' unedited presentations of suffering and need present a view of economic precarity made possible by the anti-language of children. The young voices in the Roosevelt letters invite us to listen to that which we might otherwise reject or not even notice by unsettling discursive systems and forcing us to negotiate a new discourse, one of which we are likely unsure. What these recovered Roosevelt letters offer, then, is the possibility of a child's voice that could be autonomous, expressive talk through which the child attunes a reader to a subjectivity emerging from distorting social circumstances. As a mode of representation, these letters offer opportunities for grasping the child in poverty, opportunities for eliciting a moral engagement in which we as readers learn to listen to a kind of self-presentation that is of its own making and that asks us to respond and to comprehend.

Introduction

Reading the Classed Other

Children in the Young Pioneers, a U.S.-based Communist alternative to the Boy Scouts that was active in the 1920s and 1930s, sang from the 1935 *Pioneer Song Book: Songs for Workers' and Farmers' Children*, in which familiar songs were adapted into songs of protest and education, a primer of class consciousness.[1] "Mother Goose on the Breadline," for example, is an eleven-page section in which Yankee Doodle "gets his pay in praises" so that Uncle Sam can profit, an old woman lives in a shoe because of a bank failure, and Jack and Jill are scabbing "while we were striking." Playing within traditional nursery rhymes, these songs offered young singers an anti-language of protest to "make [America] a country run by workers and for workers."[2]

While many of the songs focus on more conventionally adult narratives of class conflict and struggle, including workers' rights, most position young people as capable and active agents in the struggle and witnesses to the injustices carried out against adult workers:

> tom - tom, the striker's son
> saw his dad shot by a gun.
> when tom - tom grew up tall
> he was the bra-vest stri-ker of them all.[3]

One song, however, does explicitly direct the child performer and listeners of any age to the plight of many children in the Depression era. "Hunger Children" is accompanied by the only illustration in the songbook in which young people are not smiling and are visibly poor: They are barefoot, with holes in their clothes and hems ragged, their faces wan (see figure 2). Embedded within the lyrics of "Hunger Children" are national narratives of childhood, class, and nation that *Reading the Classed Child* will take up.

The Discourse of Childhood in American Culture

The child as a trope has long been at the center of American culture. It is well documented that children "[absorb and help] to disseminate the divergent, sometimes contradictory, ideologies that typify particular historical periods."[4]

FIGURE 2 Page 4 of the *Pioneer Song Book*, by Harry Alan Potamkin, Gertrude Rady, and Mary Morrow.

Daniel Thomas Cook languages it this way: Children often function as symbols, "conduit[s] for meaning."[5] As the colonies gained their independence from Britain, for example, characterizing "colonial Americans as children wrongfully deprived of their rights and welfare pervades Revolutionary rhetoric" and justified controversial actions separating the metaphorical mistreated children from their oppressive parent.[6] By the antebellum period, the definition of childhood was changing: The period of filial obedience had given way to the Enlightenment model of the "child as a blank slate waiting to be shaped by parental and environmental influences."[7] This change transpired parallel to economic changes, particularly the advent of the growing Northern middle class, which, of course, required the continued oppression of children under chattel slavery and educational and economic systems designed to maintain inequality.

In the antebellum period, the Lockean belief that "children are permanently marked by experience" both real and literary helped reinforce the burgeoning middle-class belief that "a child could be shaped by creating an environment that instilled appropriate values and behaviors."[8] This idyllic space also became a space of anxiety. As Anna Mae Duane argues in her 2010 *Suffering Childhood in Early America: Violence, Race, and the Making of the*

Child Victim, "[S]lavery created millions of orphaned and suffering children within the United States, and as black writers wrote of their childhood pain in the first person, childhood itself became emotionally and rhetorically linked to experiences of terror and pain. Diaries, slave narratives, and other historical sources indicate that, as white witnesses described the horrors visited on children, and as slave children sought to describe their own experience, they altered the palette of meanings attached to childhood itself."[9] In other words, the antebellum period's changing definitions of childhood—"a protracted period in which the child would ideally be protected from the difficulties and responsibilities of daily life[,] including the need to work"—were based in large part on middle-class parents' desire to differentiate their children from those who were suffering.[10] Across the nineteenth century, "national ideologies of class promised that in the United States poverty, like childhood, is merely a stage to be outgrown."[11] Thus, cultural narratives preserved childhood as a condition occupied by children sheltered from the hardships of labor and carefully shaped by the forces of right feeling fostered in a middle-class home; those children without this formative shelter were not allowed the luxury of childhood.

Increasingly, many of the bodies over which capital was king were the small bodies of children. The number of children in the workforce by the 1890s was growing faster than the number of adults.[12] Though there were labor laws in many states, they were lackadaisically enforced and—just as today—grossly ineffective. Most Americans, however, did not see child labor as an ethical problem and "assumed that, within reason, it was good for [children] to do so."[13] In low-income families, children were an economic asset and often provided up to half of a family's income.[14] Paradoxically, their income allowed many families to "secure a property stake," a beginning step in exiting the lowest classes, yet their doing so also "virtually removed [children] from the competition for middle-class jobs," another entry point needed to sustain class mobility.[15] Muckrakers and reformers railed against child labor. This was, of course, also a savvy rhetorical choice, as children were considered the "most deserving of sympathy and most entitled to generous assistance."[16]

The alternative proposed by reformers was often education, for it would enable children to escape their brutal working conditions by training for jobs that paid higher wages. Emphasis was also placed on the role education would play in the assimilation of children (and thus their families at home) into American culture. Though these ideas were progressive for the era, at the core of their intent was a nagging notion of middle-class anxiety: "[T]hey were all attempts by the dominant power groups to impose order and control on the 'other half.' The means of doing so was to view harshly and deal harshly with those members of the poor who threatened the social order and to view sympathetically and treat sympathetically those members of the poor who were already aligned with dominant group values."[17] Reform was engendered to help children in poverty become just like the middle-class ideal. As Patricia Crain's *Reading Children: Literacy, Property, and Dilemmas of Childhood in Nineteenth-Century America* illustrates, "[T]he work of schooling, of reading and writing, was increasingly (if unevenly) seen as the labor newly appointed to and appropriate for children in the nineteenth century."[18]

Though at the beginning of the nineteenth century most children worked, by the beginning of the twentieth, young people working was no longer normative, and children no longer contributed financially within middle-class families.[19] For the middle class, mothering became the primary role of women, childhood became a prolonged period of education and moral instruction, and families centered the raising of children.[20] Therefore, this "sentimentalization of childhood[,] the assertion of childhood's importance and its vulnerability to mistreatment," became a middle-class privilege.[21] As Steven Mintz notes, the protection of middle-class children resulted directly in the exploitation of poor children who were still required to work to help their families, and this protection eventually provided "a crucial vantage point for criticizing the abuse of children."[22] In fact, between 1870 and 1900 there was an increase of over one million child workers.[23] Furthermore, many families were never free from the anxiety of fearing they could unexpectedly descend into poverty. Thus, changing definitions of childhood continued to be calibrated by middle-class parents' desires to differentiate their children from those suffering and, in doing so, lay claim to a more stable class position.

The sentimentalization of childhood would not become a permanent cultural norm for all classes until the 1930s.[24] This also corresponds to a shift in public perceptions of poverty. When poverty was widely considered "a blessing in disguise or an unfortunate but inevitable necessity," child labor was largely viewed in a positive light; conversely, as poverty began to be seen as a product of failed social systems, perceptions of child labor shifted in broader cultural conversations.[25] As FDR's efforts legally ended most forms of child labor in 1938 through the Fair Labor Standards Act, the children of the poor were no longer supposed to contribute economically to their families. Although, as Viviana Zelizer notes, the Great Depression did cause some children to again become workers outside of the home, "the economically useful child became both numerically and culturally an exception." This change in public perception of child labor is due to several compounding factors in the first three decades of the twentieth century, including a growing immigrant workforce, rising incomes, the industrialization of the family wage, stricter compulsory education laws, and the advances of industrial capitalism. Reformers argued that "the economic participation of children was an illegitimate and inexcusable 'commercialization of child life'" and shamed parents who positioned their children as "agent[s] of production" who earned a wage and, therefore, "were not being properly loved."[26] Reformers' sentiments were not universally held, especially concerning older youth. Katharine DuPre Lumpkin and Dorothy Wolff Douglas's 1937 *Child Workers in America* filled an entire chapter with excerpts from primary sources outlining arguments for labor "for the child's own good."[27] Nevertheless, "[a]s twentieth-century American children became defined by their sentimental, noneconomic value, child work could no longer remain 'real' work; it was only justifiable as a form of education or as a sort of game."[28]

Popular media played an essential role in shifting public opinion as well.[29] The photography of Lewis Hine, a schoolteacher who, after he quit teaching, began working as a photographer for the National Child Labor Committee (NCLC), anticipated the popular influx of documentary photography in the 1930s.[30] Hine's photographs provide a "visual vocabulary" that conjoin "two discourses—public concerns of progressive reform and the personal, even intimate imaginings of modern childhood."[31] Clearly without a sentimental childhood, the children in Hine's photographs both actively labor and actively display the effects of labor on the developing child body. Perhaps the most subtly framed of Hine's photographs is the one that depicts boys in a cigar factory, taken in 1908 (see figure 3). A cursory glance might find the frame filled with boys at school, heads bent over their sums in front of a back wall with a map of both Indiana and the United States and a side wall whose windows have between them images of important men. However, the boys are not seated at desks, nor are their hands holding pencils; instead, they sit at the end of a table of men, and their hands are filled with tobacco or wrapping papers or labels. Ideal pupils, the boys are intent on their work, finding it more imperative to maintain production than to return the camera's gaze. Their productivity, as well as Hine's choice to give the viewer access to the entire workroom and not take a photograph that privileged a specific child or his hands marked by labor, attempts to make the image without sentiment. Furthermore, because the alternative for these boys would have been rows of desks and pencils and geography lessons with the maps, Hine's choice to evoke a schoolroom in the framing of the image only exacerbates its irony. Hine's children serve as "human documents." The hope of the NCLC was that

FIGURE 3 Lewis Hine's August 1908 photograph, *Cigar Factory, Indianapolis Ind. Boys in foreground. Witness E. N. Clopper*. National Child Labor Committee Collection, LOC 2018673700, Prints and Photographs Division, Library of Congress, Washington, D.C.

after viewing photographs presented in such a persuasive manner, viewers could not "help but to act."[32] Reform efforts, including those of Hine and the NCLC across the early twentieth century, were effective, and child labor declined.

The sentimentalization of childhood, culminating in the 1930s, positions literary and cultural representations of children in poverty of this period as a generative study of major cultural shifts in the definition of childhood in a country so deeply divided and structured by class.

The Modernist Language of the Child in Poverty

These significant cultural shifts overlap with the literary modernist period and offer rich context for reading class in literary and cultural representations of children. Many twenty-first-century literary scholars have worked to expand conventional definitions of modernism, often by insisting on modernism's ability to disrupt that which is assumed. These scholars' insistence on the work required of the reader within a modernist text and on modernist authors' attention to the effects of structures of power more broadly—specifically when considering genres and lived experiences outside what is typically considered modernist—expands the capacity of modernism as a structure for literary inquiry that explores the representation and voices of children. Much of the work to expand definitions of modernism has come from scholars focused on the 1930s, which, in turn, has brought forward the experiences of the poor and working class often through the study of the period's abundance of documentary texts.

Traditionally, literary scholarship focused on the Great Depression has emphasized the documentary form and use as a baseline according to the definitions provided by William Stott in his 1986 *Documentary Expression and Thirties America*. Stott begins by establishing two competing definitions of documentary: first, "presenting facts objectively and without editorializing and inserting fictional matter," and second, a "human document" that is "not objective but thoroughly personal." Tracing the use of the modifier "human" through the thirties "as a synonym for emotional or touching or heartfelt," Stott argues that historical documents are understood intellectually, while human documents are understood emotionally.[33] Paula Rabinowitz has noted that because of the efficacy of the documentary form in the Depression era, other genres "sought to re-create the immediacy and power offered by the direct testimony of reportage."[34] Yet this immediacy was not immediately seen as valuable by literary scholars. Alfred Kazin extensively cataloged his complaints against the documentary form in his 1942 *On Native Grounds: An Interpretation of Modern American Prose Literature*: Documentary was "a register of the learning process, an example of a new social consciousness in America whose greatest distinction was the very fact of that consciousness in itself, the sense of a grim and steady awareness rather than of great comprehension." Taking issue with what he perceived as the passivity of reading documentary texts, he argued that America was "only quoted and photographed" instead of the subject of cultural or political critique.[35]

Jeff Allred's 2010 *American Modernism and Depression Documentary* takes issue with Kazin's dismissal of documentary in an effort to redefine modernism. Though he slightly overextends Kazin's critique of documentary forms (certainly many of Kazin's valid questions and complaints initiated important critical conversations about the ethics of photography and the role of the reader), his argument is built from an odd, brief comment Kazin made about the ability of the fragments of documentary photography to "tell the truth of the times." In essence, Allred argues that documentary fragmentation is not a failure of art or expression but rather a form of modernism that "expands or explodes realist modes of representation by mediating between things themselves and the inner processes by which they are perceived."[36] For Allred, documentary modernism is "a radicalization of literary realism" in which the text serves as "a dialectic of the real and its representation."[37]

Also a central work in framing modernism as central to contemporary documentary studies, Joseph Entin's 2007 *Sensational Modernism: Experimental Fiction and Photography in Thirties America* begins by restating the widely accepted critical position that traditional representations of the poor in literature (naturalism and sentimentalism) have the effect of maintaining rigid class structures and "cast[ing] the disenfranchised as abject figures of middle-class pity, disdain, or supervision." Sensational modernists, he argues, "[combine] a sensational focus on visceral impact and social contrast with a modernist emphasis on aesthetic experimentation and cognitive disorientation [and] deploy arresting images of disfigured bodies to depict the poor and dispossessed in ways that challenge the sense of moral authority and cultural control that sentimentalism, naturalism, documentary photography, and high modernism typically grant the middle and upper classes." Entin finds that the disfigured, grotesque body of a poor or working-class person offers a disruption in which "social and epistemological violence is made legible." Similarly, *Reading the Classed Child* demonstrates that the language of the poor and working class, specifically the child in poverty, offers the same potential for disruption; however, precisely because it is not corporeal, the language of a child can differently nuance the complications of what Entin calls "the uncertainty and instability of social understanding."[38]

In an era saturated with images of suffering, especially the suffering of children, the voice of the impoverished child in modernist fiction demands a different type of response as the reader experiences an experimental modernism that is, at once, as political and complicated as highly sentimental images. Yet the purpose of this project is not to argue that Depression-era fiction is superior to documentary texts. Instead, *Reading the Classed Child* illustrates that the fictional construction of a poor child's voice does major cultural work that has been long ignored in studies of this era, work that expands discussions of poverty and teaches us how to listen to what we might otherwise reject. Taken together, these scholars' insistence on the work required of the reader within a modernist text and modernist authors' attention to the effects of structures of power more broadly—specifically when considering genres and lived experiences outside what is typically considered modernist—expands the capacity of modernism as a structure for literary inquiry. Noteworthy also are the ways these scholars refocus modernism to bring forward the experiences of the poor and the working class.[39]

Also underexplored in studies of literary modernism and, more broadly, in American literature is the figure of the child. Mason Phillips's 2016 *Representations of Childhood in American Modernism* is the first book-length treatment of the subject and responds not only to the pattern of histories of childhood neglecting modernism but also to the pattern of literary scholars disregarding works of modernists who "actively sought to widen the ways that adults think about childhood" in response to prevailing nostalgic views of childhood. While I disagree with Phillips's claim that "the writers and thinkers of American modernism [. . .] were among the first to question the universality of childhood, among the first to assert the social construction of childhood, and among the first to show concern for the damage that ideals of childhood could do to children as well as adults," my argument aligns with hers in that we both see within the modernist literary movement new approaches to childhood.[40] Furthermore, not present in Phillips's book is a consideration of class, especially the poor or working class, and the ways such nostalgic definitions of childhood hide the effects of class as central to critically reading representations of children and broader cultural conceptions of childhood.

The necessity of centering class, specifically poverty, as a mode of analysis in scholarship of American literature was the subject of the September 2022 themed issue of *American Literature.* Within the issue's introduction, "How American Literature Understands Poverty," Clare Callahan and colleagues establish the capacity of literature to "unsettle the term" and consider "conceptual problem[s] of seeing and representation." They call for continued work, as poverty "has remained marginal in literary studies." *Reading the Classed Child* responds to this gap and offers a method of reading the classed other that responds to the questions the editors raised: "What theories and methods of reading does literature about poverty demand? What language for talking about poverty does literature provide? In turn, what kinds of demands and pressures do efforts to address poverty, dispossession, and extreme economic inequality place on literary form and language?"[41]

When we look within literary and cultural scholarship focused on the Left, a space in which privileging discussions of class is central, we also find a conspicuous lack of children as subjects in scholarship focusing on the 1930s. For example, Alan Wald's 1994 *Writing from the Left: New Essays on Radical Culture and Politics* includes a call to action for the creation of a Marxist "organization that can harmoniously represent the aspirations of working people, oppressed nationalities, women, gays and lesbians, and all others who suffer the consequences of a callous, exploitative, and destructive capitalist system."[42] Unless they are represented by the good-faith effort of mentioning "all others," children are missing from Wald's list. In the works of other contemporary Marxist scholars who discuss the 1930s, such as Michael Denning's 1997 *The Cultural Front: The Laboring of American Culture in the Twentieth Century* (in which there is a one-sentence mention of the decline of child labor) and Barbara Foley's 1993 *Radical Representations: Politics and Form in U.S. Proletarian Fiction, 1929–1941* (which discusses the genre of the proletarian bildungsroman in chapter 9 but with an emphasis on the end of the formula, not its beginnings in childhood), childhood and/or children and youth as categories of analysis are largely, and ironically, absent.

Two powerful exceptions bear mention. One is Julia Mickenberg's 2006 recovery project, *Learning from the Left: Children's Literature, the Cold War, and Radical Politics in the United States,* which traces the little-known history of the Left in children's literature, specifically, the evolution of the Old Left preceding the 1930s and the New Left that emerged from the Popular Front and in response to the Cold War. Mickenberg is the first to track the pervasive influence the Left had in children's book publishing and trends. Beginning in the early twentieth century, she argues, this influence largely went unnoticed due to "women's specialized knowledge concerning children, and the feminized position of children's literature within a literary hierarchy." She also notes that the "circulation [of proletarian literature for children] was so limited" that it "escapes comment in nearly every scholarly survey" of literature of the left, a fact supported by the previously mentioned dearth in scholarship.[43]

The second exception is the epilogue to Paula Rabinowitz's 1994 *They Must Be Represented: The Politics of Documentary* and a follow-up article in 2011 published in *American Literary History,* "'Between the Outhouse and the Garbage Dump': Locating Collapse in Depression Literature." The title of her book's epilogue, "One More Thing," pauses to mention children, for "[c]hildren hold no social, economic, or political status in our culture [and] are despised, ignored, abused, and condescended."[44] Rabinowitz's purpose in her 2011 article is to return to that pause, and she admits that children "remained marginal, an afterthought noted in the book's coda." In this essay, she uses the trope of the Depression child as an "optics of depression," a way in which to examine representations of economic depression. Drawing on Carolyn Steedman's *Strange Dislocations: Childhood and the Idea of Human Interiority,* Rabinowitz proposes that "children stand metaphorically for these depression sites: they literally are below the eye line of adults, out of sight." Yet their position as marginal, she reminds the reader, is of great worth, as they "[enable] a new look at what was beneath view." Even though her argument that coming-of-age novels whose plots take place within the 1910s or 1920s "required the Great Depression to be written," as "it made childhood poverty in America decipherable—not merely as a stage, but as a condition," is compelling and complementary to my claim that the 1930s were the apogee of representations of child poverty in literature, it too sees children more as a placeholder or childhood as a metaphor rather than examining the child as an autonomous subject who might have something to say.[45]

Largely relegated to the margins of scholarship across several disciplines, representations of children in poverty challenge our most sacred myth of national exceptionalism and the often linked and unquestioned but well-intentioned commitments to upholding a sentimental childhood. "[T]he concept of childhood offers a unique lens through which to glimpse assumed, neglected, or hidden processes of cultural signification," Caroline Levander and Carol Singley argue in their introduction to the 2003 edited collection *The American Child: A Cultural Studies Reader*.[46] What we find in many modernist literary representations of young people in poverty then, I argue, is an astonishingly complex representation most powerfully linked to modernism through the child's use of language, which calls the reader into the work of examining intersectional structures of power that represent a culture's prevailing beliefs about age and class.

Languaging Poverty

In these texts and in broader cultural records is an insistence on the capacity of the language of young people in poverty. As Gavin Jones argues in *American Hungers: The Problem of Poverty in U.S. Literature, 1840–1945* (2008), "Literature reveals how poverty is established, defined, and understood in discourse, as a psychological and cultural problem that depends fundamentally on the language used to describe it."[47] This study explores the tensions inherent in the language of working-class children and children in poverty that reveal moments of resistance and resilience. These representations not only reveal the injuries of class but also place the reader in an ethically demanding position. Drawing on sociolinguistics, which takes language into account not as an ideal system but as emergent within social situations, my readings explore how apparently discordant and even deviant language reveals language formation and use as a process of compromise and discovery. If "analysis of the discourse moment of a social practice can give insights into its dynamism which are not available from other moments," literature, I argue, is one such moment.[48]

How might drawing from practices of discourse analysis help us return differently to not only language used by but also language constructed for young people in precarious class positions? Active and dialectic, this approach helps us read against assumptions, past and present, of the voices of the poor and working class, and we can hear them now as extreme but not chaotic, as demanding but not helpless, as rejected but not absent. Altogether, these voices reveal desperate circumstances even as they insist on working through them in whatever patchwork way is at hand. Building on poststructural theories that argue that language is context-driven and drawing on Robert de Beaugrande's blend of linguistics and literary theory, I argue that the complex discourses of poverty require a careful parsing of "the enactment of a dialectic between harmony and conflict, between order and incongruity, between real and potential" in which "values do not obscure or distort but constitute both precondition and ambience of the engagement."[49]

Admittedly, of course, seeing language as a site of struggle is not new to literary studies. However, when examining representations of class, there is need for continued nuance. Amy Schrager Lang's 2003 *The Syntax of Class: Writing Inequality in Nineteenth-Century America* argues that "the language of class is less stable" largely because "Americans displace the reality of class into discourses of race, gender, ethnicity, and other similar 'locked-in' categories of individual identity."[50] This is not, however, to negate the importance and power of race and gender as categories of exclusion or oppression. As Barbara Foley argues in *Radical Representations: Politics and Form in U.S. Proletarian Fiction, 1929–1941* (1993), race and gender "signal experiential realities [as] there is a limited sense in which they can be abolished. Class, however, is nothing but a social relationship; it is, indeed the quintessential social relationship."[51] Discourse analysis explores the gaps within and tensions between socially constructed positions of power and authority and the discourses that "sustain and reproduce the social status quo."[52] Language, as Fredric Jameson insisted, is never neutral and, therefore, always political.[53]

Traditionally, discourse analysis is more concerned with everyday texts such as speeches or nonfiction genres such as journalism. Roger Fowler, however, argues for an application of discourse analysis to literary studies, for literature viewed "as discourse and thus as communication rather than as object [. . .] is to see the text as mediating relationships between language-users: not only relationships of speech, but also of consciousness, ideology, role and class."[54] In other words, writers are conditioned by systems of discourse yet can innovatively push against them as well. Language is, to reference Mikhail Bakhtin's concept of dialogism, "always responding, always anticipating and eliciting responses."[55] Literature, therefore, is a process, "the communicative interaction of implied speakers and thus of consciousnesses and of communities."[56] Lang argues that the "displacement of class into the discourses of race and gender" unfairly "give[s] precedence to one vocabulary of representation over another in the interest of achieving particular ideological ends." "Writing in equality," she argues, "we write out power." Her thesis calls for literary analysis that intentionally pursues the construction and negotiation of class in literary texts: "To parse the syntax of class—to identify the ordering of language that makes apparent the mutual relationship of parts in which meaning inheres—is, then, I hope, to open a discussion of the impact of differentials of wealth, power, and prestige on the representations Americans make of and about themselves, a discussion endlessly deferred both in their literature and in the study of that literature."[57]

Reading the Classed Child focuses on analyzing the atypical language of the poor and working class, language that at first seems erratic or cumbersome or antisocial but is instead a mixture of a critique, of survival skills, and of crude efforts at a solution that together are revealed to be a fantastic (i.e., inventive yet bizarre) bulwark. Michel Foucault's idea that "to change the perspective from which things are seen is also to change what is seen and to make it possible to think, speak and do things in a new way" further amplifies texts that privilege the voices of the poor in discussions of poverty.[58] What people in poverty have to say about being poor and, furthermore, how authors construct what the poor say draw our attention to the ways all representations are highly mediated. Examining these constructions requires "mediat[ing] the connection between detailed semiotic/linguistic features of texts and interactions, as social and cultural structures and processes," always keeping in mind that many times critical insights are "revealed by absences."[59]

Within analysis of atypical discourses, characters who are given voice that is well beyond what readers have been conditioned to expect because of the characters' class position or antagonistic relationship to social norms may be said to speak in what Halliday and Fowler have called an "anti-language." Such anti-language is so powerful that it can arguably exert a dislocating effect on a text, at times decentering it and at other times exposing its commitment to a rigidly normalizing discourse. This idea was first developed by Halliday and published in 1976 in an article in *American Anthropologist*. His claim uses three different real-life examples of languages formed by a metaphorical anti-society (he draws primarily on examples from prisoners and criminals). These languages create an alternate reality in which "[i]t is not the *distance* between the two realities but the *tension* between them that is significant."

Therefore, anti-languages are created and sustained by a hyperawareness of power structures within society.[60] Though concerned with real-life examples, Halliday does propose, in the last paragraph of his essay, that the language of literature can serve as anti-language as well, though he offers neither an example nor further discussion.

Years later, Fowler expanded and modified Halliday's brief mention of literature as anti-language in his 1981 *Literature as Social Discourse* and in his 1986 *Linguistic Criticism* by extending Bakhtin's concept of the dialogic to a wider range of fictional texts.[61] For Fowler, anti-language is more than just nonstandard English. It is "a type of sociolect ('a variety associated with a particular class or social group') which relates to the standard in a radically antagonistic way."[62] It also becomes the "locus within which the norm society and the deviant group confront and negotiate." Therefore, one of the major differences between Halliday's and Fowler's theories of anti-language is Halliday's premise that anti-language is a variety, while Fowler's argument is that it is also a process. It is, after all, still connected to the standard language, serving as both a "medium of negotiation" and "a creative critique of the norm."[63]

And if literature creates its own discourse to which readers do not bring an overt set of expectations regarding its functionality in everyday life (such as we would bring to reading an instruction manual), "it teaches its own use; it is sovereign in its own domain of language."[64] Or, in other words, literature is a "dialogue between ideologies, reflected in linguistic transformations." Many times those linguistic variations are "social differences, principally class divisions." Anti-language, therefore, is more than a code, "a technique of representation"; instead, it is a process of complex negotiations of "status, identity and ideology between an official establishment and a group which diverges from its norms."[65]

Anti-language, then, is inherently a by-product of class. "The question is," Fowler claims, "whether the author is prepared to allow his working class characters any kind of free identity, freedom to challenge or even invert the middle class norms, or whether their values are submerged, neutralized by a middle class ideology." Thus, when Halliday and Fowler present the common speakers of anti-language as "'deviant' or 'criminal' or 'deficient,'" I would suggest that "deficient" is analogous with common perceptions of people in poverty and the working class.[66] Furthermore, when they claim that anti-language is a "secret language" and, therefore, hidden from dominant cultural forces, I would argue that the anti-language of poverty, especially the child in poverty, gains its status as subversive in part because so few are listening.

The anti-language of economic precarity at times both upholds the standard cultural discourse and subversively challenges it. Thus, I read these moments of language not as failures or oddities. Instead, they demand a response from the reader, and in turn they expand our understanding of class and poverty, or at least their complications. I'm not interested in proposing how class inequalities should be fixed (that is a structural conversation beyond the scope of this project); instead, I question what in the way that these inequalities have formerly been described has kept them from even being approached. Even a text intended plausibly to arouse sympathy for the poor or working class can include language that works in a contrary manner, both alarming and alienating readers. Furthermore, in texts that privilege the child in poverty, we can also see more powerfully how anti-language as a complex rendering of the process of language formation within a rigidly classed society. After all, in the words of Fowler, the poor "mean differently."[67]

Premodernist Examples of Anti-Language

Within American literature, the dynamics of class are often most pronounced within narratives of poverty and the child. What follows are two examples of anti-language in well-known works of American literature prior to the 1930s. Horatio Alger's *Ragged Dick*, for example, published serially in 1867, represents hegemonic cultural narratives of want and work ethic using language that keeps the reader at a distance from the child in poverty. Conversely, Mark Twain's 1885 *The Adventures of Huckleberry Finn* unsettles this type of cultural narrative by placing the reader inside the head of a homeless child who sees the world in a way that allows him to doubt, question, and create alternative possibilities. By using language that engages the reader differently, Twain created a literary public sphere where grasping the language of the child in poverty is essential.

Ragged Dick is a jeremiad, a cyclical rhetorical formula from the Old Testament, interestingly housed in the body of a poor child.[68] Alger's distillation of the tripartite sermon (first, pinpointing present problems of decline, second, identifying a turning point by demonstrating what was right in the past and precisely where it went wrong, and third, calling for reform) into the remarkably self-reflexive child protagonist utilizes many of the same tropes employed by sentimental literature earlier in the nineteenth century. Chapter 1 begins to establish sympathy for Ragged Dick, an orphan who sleeps in "a wooden box half full of straw"; who, despite the propensity of other street boys to do so, would not steal; and who, "if he had been clean and well dressed[,] would have been decidedly good looking" (*RD*, 40). Yet, true to the jeremiad, Alger's trustworthy third-person narrator faithfully catalogs

Dick's flaws so that the reader knows he "[doesn't] consider him a model boy" (43).

In chapter 8, the reader learns the initial reason for Dick's decline. While his father was likely lost at sea, his mother died when he was three. Until the age of seven, his mother's kindly boarders took him in, but after that he has "to scratch for himself" (*RD*, 85). As Lang notes, "In order to recover the possibility of Dick's ascent to respectability, Alger must render his poverty accidental, not structural, the consequence of his orphaning, not of his oppression at the hands of a capitalist class."[69] The turning point of the jeremiad comes when Dick meets Mr. Whitney, and his nephew Frank prophetically offers Dick the myth of class mobility: "If you'll try to be somebody, and grow up into a respectable member of society, you will. You may not become rich,—it isn't everybody that becomes rich, you know,—but you can obtain a good position, and be respected" (75). Converted, Dick spends the next twenty chapters correcting his sins.[70] When Dick begins to go to church, rent a room, bathe properly, and go early to bed, his reformation—the longest and third portion of the jeremiad—does in fact lead to his renewal, for by the end of the novel he is finally granted the middle-class parent he desires.[71]

For Alger, Dick is worthy because of his character, not because he is a child in a vulnerable and precarious class position. Alger's narrator describes young Dick (at this point in the book he is roughly fourteen) as an adult throughout the entire text. Though partially in jest and also in the spirit of the business metaphors that govern the book, the narrator tells the reader in chapter 1 that Dick has "no office to open," and in chapter 6 Frank counsels him to take up a new profession (*RD*, 41). Though Alger correctly emphasizes the economic burden of survival that is the daily reality of Dick and other street orphans, his flippant characterization of Dick as an adult removes the attention the novel could draw to the effects of poverty on children.

Alger's third-person narrative style also carefully frames Ragged Dick's thoughts within the parameters of the novel's tidy plot, keeping the reader at a comfortable distance from his suffering. Where there is language that might represent for the reader Dick's life on the street, it is accompanied by a tidy translation:

> "You're a brick," [Ragged Dick] said [to Frank].
>
> "A what?"
>
> "A brick! You're a jolly good fellow to give me such a present." (*RD*, 58)

Such dialogue does not occur in the novel between Dick and his bootblack friends; in fact, the vast majority of conversations Dick has in the novel are with persons in a higher class position. Alger does not allow the reader to see any parts of Ragged Dick's anti-society that are not carefully juxtaposed to show the reader its direct and deserved position below the middle and upper classes. Even in language ripe with subversive potential, Dick only speaks with a kind of specious anti-language. In chapter 6, when Dick dons Frank's clothes, Dick's propensity for comic hyperbole is labeled by Frank as unusual. "Well, I've been brought up queer," Dick replies and then offers a metaphor as explanation: "Some boys is born with a silver spoon in their mouth. Victoria's boys is born with a gold spoon, set with di'monds; but gold and silver was scarce when I was born, and mine was pewter" (*RD*, 74). Metaphors such as this one reveal both an awareness of class and an odd acceptance of social position on Dick's behalf, as they sustain rather than disrupt the status quo.

Instead of, as Fowler describes, Ragged Dick's language "emphas[izing his] freedom from the patterns of the language [. . .] and from the norms of the society," Dick strives in his language to emulate the norm.[72] Dick's letter to Frank at the end of the novel, for example, retains some of the slang and conservative figurative language evident in earlier chapters; however, Dick is eager for its grammar to be corrected. Before drafting it, he asks Fosdick, his roommate, who is also an orphan, to "look it over afterwards, and shine it up a little" (*RD*, 201). Fosdick's insistence after reading the letter that, despite "some mistakes," "it sounds so much like you that I think it would be better to let it go just as it is. It will be more likely to remind Frank of what you were when he first saw you" suggests Alger's desire for Ragged Dick's linguistic progress to be recorded and noted by the reader as impressive but still clearly marked with difference (203). Alger uses the language of Dick's poverty only to mark the impressive height of "Richard Hunter, Esq.['s]" ascent to the back door of the middle class (216). After all, though not everyone "becomes rich," to be "a respectable member of society" is accessible to all (75).

Twain's *Adventures of Huckleberry Finn*, eighteen years later, found an opposite use for the language of the child in poverty. Huck Finn, Twain's "malleable emblem of [American] childhood," has been interpreted differently by many.[73] For Leslie Fielder, for example, the young boy opened up a repressed homoerotic trend in American fiction; for Mark Altschuler, he is instead a motherless child who must piece together his own moral instruction; for popular culture, Huck represents the freedom encapsulated by our frontier past.[74] What has been neglected, strangely, is Huck's poverty. Huck's hungry and bruised body stubbornly houses a lingering debate between degrees of sentimental right feeling as it gestures toward stylistic developments that foreshadow modernist literature, such as the ability to pause within the mind of the poor child and witness the decisions made amid a prodigious lack of resources.

Huck is a child from a poor class position who always offers a critical point of view, and his anti-language is especially evident in the way he processes the moral dilemma of aiding Jim's escape in chapter 31. The ethics of a religion that justifies the enslavement of human beings, a tension throughout the novel, comes to the forefront when Huck debates his response to the King and Duke selling Jim "for forty dirty dollars."[75] Having previously felt guilt for not alerting Tom's owner, Miss Watson, of his whereabouts, Huck applies a strange blend of Pa's superstition and Miss Watson's hellfire and brimstone Christianity to come to the conclusion that, although he was "brung up wicked," he should adhere to the "plain hand of Providence slapping [him] in the face and letting [him] know that [his] wickedness was watched" (*HF*, 213, 212). Yet after a quasi-stream-of-consciousness catalog linked with polysyndetic coordination, Huck realizes that Jim's quiet kindnesses offer a different kind of moral code, one that justifies runaway slaves accompanying runaway boys down the Mississippi. The way he describes this decision, "It was a close place. . . . I was a-trembling, because I'd got to decide, forever, betwixt two things, and I knowed it," frames the dichotomous relationship Huck sees between his (im)morality and the accepted moral code of society (214). Yet Huck lacks the language for this realization. "All right, then," he says, "I'll *go* to hell" (214, emphasis in the original). Huck Finn uses the religious language of the Widow Douglas to negate the very moral code her version of Christianity upholds. In other words, his use of the word "hell" signifies its relexicalization. For Fowler, relexicalization is "the adaptation of an existing [vocabulary] item in such a way as to make it clear that a shift or an inversion of values has occurred."[76] For Huck, hell is rescuing the man who has provided for his basic needs since he escaped the wrath of his pa, a fate far preferable to the Widow Douglas's insistence on shoes on his feet and prayers in the closet.

While they are on the raft, Huck and Jim live within an anti-society, "constantly striving to maintain a counter-reality that is under pressure from the established world."[77] The final nine chapters, when Tom Sawyer returns to the narrative and offers to help Huck steal Jim out of slavery again, illustrate how impossible such an anti-society is once they are on the banks of the Mississippi. Huck's plan for securing Jim's freedom is the same as before: steal the key, run to the river, and "shove off down the river on the raft with Jim, hiding daytimes and running nights, the way [they] used to" (*HF*, 302). Tom's plan, however, grows in elaborateness with each chapter. After three weeks of planning and Jim's own admission that "if he ever got out this time he wouldn't ever be a prisoner again, not for a salary," the escape hurriedly happens (342). As the trio reaches the raft, Tom, "gladdest of all," reveals that he has a bullet in his calf, and Jim refuses to go farther until Tom is attended to by a doctor (352).

Huck's immediate response to Jim's humane demand again demonstrates his frustration with language, this time for the ethical paradigm of their anti-society: "I knowed he was white inside, and I reckoned he'd say what he did say—so I was all right now, and I told Tom I was a-going for a doctor" (*HF*, 353). Huck's use of the word "white," a racially charged word in any postbellum text, is another example of relexicalization, which "only works, semantically, if the original meaning is not completely erased; that which is refused legitimation by your society is precisely that which receives honour and legitimation in ours."[78] To the Widow Douglas, Aunt Sally, the Duke, or even Tom Sawyer, "white" signifies an automatic moral high ground whose inverse is invariably the enslaved Black person. To Huck, Jim's whiteness erases racial boundaries; it does not define them: Jim is white because he is good. The tension between language and anti-language, what Fowler calls "an official and an unofficial voice," provides "an unresolved, unmediated, antithesis which preserves a critical, dialogic openness in the novel's examination of its central ethical or social or psychological (or whatever) concerns."[79] Just as Huck's earlier relexicalization of the word "hell" signifies his distrust of the moral code provided by the Widow Douglas's Christianity, Huck's relexicalization of the word "white" upends the parameters of the system of human commerce that necessitates stealing Jim (who, of course, is unknowingly already a free man). Most importantly, though, Huck's anti-language engages the reader and requires them to see the text as a site of struggle.

Perhaps this is also a way of rereading the problematic ending of Twain's novel. George Saunders argues that the reintroduction of Tom Sawyer in the last chapters positions the two young boys as the "two viable models of the American character":

> They exist side by side in every American and every American action. America is, and always has been, undecided about whether it will be the Unites States of Tom or the United States of Huck. The United States of Tom looks at misery and says: Hey, I didn't do it. It looks at inequity and says: All my life I have busted my butt to get where I am, so don't come crying to me. Tom likes kings, codified nobility, unquestioned privilege. Huck likes people, fair play, spreading the truck around. Whereas Tom knows, Huck wonders. Whereas Huck hopes, Tom presumes. Whereas Huck cares, Tom denies. These two parts of the American Psyche have

> been at war since the beginning of the nation, and come to think of it, these two parts of the World Psyche have been at war since the beginning of the world, and the hope of the nation and of the world is to embrace the Huck part and send the Tom part back up the river, where it belongs.[80]

The end of the novel, therefore, when Tom reenters and dominates the narrative, offers the reader a world that is the opposite of Huck's world of childhood. In other words, Tom mimics adult control of events with his elaborate plans and executive decisions. Huck, on the other hand, quickly sees Tom's plans as useless and impractical. Huck prefers actions that bring the least harm to both Jim and Aunt Sally, and his penultimate sentence of the novel—"But I reckon I got to light out for the Territory ahead of the rest, because Aunt Sally she's going to adopt me and sivilize me and I can't stand it"—is his refusal to submit to the world of adulthood (*HF*, 375). It is not that Huck refuses responsibility but that he refuses to live in a world structured by the Widow Douglas or Aunt Sally, the Grangerfords or the King and the Duke, or even his father or Tom Sawyer, all adult ways of structuring the world that Twain has satirized throughout the novel. Is Huck's decision to "light out for the Territory" the ultimate expression of an anti-society? He does, after all, refuse to live under its rules, to speak its language. Once we learn to hear Huck's anti-language, then we too are equipped to reapproach the novel's tensions. Perhaps most importantly, we can reapproach the language of Twain's child narrator, whose inventive dialect relexicalizes societal rules to recover ethical ones.

Reading the Social Other

Just as anti-language insists on the capacity in nonstandard language, the work of scholars across disciplines offers models of what becomes possible and what crucial questions emerge if we insist on the child's capacity. *Reading the Classed Child* builds from Marah Gubar's kinship model, which both builds from what Sánchez-Eppler and others have claimed—that children "begin life [. . .] immersed in discourses not of their own making that ineluctably affect how [they] conceive of [them]selves and the world"—and insists that children are "simultaneously scripted and scripting. This way of thinking about what it means to be a child has significant benefits. It accords children agency without denying that they are shaped by a classification that pre-exists their arrival in the world, one that has spawned a matrix of adult-controlled discourses and practices that affect how young people perceive themselves and their relationship to the world they inhabit."[81] Looking at variations in the enactment of these scripts as within the realm of possibility of children's design and choice suggests what Rachel Conrad invites us to consider in her 2020 book *Time for Childhoods: Young Poets and Questions of Agency*: "[C]ultural conceptions of youth that neglect appreciating young people's lives in the present" overlook the ways children's agency is "an active practice" in which the "ideas, desires, and strategies that children envision, rehearse, practice, or enact" can manifest in everyday practices that might not be highly visible to adults.[82]

Children, as subjects, have traditionally inhabited the margins of Americanist scholarship. Powerful works that are wholly devoted to moving children from the margins to the center—most notably, Anna Mae Duane's 2010 *Suffering Childhood in Early America: Violence, Race, and the Making of the Child Victim,* Karen Sánchez-Eppler's 2005 *Dependent States: The Child's Part in Nineteenth-Century American Culture,* Robin Bernstein's 2011 *Racial Innocence: Performing American Childhood from Slavery to Civil Rights,* and Patricia Crain's 2016 *Reading Children: Literacy, Property, and Dilemmas of Childhood in Nineteenth-Century America*—have changed conversations in the field. They are all also rooted in the study of the nineteenth century.[83] *Reading the Classed Child* extends these efforts into the twentieth century, directly addressing the lack of critical studies of the language of the child in poverty in early twentieth-century culture and modernist literature.

My efforts to address this lack build on the work by the philosopher John Wall and literary scholar Gabrielle Owen. While neither scholar is focused on the intersections of class and childhood, both invite critical conversations about young people to move beyond notions of agency, a debate that is well cataloged in the field of children's literature.[84] Owen's 2020 work, *A Queer History of Adolescence: Developmental Pasts, Relational Futures,* argues that notions of dependency have wrongly construed perceptions of childhood and youth by disregarding the "profound degree to which *all* relationality involves interdependency and mutual entanglement" and, therefore, bring forward possibilities "to reshape ethical considerations for all human relationships."[85] Similarly, Wall languages his ethics of relationality as "childism," a framework within which "understanding and practices for all" shift in response to the "experiences of children."[86] In other words, we are inextricably bound to one another.

"Class and childhood are both highly visible yet often undertheorized," Sánchez-Eppler notes.[87] More recently, Jason Hart and Jo Boyden have echoed this claim, though on behalf of a different discipline: "[C]hildhood studies scholars have paid relatively scant attention to the issue of class."[88] *Reading the Classed Child* offers a model for bringing together these areas of inquiry by enacting an interdisciplinary theoretical conversation through which we can read literary and cultural representations of and by young people from the 1930s that depict the Other that is actually other, disorienting and confusing and odd. After all, it is tenable for a child in poverty to choose silence or for a working-class child to choose bitterness, yet these representations give the reader access to the voice of the classed child, a voice that sensitively displays great ingenuity and practicality. The anti-language of this vulnerable Other prompts the reader to see overlapping registers not as chaotic or nonsensical but as the child's efforts to shape order from clutter and to engage others in the problems of their world, a world marked but not wholly defined by lack, loss, and damage. For Wall, the "more fundamental ethical fact is not agency but disruption," as we are "called upon not only to be disrupted by the other but also to disrupt and recreate [ourselves] in the process."[89] How, then, can we take up the work of ethically engaging with the classed child? As we read we must first assume a purposefulness to children's language.

I believe that if we can learn to read differently the language of working-class children and children in poverty, then an ethical response is possible because what we have thought or understood previously has been disrupted. Stopping to listen, I would argue, helps us to see—then and now—a society woefully out of balance. By unpacking the disorder within the language of the poor child, the limit case for depravity, readers undertake an empathetic engagement: Because they see the child as other, they attempt to imagine the child's interiority. The child in poverty models for us a way to see the world anew and invites a call for an ethical understanding that brings forth imaginative proposals to solve problems that are devastatingly simple—a lack of basic needs—yet made complex not only by the magnitude of those suffering and the systems that propagate such suffering but also by the fact that the one suffering is a child. In other words, the anti-language of the child in poverty can teach us how to read ethically.

If we read this way—as readers and scholars and teachers and citizens—we must first acknowledge young people's capacity for and understanding of language. It is then that the work becomes ours: The discord or difference we often find in the language of poor and marginalized children prompts us to stop and listen again. In the aforementioned 2022 special issue of *American Literature*, the editors propose that new ways of reading poverty "might help us to recognize the forms of social, epistemological, and even material power the poor possess despite their active dispossession."[90] I would add to their list *linguistic* power. If we are taught how to listen to that which we might otherwise reject, then the anti-language of the poor or working-class child—articulated or silent, stream-of-consciousness or formally narrated, fictional or epistolary—demands a response. Poverty, after all, is deeply embedded within our denials, and America, quite frankly, does not know what to do with the poor. A call to develop an ethical understanding that elicits our engagement moves young people in poverty from the outermost margins to the center, where we are made aware and can begin the arduous work of unpacking the complicated dialectic of their language.

In sum, *Reading the Classed Child* works to unpack illustrative examples of the linguistic ingenuity that is the voice of the child in poverty within literary and cultural representations from the Depression era, a disorderly but comprehensible depiction of the stresses that poverty delivers and the shrewd efforts of resistance by those with the resources of their own patchwork inventiveness.

"[C]hildren [were] prominent markers of national and individual duress during this period," and many 1930s novels take up the child in economic precarity.[91] Many depict the somatic and linguistic experiences of first- or second-generation immigrants whose economic hardship preceded the Depression. The third-person omniscient narrator in Pietro Di Donato's *Christ in Concrete* (1939), for example, tells the reader how Paul, orphaned at age twelve, quickly takes his father's place working concrete. In doing so, Paul "*belongs no more to the world of children, who play and laugh and sing.*" After hearing the news of his father's grotesque death by being buried in concrete, Paul relexicalizes the word "father" to scale: "*I shall be the father.*"[92] David Schearl is also isolated from others his age in Henry Roth's *Call It Sleep* (1934), in which he is immersed in the Yiddish of his home. Roth's novel shows "the importance of language in the construction of David's self, but also the unstable referent of the different language that make up his world," and the child spends more time navigating the tension between the Yiddish of his home and the dialects and immigrant languages he encounters occasionally on the street or when visitors enter their home.[93] Leane Zugsmith's *The Reckoning* (1934) at times offers quick examples of the street language of the young boys in teacher Carolyn Muller's class. The text does not linger long enough in the world the boys are trying to create to give the reader fuller access beyond a short list of the children's cant, a conventional use of anti-language: nest, bulls, sally, pipe, cull.[94]

What we find in many modernist literary depictions of the child in poverty, then, is an astonishingly complex set of representations most powerfully linked to modernism through the child's use of language that may seem bizarre, ill-fitting, and outrageous. Such representations, I argue, are artistic and political triumphs that call the reader into the work of examining intersectional structures of power that reflect a culture's prevailing beliefs about age, race, and class.

Drawing from my research in multiple archives, each of the following four chapters sets up the reading of epiphanic moments within seminal 1930s texts in which the construction of the language of the child in poverty functions as a deeply mediated recovery project, a project made possible by the authors' sustained engagement with the language of young people in economic precarity and the ways that authors move within the parameters of the documentary, modernism, and realism to pause within the language of the child. Each chapter also includes the linguistic cultural productions of young people in which their language is a dynamic through which mainstream language and anti-language emerge. While some representations of the language of children diminish and even erase the disorder within that speech, many literary and cultural depictions of the child's anti-language open the child's interior complexity and make visible that which has been long ignored in studies of this era, cultural work that expands discussions of childhood and class, positions young people in poverty as active producers of political and cultural meaning, and prompts the reader's ethical engagement.

Chapter 1, "The Silences of Southern Poverty," takes up the youngest children of the oddly parallel families central to William Faulkner's *As I Lay Dying* (1930) and Erskine Caldwell's *Tobacco Road* (1932) to consider the interiority of the child by exploring the child's silence. For Faulkner's Vardaman, silence comes with resignation; for Caldwell's Pearl, it is a subversive silence of choice. Building from Jeff Allred's definition of radical realism as a form of modernism, I argue that these silences prompt the reader to read analytically instead of realistically, Faulkner through stream-of-consciousness narration and Caldwell through the strange marriage of the sentimental and the grotesque. From within the modernist stream-of-consciousness narration of Faulkner's Vardaman Bundren emerges an aesthetics of interruption that juxtaposes—at the very least—the vivid interior world of the poor child and the oppressive weight of the external world. This juxtaposition forms the context in which the reader must read the child and his language. My rereading of Vardaman centers the poor child's ability to resist the limitations inherent in the parameters of his world through agential and inventive language. Faulkner's attention to Vardaman's place in the margins of the family's narrative brings forward not only the vulnerability but also the capacity of the child.

Chapter 2, "Discourses of Play and Control," catalogs a similar hyperawareness in the poor Black child's acquisition of language. Joseph Entin finds that within the documentary work of the 1930s the bodies of the poor or working class offer a disruption in which "social and epistemological violence is made legible." I similarly demonstrate that the language of the child in poverty offers the same potential for disruption; however, precisely because it is not corporeal, the language of a child can more powerfully nuance what Entin calls "the uncertainty and instability of social understanding."[95] Richard Wright's autobiographical *Black Boy* (1944) demonstrates this with the presence of carefully controlled anti-language that remains hauntingly present in later chapters as he migrates from the South to Chicago, a tension between his efforts to control a narrative that is itself all about being unable to control. By reading the anti-language of the novel's first three chapters alongside the anti-language that Ralph Ellison recorded in his ethnographic notes from Black children playing at Harlem playgrounds for his work for the Federal Writers' Project and in his early short stories, I demonstrate that the poor Black child's language continually makes meaning through carefully ordered, structured, and controlled anti-language.

Chapter 3, "The 'Damaged' Child's Polyvalent Language," examines texts adhering to and resisting partially the parameters of Michael Gold's call for proletarian realism. I contrast the rhetorical and polemical use of the poor child's body—consistently and sentimentally presented as damaged—in the propaganda of the Popular Front and proletarian novels and short stories written by women with the way Tillie Olsen's Mazie in *Yonnondio: From the Thirties* (1974) shifts the reader's focus from the body of the child to an account of how the child learns to articulate her suffering. By examining the development of Mazie's polyvalent anti-language, a dialectic bound to the corporeal, I illustrate the way language emerges from a life of violence and profound discontinuity. Olsen depicts the way a single voice can speak against inherent power structures even as the speaker is becoming more fully aware of their existence, always showing how life can be sustained amid such damage.

Chapter 4, "Reading (in) Class," takes up Depression-era literature written for children to consider the relationship between a marked growth in radical literature for young people in the beginning decades of the century and the shifts that emerged parallel to a growth in realism in children's literature and changes in broader cultural beliefs about young people and the purpose of texts for children as the Depression lingered and the Popular Front grew. I begin with close readings of articles and children's writing within early issues of the leftist *New Pioneer* magazine. I then discuss school readers developed for young people in New York City public schools, as well as popular commercial children's novels such as the Newbery Award–winning *Thimble Summer*

(1938). By examining how adults illustrated and languaged cultural narratives of age and class in texts for children, as well as children's linguistic choices in child-authored texts, I offer close readings of the rare moments in which anti-language emerges, particularly in children's adaptations, "manifestation[s] of intertextuality."[96] By considering how narratives of class and language acquisition are presented, I argue that even as these genres strove to widen class representation, these texts illustrate concerns that literature for young people continues to struggle with today.

I conclude by pausing briefly to reflect on the ethics of reading the language of the classed child in an epilogue, "Rereading Depression-Era Children."

BY MAPPING THE LANGUAGE of the poor child not as disorder but as a search for order, the reader is elevated into engaging with a figure who is newly subjective, not lost but finding and developing an interiority under inimical conditions. John Wall's contention that children "occupy the periphery [of] contemporary humanities scholarship, arguably more than any other group," coupled with the lack of critical literary studies of the language of classed children in American literature and culture, calls us to make space for the child too easily excluded from larger conversations about poverty in the humanities and our public sphere.[97] Responding to the need to examine poverty as an area of cultural inquiry in its own right, *Reading the Classed Child* centers representations of the language of the child in poverty.

CHAPTER ONE

The Silences of Southern Poverty

You Have Seen Their Faces was the most popular documentary text published in the 1930s.[1] From our vantage point in the present, Erskine Caldwell's fictitious captions for the photographs Margaret Bourke-White took during their travels in the Deep South put words in the mouths of children, words that make the children's suffering more palatable by reinforcing what the viewer expected them to say. By his own admission in the book's prefatory material, the "[l]egends under the pictures are intended to express the authors' own conceptions of the sentiments of the individual portrayed; they do not pretend to reproduce the actual sentiments of these persons."[2] Caldwell's caption for the opening image reads as follows: "My father doesn't hire any field hands, or sharecroppers. He makes a lot of cotton, about sixty bales a year. Me and my brother stay home from school to work for him."[3] The factual nature of this child's sentences when taken in tandem with the angle Bourke-White chose for this photograph presents the child as far older and stronger than what his beardless face and aviator cap and goggles suggest. His furrowed brow and the shadows that hide his eyes imply not only concentration but also the amount of work the child and his brother must do to produce sixty bales a year with a hand plow. Caldwell writes onto the child a narrative of familial loyalty and sacrifice, a boy's duty to his father and the land. While this caption might be akin to the child's response if he were asked a question by a female photographer and her companion who were clearly not from Elbow Creek, Arkansas, Caldwell's words provide no glimpse into the interiority of the child.

James Agee and Walker Evans, whose 1941 documentary text *Let Us Now Praise Famous Men* is a stark contrast to *You Have Seen Their Faces* both in its experimental approach to documentary realism and the struggle to get the work published, were disgusted with what they considered the ethical violations of Caldwell's prose.[4] Agee and Evans intended to "translate the experience of inhabiting the lives of poor rural dwellers to readers in as intact a state as possible," so they created a detailed catalog of their 1936 summer foray into the lives of poor sharecroppers in Alabama in an effort to shift the reader's "consciousness" from the "imagined, the revisive, to the effort to perceive simply the cruel radiance of what is."[5] Because of Agee's self-consciousness and his parallel insistence that the reader not "think of it as Art" (*LUN*, 12), this documentary work illustrates Rabinowitz's description of the complications of documentary texts, "a paradigmatic instance of the problems intellectuals face when they search out and describe their social others."[6]

Within the parameters of this project, perhaps the most unsettling of Agee's pages are the beginnings of section 3, "Inductions," which return the reader to the start of Agee and Evans's time with the Ricketts, Woods, and Gudger families, from meeting the male heads of household at the courthouse in town to first photographing them with their wives and children. Agee's retelling of this initial photography session parallels the representations of the poor child in the 1930s that are the focus of *Reading the Classed Child,* children who, from the margins of texts, make great efforts to communicate, efforts riddled with distracting mistakes and real and imagined fears. "I shall not forget you soon," Agee writes, then, rhetorically turning to children who will likely never read his words, "nor you children: you started out from behind bushes and hid behind one another and flirted at us and ridiculed us like young wild animals, and even then we knew you were wonderful, and yet it is amazing to me now how relatively lightly we realized you then" (*LUN,* 321). Appropriately, then, Agee's ironic retelling of these initial family photographs initially leaves the "barefooted and slaver-mouthed" children in the background and focuses instead on their mothers. The reactionary urgency of Mrs. Ricketts, who "washed the faces of [her] children swiftly and violently with rainwater, so that their faces were suddenly luminous stuck out of the holes of their clothes," is juxtaposed with the careful preparations of Mrs. Gudger, who "had taken time to wash [her children] and to put a clean dress on [her daughter,] Louise, and a ribbon in [her] hair" (322, 324). This ten-year-old child, Maggie Louise, becomes Agee's focus as he continues to directly address the child with the informal "you."

Agee's attention to the child's body—the flimsy party dress "through which your body was visible," "the animal litheness of your country body," the glowing skin that comes "only to those who came straight out of the earth"—is secondary only to his page-long explication of her eyes in which he attempts to rationalize the pleasure he finds in looking at her (*LUN,* 324). "There is no other blankness like you," Agee continues, intent on narrativizing Louise's blankness as "temperatureless, keen, serene and wise and pure" and culminating with the admission that "suddenly yet very quietly I realize a little more clearly that I am probably going to be in love with you" (325–26).

A little more than twenty-five pages later, Agee first sits in the Gudgers' house and devotes another two pages of description to the way Louise looks at him "without smiling" with eyes he "cannot look into [. . .] long at a time without panic and quick withdrawal" for "such a vibration increasing between [them] as drove [him] half unconscious" (*LUN*, 352–53). Though the gaze of the child remains "without fear nor wonder, but with extraordinary serene reception and shining and studiousness, and yielding of no remotest clue, whether of warmth, hatred or mere curiosity," Agee feels the need to offer (nonverbally, of course) an apology of sorts:

> [I]t is as if I were telling her, good god, if I have caused you any harm in this, if I have started within you any harmful change, if I have so much as reached out to touch you in any way you should not be touched, forgive me if you can, despise me if you must, but in god's name feel no need to feel fear of me; it is as if the look and I had never been, so far as any harm I would touch you with, so far as any way I would not stand shelter to you[.] (*LUN*, 353–54)

Louise's response is the "same blank, watchful, effortless excitation," and Agee looks away (*LUN*, 354). Rabinowitz reads this highly sexualized moment as a reversal: Louise's gaze "becom[es] in a sense the camera that had earlier fixed on her," and "her gaze functions as the camera's—implacable, central, invariable—and able to transfix him with its power." Because Louise "looks differently," her gaze functions as resistance, an anti-language of silence to which Agee feels compelled to give language.[7] It is of note that his apology assumes for Louise a sentimental childhood in which he is the first threat to her innocence, whether corporeal or cognitive.

Claiming a place for the documentary form in American modernism, Allred finds essential modernist qualities in the fragmented documentary photograph and its complicated relationship "between reality and representation, self and other, reader and text." In conversation with the work of other contemporary critics arguing for a relexicalization of modernism, Allred argues that modernism is "a radicalization of literary realism" that "expands or explodes realist modes of representation by mediating between things themselves and the inner processes by which they are perceived."[8] Just as Fredric Jameson urges us to "explore the multiple paths that lead to the unmasking of cultural artifacts as socially symbolic acts," Allred argues that a documentary text must be considered "in the public sphere of [its] moment."[9] Allred's reading of modernism is built on the critical premise that documentary texts are contested sites too commonly and incorrectly framed as simple and direct.

To situate modernism as a form of radical realism, Allred notes the parallel development of advancements in modern fiction and documentary, claiming the earliest American example to be the documentary photography of Jacob

Riis and the premodernist qualities of Stephen Crane's novella *Maggie: A Girl of the Streets* (1893).[10] Riis and Crane also both insisted on the centrality of the child in their depictions of 1890s tenement poverty. The parallels within Riis's photographs and Crane's *Maggie* and the central Depression-era works of this chapter, namely, the documentary photography of Ben Shahn and the fiction of William Faulkner and Erskine Caldwell, are pronounced. Here I will examine how these premodern texts foreshadow Depression-era documentary photography and fiction to ask what was at stake when poor children were the focus in Southern literature of the 1930s, "a decade when the region's problems magnified those of the nation more broadly."[11]

In his 1982 discussion of William Dean Howells's oft-referenced definition of realism, *The Incorporation of America: Culture and Society in the Gilded Age,* Alan Trachtenberg argues that Howells saw realism as political, a "democracy of literature [that] wishes to know and tell truth," yet Howells often turned to romance to ensure that his realism ended with the moral force he desired.[12] When Trachtenberg, therefore, titled a chapter "Fictions of the Real," he meant the label pejoratively. Allred's modification of the phrase, adding the adjective "plausible," shifts its meaning "away from its mimetic role in reflecting or translating the real and towards its rhetorical dimension."[13] Allred sees this shift as prioritizing audience. My return to Trachtenberg's phrase agrees with Allred's insistence on moving away from mimesis but insists upon a different rhetorical focus. In what way, I argue, are such fictions constructed? Who speaks and to whom? Who remains silent? What shifts occur, in other words, when modernism radicalizes realism?

The Shifting of Place in Modern Depictions of Poverty

From tenements to rural spaces, the documentary photography of Jacob Riis and Ben Shahn presents poverty as firmly grounded in place. Riis, like many in the latter half of the nineteenth century, found children to be not only ideal protagonists but also formative social platforms. Writers and journalists in New York latched onto the appeal of a city in decline comprised of "dangerous interiors [and] children playing in the mean streets."[14] The Bowery, specifically, was ripe for representation. Already familiar with the Bowery from his job as a police beat reporter and earlier as a jobless and unhoused immigrant on the streets of Manhattan, Jacob Riis created *How the Other Half Lives,* his 1890 collection of photographs and essays chronicling the problem of poverty in New York City.[15]

Riis carefully composed his images. He often paid subjects to pose in certain ways and took many photographs at night.[16] Riis's most persuasive images in both lecture and print focused on children. He claimed that for slum children, "[h]ome [. . .] is an empty name" and the "joyless" precursor to "lives of wearisome toil that claims them at an age when the play of their happier fellows has but just begun."[17]

Riis photographed children in positions of vulnerability. In *Portrait of Poverty*, for example, a small child is holding a smaller child (see figure 4). Often referenced as *Organized Charity—a Little Girl Minding a Baby*, this secondary title positions the children as siblings, as the girl's hands tightly grasp the younger child in a gesture that is equal parts function and protection. Her eyes meet the camera directly and with suspicion, almost daring the uninvited audience to wake the baby, who has finally fallen asleep. The children are sitting in a doorway, and framing the left of the image is a garbage can, an environmental hazard that offers further reprieve from passersby. Furthermore, the first word of Riis's title, "portrait," suggests a formality within this photograph; the third word, "poverty," is positioned here as signifying the unnatural care of one child for another. Some of Riis's other photographs of mothers and children utilize the Madonna-and-child theme, but the bodies of this prepubescent Madonna and the child in her care are too similar in size to allow a proper ratio of reverence.[18]

Ben Shahn was employed by the New Deal's Farm Security Administration from 1933 to 1938. Patsy Watkins argues that he originally took photographs to use as "visual research" in the composition of his commissioned relief posters and murals, though Shahn's partner, Bernarda Bryson Shahn, wrote that "[h]e respected the camera, and did not set out to use it as a prop for painting."[19] Nevertheless, Shahn's photographs differ in composition from those of many other FSA photographers. As was standard FSA practice, his captions serve more as a marker of place and of the basic categorization of the bodies (e.g., wife, child, sharecropper) in the frame. Of note is Shahn's use of the adjective "destitute" in over one-third of the captions for his Arkansas photographs. Furthermore, roughly 40 percent of the photographs taken on his trip south with photographer Arthur Rothstein were taken with the subject slightly off center, a technique decidedly "non-journalistic."[20] Amanda Coleman's analysis of Shahn and Rothstein's 1935 Arkansas photographs reveals that of the 168 photos taken, only 2 contain a complete family unit; more common, she notes, is a photograph of "the children alone or in the presence of only their mother," further "disaggregates the family unit and denies poor white southerners a conventional family identity."[21]

Shahn's *Children of Destitute Ozark Mountaineer, Arkansas 1935* is one such off-center and fatherless photograph. The young girl is framed by her brother

FIGURE 4 Jacob Riis's photograph *Organized Charity—a Little Girl Minding a Baby,* which is sometimes published under the title *Portrait of Poverty*. LOC 2002710270, Prints and Photographs Division, Library of Congress, Washington, D.C.

and mother, with the family's porch in the background (see figure 5). All that is visible of her mother are a few folds of her skirt, and the girl's brother remains secondary largely because of Shahn's decision to include only the bottom half of his face in the image. Because of this choice, as well as the relative positioning of the girl's face as the photograph's focal point, the boy's hands and chest become his most prominent features. His hold on the kittens contrasts with his sister's grasp of her doll.

Something about the girl, though, drew Shahn's lens. Both children wear clothes equally ragged; both bodies are significantly smaller than the understated presence of their mother at right; both mouths are turned slightly downward; both children hold childhood objects of play. Perhaps it was the girl's careful attention to the remaining arm of the doll, which she holds as if they are playmates pausing between games. Perhaps it was the contrast of the girl's pristine skin with the scars on the doll's face and arm, flesh that looks as though it has been burned, especially in contrast with the doll's smooth torso. Certainly, the juxtaposition of the girl's downturned mouth to the doll's

FIGURE 5 Ben Shahn's FSA photograph *Children of Destitute Ozark Mountaineer, Arkansas 1935*. Farm Security Administration, Office of War Information Photograph Collection, LOC 2017729984, Prints and Photographs Division, Library of Congress, Washington, D.C.

permanent smile was of interest to a painter who actively encouraged other artists to join the Left.[22]

The grotesqueness of the doll's smile in contrast to its own lack—of arm, of clothes, of unblemished skin—and the absence of the rest of this destitute Ozark mountaineer's family are unsettling. The photo was taken with the explicit intent of visually representing Shahn's overused epithet, "destitute," for the American masses, and it asks the viewer to consider the doll as another victim of poverty. The little girl lacks the dark circles under her brother's eyes, and her full cheeks and wispy blond curls seem the antithesis of poverty. If she were drawn wearing different clothes and with an upturned mouth, for example, she could easily adorn the envelope of a 1930s Simplicity sewing pattern; these patterns often included miniature versions of girls' fashions for their dolls. Instead, the doll's pants, as desperate for patches as the boy's overalls, almost blend in with the girl's dirty shift. Neither one, the girl or her doll, represents what an American childhood should be.

The scarred doll returns in another of Shahn's photographs of the same family, *Wife and Child of Destitute Sharecropper, Arkansas October 1935*.[23] This time the mother holds both the doll and a young child, but the smile of the doll again contrasts sharply with the solemn face of the child, as well as with the hesitantly smiling face of the mother (see figure 6). The soot or dirt on this doll is considerably darker from this angle, and again the doll's arm is missing. Much later, in 1957, Shahn wrote that "[t]he incidental items of reality remain without value or common recognition until they are symbolized, recreated, and imbued with value. The potato field and the auto repair shop remain without quality or awareness or the sense of community until they are turned into literature by a Faulkner or a Steinbeck or a Thomas Wolfe or into art by a Van Gogh."[24] The motif of the poor children's playthings in his work illustrates his own claim.

The rural as a place of health and wellness was the solution proposed by Riis and other 1890s reformers to the problems of the masses of tenement children. While the Great Depression did not bring rural poverty into existence, it did shift the nation's attention to the rural neither as a place immune to poverty nor as a cure-all. The photographs of both little mothers, Riis's with a living doll and Shahn's doll whose body bears more visible scars of poverty, ask their viewers to find this type of motherhood unnatural and discomfiting. Both photographs rely on the sentimental in a persuasive exercise intended for adults. Yet the 1930s photograph, through the presence of a visibly scarred doll, adds the grotesque.

A vein of the Southern Gothic tradition, the grotesque relies on "incongruous, abnormal, [and] 'monstrous' characters, situations, and events" to present an "unflinching portrayal of human frailty, degradation, violence, and suffering."[25] Yet the grotesque is more than just that which is "bizarre or perverse."[26] In *Modern American Grotesque: Literature and Photography* (2009), James Goodwin makes an argument for a rereading of the grotesque by arguing that the American literary tradition of the grotesque is subversive because it "deploys a willfully oblique, partial, deforming, and contentious perspective that yields a comprehension of society and culture not otherwise possible."[27] Denning, twelve years earlier, had also argued that the political power of the grotesque was revolutionary, as writers used the grotesque as "an attempt to wrench us out of the repose and distance of the 'aesthetic.'"[28]

While no viewer was intended to see Riis's child mother as acceptable, Shahn's image—which juxtaposes the smooth skin and frowning mouth of the child with the pocked skin and grotesque smile of the doll—captures differently the vulnerability of the child. This is not to privilege the work of Shahn; instead, this is to say that the viewer is allowed to see Shahn's subject more closely. And as Riis's photographs were enveloped with sentimental prose, Shahn's received generic, placeholding captions.

FIGURE 6 Ben Shahn's FSA photograph *Wife and Child of Destitute Sharecropper, Arkansas October 1935*. Farm Security Administration, Office of War Information Photograph Collection, LOC 2017729982, Prints and Photographs Division, Library of Congress, Washington, D.C.

Without narrativizing prose, poverty becomes more grotesque and requires the reader to navigate the image without the language ordained for such a purpose. Shahn's *Children of Destitute Ozark Mountaineer*, for example, lacks the sentiment of Riis's preordained narrative of slum life for children: "With such human instincts and cravings, forever unsatisfied, turned into a haunting curse; with appetite ground to keenest edge by a hunger that is never fed, the children of the poor grow up in joyless homes to lives of wearisome toil that claims them at an age when the play of their happier fellows has but just begun."[29] The gap between the photographs of Riis and Shahn is not one of realistic construction, as both took care to situate the poverty on display. Instead, by "expand[ing . . .] realist modes of representation by mediating between things themselves and the inner processes by which they are perceived," Shahn's work attunes the reader to read analytically, and the framing of his photographs raises questions that insist on the centrality of the child.[30] Riis shows the viewer an ironic Madonna and child and insists on the role the city plays in the child's poverty. The photograph is centered and framed for the viewer in order to create the greatest amount of sympathy. Shahn, conversely, by excluding the mother and brother from fully entering the frame, highlights the contrast between the doll and the child's facial expressions and the inability of this little mother to protect her child. In other words, if Riis's photograph were cropped the same way, the foregrounded garbage can becomes bigger than the child, and the viewer no longer knows who else is close enough to help when the baby wakes. Riis presents a single, digestible reality that controls the narrative of the photograph. Shahn's viewer must engage with the photograph because of its composition, even if only to ask the series of questions it prompts: Why crop off the boy's eyes? What is the mother holding? Where is the father, to whom the photograph's title alludes? What has grotesquely marked the face and arm of the doll?

Many similar parallels—a narrative of a poor child grounded in place, the centrality of a mimetic object, carefully arranged ways of seeing poverty, the emergence of the grotesque—transpire in the fiction contemporaneous to the documentary photography of Riis and Shahn. Riis's contemporary, Stephen Crane, is most known for his novella *Maggie: A Girl of the Streets*. Immediately after *Maggie* was published, Crane wrote three sketches in which he chronicled the adventures of a young, impoverished child who was later identified in manuscript material as Tommie, Maggie's little brother, who dies in the novella.[31] Critics have dismissed these sketches or even considered them "an afterthought, when [Crane] was looking for a market for work already completed."[32] In them, however, Crane draws the reader's attention to the sparse language of the poor child.

"An Ominous Baby" begins by blatantly labeling the "toddling" protagonist an outsider—"A baby was wandering in a strange country"—though logically it is improbable that he could be too far from his tenement home.[33] Crane controls the gaze of both the protagonist and the reader: passive, primarily immobile, and silent, the child observes the scene before him as Crane draws the eye of the reader up to notice the "glancing sun-rays [that] changed cornices to blazing gold and silvered the fronts of windows" high above the "brown street filled with dull gray shadows" on which the child walks ("OB," 167). It is only when the child responds to the greeting of another child that he is noticed and told to "[g]o 'way," for he is "all dirty" (168). Nonetheless, Tommie continues to watch, and Crane's descriptions contrast the middle-class neighborhood with his "intent baby face covered with scratches and dust as with scars and powder smoke" (168).

A brightly painted toy finally moves Tommie to action. He moves closer and softly asks the owner of the fire engine if he can "play wif it"; the request is, unsurprisingly, denied, and the conflict escalates until Tommie steals the toy ("OB," 169). Described now by his deviance, the "small barbarian" and "little vandal" runs away with the loot. It is here that Crane shifts to Riisian sentiment: "He was weeping with the air of a wronged one who has at last succeeded in achieving his rights" (170). If such rights exist, the child is unaware of them, and such knowledge did not predetermine his wanderings. It is the allure of objects—chrysanthemums, perambulators, and soft things, "heaps of rugs and cushions"—that did (167). As the story closes, the child "turned and vanished down a dark side street as into a swallowing cavern" (170). In typical Crane fashion, the city and its shadows inhale the poor.

Crane stains his stories with colors that did not transfer to film. Absent in Riis's photography is the upper half; yet by incorporating so much color, Crane's fiction demonstrates the close proximity in which the two halves lived. The middle-class neighborhood Tommie wanders through is full of color, and the vibrantly colored fire engine, as Bill Brown notes, "provokes conflict and the tragedy of mimetic desire."[34] This hypnotic allure of middle-class objects is a staple of Crane's *Maggie* and New York tales.

The first story about Tommie describes a child's early conflict with class. The second, "A Great Mistake," follows a similar plot: an object of mimetic desire, a lemon, in the possession of an adult with power. In the final Tommie sketch, "A Dark Brown Dog," a neighborhood stray follows Tommie home, and his drunk father "held carnival with the cooking utensils, the furniture and his wife."[35] Crane's casual presentation of all three items in the list as objects that can be thrown at will foreshadows the dog's imminent doom: Days later, Tommie's father "[flings the dog] with great accuracy through the window," from which he falls five stories onto the roof of a shed and "roll[s] to the pavement of an alleyway" ("DBD," 181).

In the other Tommie tales, only the reader watches Tommie until his actions force others in the scene to acknowledge his presence. This tale differs from the first two because of the death of the dark brown dog. Crane narrates a paragraph-long description of the intertextual audience of the dog's fall. At the height of this climax, Tommie, "uttering loud cries, [comes] valiantly forth like a knight," though his valor is rendered mute, as "[t]he father of the family paid no attention to [the] calls of the child" ("DBD," 180). Only at the end of this sketch is Tommie willing to leave the table, under which he finds protection from familiar familial battles. He "burst into a long, dirgelike cry, and toddled hastily out of the room. It took him a long time to reach the alley, because his size compelled him to go downstairs backward, one step at a time, and holding with both hands to the step above" (181). Miniature once again, Tommie was but a moment before a chivalrous knight. Crane assiduously reassembles the most salient details of his sketch in the tiny, vulnerable body of Tommie. As he prolonged the fate of the dark brown dog by noting other tenement witnesses to the fall, Crane again slows the narrative. In the length of time it takes for Tommie's unsteady legs to reunite with the body of his dog, Crane wants the reader to dwell on the vulnerability of a child who is not yet big enough to go forward down five flights of stairs and the knowledge of a child who can quickly find the dog's body.

How quickly Crane's desired middle-class reader had sympathy for the innocent dog. Yet Crane redirects the reader by focusing on Tommie's compact frame. How easily the "small rug of a dog['s]" body could have been replaced with Tommie's. The reader, like the other tenement spectators, marvels at the act of violence committed against a dog; Crane simply wonders if the response would have been the same for a child. There is a gravity to this sketch that the others lack.[36] Tommie sits so long that his family has to come get him. It is no wonder that in the novella young Maggie stole a flower for "his small waxen hand" to hold inside of his "white, insignificant coffin."[37] For a child so enamored with color, its absence in the final Tommie tale is bleak. Crane resurrects Tommie only to prepare him to die.

"An Ominous Baby" focuses on Tommie's obsession with the toy fire engine, a shiny object that serves as a distinct placeholder of the middle class. Similarly, William Faulkner's youngest character in the novel *As I Lay Dying*, Vardaman, greatly desires the train "red on the track" displayed in town "behind the glass."[38] Unlike the burned dolls in Shahn's photographs, Tommie's fire engine and Vardaman's train remain pristine. Nevertheless, Tommie is in possession of the fire engine, but Vardaman's train, not for lack of trying, remains out of his grasp and thus serves as a permanent marker of rigid class boundaries. Just as Shahn's 1930s photographs demonstrate a modernist reframing of poverty, *As I Lay Dying* reconsiders the limitations of realism's attention to the language of children in poverty. Specifically, the greatest difference between Crane and Faulkner is Tommie's relative silence and Faulkner's rapt attention and sensitivity to Vardaman's language.

A third-person objective narrator recounts to the reader Tommie's theft but gives more attention to his miniature body, taking care to describe his "gaping shoe [wherein] there appeared an array of tiny toes" or how his "little form curved with pride" over the stolen fire engine ("OB," 167, 170). In this sketch, Tommie only speaks seven times and only to repeat the same slightly modified phrases: "Well, le' me play wif it?" and "It's mine!" (169). The allure of mimetic objects moves Tommie to speak and to act outside of the claustrophobic tenements. (Noteworthy is the fact that he does not speak within the other two sketches, both of which largely take place within the shadows of the tenements.)

Crane's insistence on Tommie's near silence contrasts with Faulkner's insistence on the intricacies of Vardaman's language. The developments of modernist modes of representation, specifically stream-of-consciousness narration, allow the reader to read the child in poverty differently by accessing their thoughts. Useful here is Allred's application of Ástráður Eysteinsson's discussion of the ways in which modernist texts force an engagement between the reader and the text, what Eysteinsson calls an "aesthetics of interruption": "[T]he modernist text appears to its reader as a kinked chain of signifiers whose sense must be teased out through a painstaking interpretive process. Modernism, in this light, is an insubordinate mode of expression that frustrates the expectations readers develop through everyday engagement with the language of bureaucracies and the mass media, thereby rendering the usually unconscious protocol by which language makes sense to us as a problem, as an object of analysis." Drawing on Roland Barthes and Walter Benjamin, Eysteinsson argues that modernist texts are "coauthored in some sense by reader and writer, both of whom generate a contingent set of meanings from a fragmentary world/text." An aesthetics of interruption argues that the text (or the image) is a site of struggle that holds the potential for multiple readings, or what Allred calls "aesthetic construction in the subjunctive mood, one that recruits readers in a shared project of thinking through plausible pasts, presents, and futures."[39]

Therefore, from within the modernist stream-of-consciousness narration of Vardaman emerges an aesthetics of interruption that juxtaposes—at the very least—the vivid interior world of the child in poverty and the oppressive weight of the external world, the context in which the reader must read the child and their language. In other words, Vardaman sees the red train as already his, though it is behind glass, but the reader knows that the red train has little chance of ever being his. The glass might as well be impermeable. Where Crane carefully controls the reader's gaze and tidily frames Tommie's red fire engine within a middle-class world exempt from the child's familiar and colorless tenements, Faulkner sets before the reader multiple layers of narration, awareness, and language, and the reader must find a way to piece those discourses together. The premodern work of Crane is, to borrow Allred's metaphors, written in the indicative mood, where the radical modernism of Faulkner occupies the subjunctive; both, however, place before the reader the limitations inherent in the parameters of the poor child's world, as well as insist that the reader see the child's efforts to resist such parameters.[40]

The Unexpected Discourse of Faulkner's Vardaman

Faulker's *As I Lay Dying* demonstrates the possibilities within modernism to insist on the capacity of the child in poverty. Allred's definition of modernism, a radical realism that increases the capacity of "modes of representation," draws the reader's attention to the ways in which such representations are constructed and navigated. Within the novel, Faulkner invites the reader to explore the Bundrens through each character's stream-of-consciousness narration.[41] Though Faulkner attends to the anti-language of each member of the family, his attention to Vardaman's place in the margins of the family's narrative brings forward not only the vulnerability but also the capacity of the child.

Vardaman's first narrative section illustrates this clearly. Within the quoted dialogue, short, fragmentary sentences built of repetitive slang and occasional swearing occur once every few paragraphs in ways that mimic the syntax and diction of the other Bundrens. The contrast between the sensitive and intricate language of the interior monologue versus the rough and staccato verbal speech quoted there is, for many readers, one of the most discomfiting contrasts of the novel. Surely the child who says the word "kilt" four times in four sentences totaling only thirteen words cannot also be the child who uses words such as "integrity" and "ammoniac" within one sentence of fifty-four words (*AILD*, 54–56)? As do many others, I build from Dorothy J. Hale's explanation: "Faulkner [. . .] establishes a spectrum of symbolic meaning for narrative discourse. Quoted dialogue represents the most extreme public expression; it stands as an objective record of a character's public language. First-person narration that is composed and mimetic shows the integration of the private and public self; the self represents its experiences to itself in public language. Mimetic stream-of-consciousness represents what a character might say if he could compose his thoughts. Private language, wholly unsayable language, is figured by nonmimetic vocabulary and tone." This "stylized representation of consciousness" is one way Faulkner radicalized realism, crafting prose that conveys that which representational dialogue cannot. And while Hale's essay does not fully consider the complications of class, she reads the novel as demonstrating a "struggle against the normative power of social language."[42]

I read the raw and unprocessed nuances within the language of Vardaman as anti-language, which responds to previous scholarship in an effort to be more aligned with Faulkner's expressed intent. Faulkner treats the child with such sensitivity that his enigmatic words are allowed to stand alone as a chapter: "My mother is a fish" (*AILD*, 84). And as the narrative unfolds and Faulkner entrusts to Vardaman more chapters of narration, his place in the novel's margins becomes more visible. Through metaphor and associative syntax, Vardaman questions, speculates, and synthesizes as he works through his understandings of loss. Because of Faulkner's experimental modernist language, the reader is privy to this process within a child who oscillates between language nearly incoherent—"and then I can cry then I vomit the crying" (54)—and language copied from the others in his family.

It is imperative to note that Vardaman does not narrate until after his mother's death. Addie's death takes place within the fifth section of Darl's narration, and the first of Vardaman's ten sections directly follows this account of Addie's passing. (Darl is the second oldest of the Bundren children.) The last sentence of Darl's section—"*Addie Bundren is dead*"—ends with no punctuation, serving as an open-ended simple sentence that the rest of the novel makes compound and complex as each Bundren articulates their response to this fact (*AILD*, 52, emphasis in the original). Akin to Tommie's aggressiveness yet narrated from first instead of third person, Vardaman's narrative entrance into the novel is both factual and lyrical. This section makes the reader painfully aware that Vardaman is a child, a child who cannot make literal sense of death. Within the first paragraph, for example, Vardaman worries that "[Addie] is getting so far ahead [that he] cannot catch her" (53). It is as though when, just a few pages earlier, Anse, Addie's husband, says to Dr. Peabody, "She's goin, is she?," Vardaman understands that at her death, his mother will go on a literal journey (45). Faulkner represents the questions Vardaman asks of his family in quick successive fashion, not explicitly identifying the speaker: "'Did she goes as far as town?' [. . .] 'Did all those rabbits and possums go further than town?'" (66). This child's experience with death is killing animals for food. His conclusion—"Why must [God] make a different place for them to go if she is just like a rabbit"—is logical according to his experience (66). Vardaman's incessant questioning, here and elsewhere in the novel, seems inane unless we understand that he is perpetually constructing a linguistic framework within which inexplicable events begin to make some sense.[43]

Nevertheless, the overwhelming majority of critical attention paid to Vardaman rests disproportionately on the five-word sentence that is the entirety of his third narrative section: "My mother is a fish" (*AILD*, 84). For some, the sentence is an illogical syllogism, a "youthful misapprehension."[44] Others find greater significance but disagree on what is signified. Is Vardaman's logic "in direct opposition to the dichotomy of words and meaning, speaking and doing expressed by Addie," as Benjamin Widiss argues, or is Vardaman, as

Mark Edelman Boren contends, "a simple Addie Bundren"?[45] Others read the sentence as a classic case of transference, while still others argue that Vardaman's repetition of the phrase deems him a "pathological figure."[46] More recently, Justin Mellette has reductively argued that Vardaman's earlier "desperate, impassioned thoughts [were] too difficult to sustain," and he "sinks instead into a bewildered trance regarding the belief that he played a role in his mother's demise."[47]

Collectively, these critical discussions of Vardaman's language almost exclusively begin and end with the enigmatic sentence, neglecting how Vardaman gains more narrative responsibility or how his language changes as the novel proceeds and, furthermore, dismissing and discounting these complex shifts as pathological. It is as though because the five words stand alone on the page, great effort has gone into filling the surrounding white space with explication of their significance. Yet Faulkner himself, on two separate occasions, erased the need for such interpretations. In May 1958 he explained the transference as "a child's rationalizing" with "no symbolism intended."[48] More extensively, he also explained that Vardaman says his five-word sentence because he was a "child [and] nobody had paid any attention to him. He saw things that baffled and puzzled him, and nobody—none of the adults would stop long enough to show him any tenderness, any affection[. . . .] He was a child trying to cope with this adult's world which to him was, and to any sane person, completely mad."[49] The inordinate amount of critical attention paid to this stand-alone sentence detracts from the variety of language Faulkner used to show Vardaman's interiority throughout the rest of the novel, as well as the complex way the child makes meaning through language here.

The first thing Vardaman does in response to his mother's death is to begin to relexicalize that which is new and unfamiliar. This happens largely through questions of semantics, what words mean and how they mean, a tension Vardaman (and others, Darl and Addie especially) revisits throughout the novel. After he flees from the room in which Addie has just died, for example, he stops at the place where earlier he had killed the fish. For Vardaman, "[i]t is cut up into pieces of not-fish now" (*AILD*, 53). By setting up "fish" and "not-fish" as relational antonyms, he insists that the two are opposites. He cannot grasp that when something is dead, it can still be what it was. Perhaps this is why Vardaman's language relies so heavily on metaphor in his earliest narrations. From "trees [that] look like chickens when they ruffle out into the cool dust on the hot days" to how in Jewel's horse "[t]he life [. . .] runs under the skin," the child's language requires the nuances of metaphor to parse the ways in which language works contrary to his literal experience (53, 54).

More than inane chatter, Vardaman's anti-language is imbibed with forms of thinking, acts of understanding, and dealings with reality that insist on a child who has a rich interiority but who is also increasingly aware of burdensome limits. Within the first two narrations of Vardaman, Faulkner carefully establishes the child's awareness of the family's poverty and displays the inner workings of his struggle for language to represent his experience and understanding. Susan Willis argues that while Vardaman's older sister, Dewey Dell, understands the family's class position, "Vardaman cannot yet know" that the toy train will remain behind the glass window in the Jefferson store.[50] While Vardaman still hopes for the train, he is also fully aware early in the novel of the difference between country boys and city boys, an awareness evidenced by the following passage:

> Dewey Dell said we will get some bananas. The train is behind the glass, red on the track. When it runs the track shines on and off. Pa said flour and sugar and coffee costs so much. Because I am a country boy because boys in town. Bicycles. Why do flour and sugar and coffee cost so much when he is a country boy. "Wouldn't you ruther have some bananas instead?" Bananas are gone, eaten. Gone. When it runs on the track shines again. "Why ain't I a town boy, pa?" I said. God made me. I did not said to God to made me in the country. If He can make the train, why cant He make them all in the town because flour and sugar and coffee. "Wouldn't you ruther have bananas?" (*AILD*, 65–66)

For Vardaman, class differences are obvious (one is either a country boy or a city boy, relational antonyms he categorizes as complementary), and class differences are illogical: He is not fooled by the offer of a banana, something that, once it has been consumed, is gone, nor does he understand why he was "made" in the country, something he did not request of God. Vardaman is all too aware of the restrictive limits pressed on him, yet he opposes them with his questions to others and his ability to draw on metaphors unique to him to grasp his shifting contexts. If Vardaman is aware that everyone needs flour and sugar and coffee and recognizes the inconsistency of making flour and sugar and coffee accessible only to town boys, then his question of birth (not as a Bundren but as a country boy) signifies an astute awareness of class for a young child.

It is tempting to argue that Vardaman's language by the end of the novel is broken or has regressed, an argument supported by a surface analysis of his syntax and the decreasing presence of figurative language in his later narrative sections (especially for the twenty-five pages, 206–31, when only he and Darl narrate and when Vardaman's narrative sections contain more of the family's dialogue and less of his internal thoughts). But in his final narration, he again begins to restructure the unfamiliar. The night after Addie's burial, Vardaman waits outside the drugstore for Dewey Dell. Some of the lyricism and metaphor returns in his stream-of-consciousness paragraphs, largely through his continued juxtaposition of rural and urban objects. One short paragraph, for example—"There is a light in the store, far back. In the window are two big glasses of soda water, red and green. Two men could not drink them. Two mules could not. Two cows could not" (*AILD*, 250)—demonstrates a logical progression of comparisons: Cows are bigger than mules, and mules are bigger than men, and none are big enough to, in tandem, drink the contents of the two glasses.

Metaphor also returns. Comparing two chicken metaphors, for example, one from his first narration and the other from his last, demonstrates this shift. In his first narration, "[t]he trees look like chickens when they ruffle out into the cool dust on the hot days" (*AILD*, 53); in his last, "[w]hile we walk the lights go around, roosting in the trees" (65–66, 250). In the first, both the tenor and the vehicle of the metaphor are rural objects; in the second, the tenor is urban and the vehicle is rural. Furthermore, the second vehicle is unstated, which demonstrates the child's great grasp of the involutions of his metaphor. What Vardaman's restructured metaphors demonstrate is that the pole of an electric light is as common to a town boy as the trunk and branches of a tree are to a country boy.

In other words, Vardaman's rural renderings of the urban would read as nonsense, illiteracy, or even a linguistic deficiency to town boys and their parents, but those renderings actually function as an anti-language for city life. For Jolene Hubbs, a rural modernism requires decentering urban spaces and people to make clear the ways in which the rural poor are often presented as obsolete in order to "establish a claim of radical and irrefutable cultural superiority" of urban whites.[51] Vardaman realizes at the end of the novel that city life is inaccessible to him. This realization is facilitated by Darl's arrest. To mourn the loss of Darl, the only brother the reader really witnesses conversing with the youngest of the Bundrens, Vardaman echoes his earlier refrain of labeling his brothers: "*Darl he went to Jackson is my brother Darl is my brother*" (*AILD*, 249, emphasis in the original). Each time this recontextualizing refrain repeats, Vardaman pushes further into that which now differentiates Darl from the rest of the family, whose names could be substituted for Darl's. Near the end of the narration, for example, Vardaman's thoughts elucidate the major difference between the rest of the Bundrens and Darl: "*He went to*

Jackson. He went crazy and went to Jackson both. Lots of people didn't go crazy. Pa and Cash and Jewel and Dewey Dell and me didn't go crazy. We never did go crazy. We didn't go to Jackson either. Darl" (251, emphasis in the original). We know that Vardaman mourns the loss of his brother, for Darl's absence seems so permanent when Vardaman comes to the conclusion that "*Jackson is further away than crazy*" (252, emphasis in the original).

The way Vardaman mourns the loss of his brother is syntactically knitted with his mourning of the train. In the same paragraphs throughout this section, back-to-back sentences move without transition between the two ideas. (Part of this seamless connection is that Darl is taken away on a train, a larger-than-life manifestation of Vardaman's fetish: "*I have not been on the train, but Darl has been on the train*" [*AILD*, 252, emphasis in the original].) At the beginning and the end of this section, Vardaman asks Dewey Dell to walk by the storefront with the train. Both times, however, she denies his request, the first time saying that the train will "be there [at] Christmas" and the second asking the rhetorical question, "Hadn't you rather have bananas?" (250, 252). Vardaman's answer to this question—"All right"—abruptly signifies his resignation, his acquiescence to the restrictive discursive practices always surrounding the train (252). Immediately following this two-word sentence is Vardaman's comparison that "*Jackson is further away than crazy*," which demonstrates that, to this child, that which he desires and loves is no longer within his reach. In a grotesque twist, only Darl has access to the train of the town boys.

After we witness the rich interiority of the poor child, we perceive his resignation as devastating. In the final scene of the novel, the reader sees Vardaman and Dewey Dell sitting in the wagon the next day waiting for Pa to return. They are, of course, silently eating bananas. At first, it seems as though pharmacy clerk Skeet MacGowan's earlier claim that "[h]alf the time [country people] dont know what they want, and the balance of the time they cant tell it to you" is correct (*AILD*, 243). Here sits Dewey Dell and Vardaman, neither obtaining what they desperately desired in town. Yet they know exactly what they want. Their journey to town, however, has taught them the futility of articulating said desires, so they sit silently.

As noted earlier, Willis reads this moment as indicative of that which "Dewey Dell understands, but Vardaman cannot yet know[:] neither of her brother's desires will be met and that bananas will be the convenient substitute," a substitute she claims "soft[ens] the hurt of his soul."[52] This reading neglects the awareness present in Vardaman from the beginning of the novel and lessens the gravity of his resignation. If any hope at all for the train remains—and there is no mention of the train after page 252, when Vardaman says, "All right"—it has been placed at the feet of Santa, who would probably have as hard a time accessing the Bundrens' hill as Dr. Peabody does.

Vardaman has learned to make meaning through language; however, that meaning will remain silent, an internal world of rural metaphors that, if articulated, would be characterized as inferior. In the trauma of his mother's death, the journey of the family and her corpse to Jefferson, and Darl's arrest, Vardaman's language does regress, if regression is measured mathematically by complexity of syntax and proportion of figurative language. But to dismiss that regression as a measure of awareness or intelligence or ability is to deny the child's capacity.

If anti-language "facilitate[s] an alternative social and conceptual reality for [its] speakers," what is conservative, then, about the anti-language Vardaman creates by the end of the novel is that it acquiesces to the role the nation perpetually assigns to the rural poor in the South.[53] We are left wondering if Vardaman's realization of class differences, that "flour and sugar and coffee cost so much when he is a country boy," will grow up to become Anse's ironic observation that "[i]t takes them that runs the stores in the towns, doing no sweating, living off of them that sweats" or something else entirely (*AILD*, 66, 110).

For Fowler, because a "novel is consumed largely by a literate middle-class readership, [. . .] the novelist who chooses to depict a deviant hero or minor character knows that their voices, and the world-views which they project, are going to be perceived as alien, as objects for inspection rather than subjects for sympathy."[54] The anti-language of Vardaman, therefore, is doubly removed, as he is both poor and a child. Furthermore, the counter-narrative he articulates by the novel's end—class rigidity—offers a critique of our national narrative of social mobility. Yet while Vardaman offers this critique, the fact that the novel ends with his silent consumption of the banana makes his awareness a discordant lack. Faulkner's Vardaman does not steal the red train, rise out of poverty, move to the city, or organize his siblings against the town boys; instead, his stream-of-consciousness narration is a radical representation of the deafening silence of the rural poor child aware of the parameters of his poverty. Yet by endowing the child with anti-language, Faulkner upholds Vardaman's capacity for speech, for metaphor, and for creative self-expression through whatever patchwork means are at hand. And the reader, in reading with a willingness to pause in the discordant language of Vardaman, has also realized Vardaman's ability to creatively respond and restructure language to begin to make sense of the grotesque chaos of being poor. Because the reader now knows Vardaman's interiority—a mind that is inventive, yearning, questioning—his silence at the end of the novel is all the more disquieting.

There are two common yet oversimplified ways of thinking about class positions in America: first, as just and deserved, and second, as irrevocable, permanent, and hopeless. Neither serves us well. Faulkner, I believe, had a hard time resolving those tensions, which live powerfully within the character of Vardaman. Ted Atkinson's *Faulkner and the Great Depression: Aesthetics, Ideology, and Cultural Politics* (2006) offers us the generative methodology of "approaching the political Faulkner by accepting, rather than trying to resolve, the dialectical forces of contradiction, thus reading his texts as sites of intense ideological negotiation and political struggle."[55] What resistance is available to the child in poverty here? Through Vardaman, Faulkner demonstrates that class consciousness alone does not shift systems of oppression. But language offers an entry point, a means through which to resist.

The last we know of Vardaman is that he is eating a banana. He has not mentioned the train again. Surely, though, he will be the one to introduce Dewey Dell's baby to how "the trees look like chickens when they ruffle out" (*AILD*, 53). More than inane chatter, Vardaman's modernist anti-language insists on the child's capacity.

Caldwell's Curious Concomitance of Beauty and the Grotesque

There are remarkably tidy parallels between Caldwell's grotesque Lesters and Faulkner's grotesque Bundrens. These parallels are not only grotesque but also gendered. Caldwell's Jeeter Lester and Faulkner's Anse Bundren bemoan the injustices of Southern farming. Jeeter is unwilling to give up farming and is highly critical of the rich, who have "got all the money that ought to be spread out among us all and won't turn it loose and give me some credit to get seed-cotton and guano with."[56] Though the Bundrens are not starving, as the Lesters are, Anse is likewise critical of the fact that "[n]owhere in this sinful world can a honest, hardworking man profit. It takes them that runs the stores in the towns, doing no sweating, living off of them that sweats" (*AILD*, 110). *Tobacco Road* portrays its patriarch as sitting, and Anse is immobile as well, his humped back, splayed feet, and hands "awkward as a claw" unable to perform labor (52). Both of the matriarchs of these novels are obsessed with dying: Caldwell's Ada "was usually surprised to wake up in the morning and discover that she was still alive" (*TR*, 71), and Faulkner's Addie believes "the reason for living was to get ready to stay dead a long time" (*AILD*, 169). Ada bears seventeen children and Addie seven, personal narratives of production also marked with loss. The Lesters' history on tobacco road, a seventy-five-year stretch that began with "the most desirable soil in the entire west-central part of Georgia" (*TR*, 63), becomes the same land that consumed the bodies of Ada's five deceased children: "The children who had died were buried in different parts of the farm. The land had been plowed over since their deaths, and as the graves were unmarked, no one would have known where to look for them if he had wanted to find them" (66). Hope in a better life is conspicuously absent from these narratives. None of the Bundrens talk about leaving, and leaving seems an option not available to the Lesters remaining after the fire. Faulkner's use of the grotesque seems so restrained only when juxtaposed with Caldwell's writings.[57]

A notable difference, however, between these novels is the curious absence of thirteen-year-old Pearl (Lester) Bensey, a character who is central to the plot of *Tobacco Road* but, because of how Caldwell structures the novel, who is never physically present in its scenes of unfolding chaos. The plot begins, in fact, because of her silence. It takes the first four chapters to tell the happenings of one particular afternoon at the Lesters' house when their son-in-law, Lov Bensey, walks by with a bag of turnips. Though Lov comes with the intent of soliciting Jeeter's help—or at least his permission—to "tie Pearl in the bed" so his marriage can be consummated, his requests are ignored, as Jeeter steals Lov's bag of turnips while Lov is seduced by Pearl's older sister, Ellie May, whose "harelip" Jeeter had been going to have "sewed together" for the last fifteen years but "had not yet got around to doing it" (*TR*, 6, 21). These beginning chapters not only establish the grotesque as the rule, not the exception, but also provide the backstory for Lov's disturbing request. "[O]nly twelve" the previous summer, Pearl is purchased by Lov for "some quilts and nearly a gallon of cylinder oil, besides [...] all of a week's pay, which was seven dollars" (25). Yet, much to Lov's dismay, Pearl neither talks to him nor sleeps in the same bed with him. Caldwell's usually affectless and occasionally omniscient narrator presents to the reader Lov's cruelties to Pearl casually: "Lov asked Pearl questions, he kicked her, he poured water over her, he threw rocks and sticks at her, and he did everything else he could think of that he thought might make her talk to him. She cried a lot, especially when she was seriously hurt, but Lov did not consider that as conversation. He wanted her to ask him if his back were sore, and when was he going to get his hair cut, and when was it going to rain again. But Pearl would not say anything" (3). The narrator also records Lov's kindnesses, such as "buy[ing] her a pretty" or snuff on pay days (3). After all, "[h]e had tried everything that he could think of so far, except force, and he was still determined to make her act as he thought a wife should" (5).

Again, Pearl is never physically present in the novel's scenes, and she does not speak. In fact, after the first four chapters she is not mentioned for over 150 pages. Pearl, who "became more beautiful day by day," remains an absence whose body is devoid of the grotesque markings of poverty her siblings and parents casually wear (*TR*, 25). For Lov, "[i]t would have been impossible for her to dress herself, or even to disfigure herself, in a way that would make her plain or ordinary-looking" (25). Though her different patrimony is offered as the reason for not only her blond hair and blue eyes but how she "had far more sense than any of the Lesters" (31), and Lov's eight months of rations made possible her addition of three to four inches and fifteen pounds, she still grew up in a house that "[w]hen the roof leaked, the Lesters moved from one corner of the room to another" and was born of a mother whose body is ill with pellagra (7). Why is Pearl so decidedly not grotesque? Why is she silent? Is it her age? Or is Lov's request for Jeeter's permission to, essentially, tie her up and rape her too grotesque for Caldwell?

For Denning, the grotesque "wrench[es] us out of the repose and distance of the 'aesthetic.'"[58] This supports Jones's claim that the "1930s may have been the decade in which the 'luxurious' and 'aesthetic' functions of literature came to seem most inappropriate in the face of widespread suffering," which, ironically, allows writers to move "*toward* the aesthetic significance of poverty—its power as a category to structure literary technique and to provide the foundation for theories of representation."[59] If, according to Goodwin, the grotesque facilitates understanding otherwise lost, then melding Denning's and Jones's premise that the grotesque is defined as the opposite of the aesthetic, or in other words, beauty, demonstrates that Caldwell's use of the grotesque depends on beauty existing only as a lack or absence, a duality that allegorizes the tension between the two—the distorted, fragmented, and excessive juxtaposed with the poised, symmetrical, and balanced.

We see this in "Rachel," a 1933 short story in Caldwell's short story collection *We Are the Living* narrated by Frank, a middle-class boy whose paper route funds his nightly date to the movies or ice cream with the title character. Rachel secretly eats dinner each night from the garbage can behind Frank's family's home, and the fact that her poverty largely exists outside of Frank's narrative reach sets up the ironic climax of the story: Frank's mother asks him to put rat poison in their garbage can, which results in Rachel's death during one of their dates. Most disturbing, however, is not Rachel's death but Caldwell's grotesque and carefully framed presentation of it, overtly drawing the reader's attention to the act of seeing the child. Frank watches the poisoned Rachel drink water in a drugstore mirror by looking at "Rachel's beauty [. . .] revealed in a way that only a large mirror can show."[60] As Rachel suffers, the reader must endure two cumbersome paragraphs ruminating on "a new and unrevealed charm in the sinuous grace of her breasts," a "charm that had lain undiscovered and unseen during all the time [Frank] had known her" ("R," 68, 69). Frank's discovery, unseen before, is facilitated by the "mysterious roundness rising from [Rachel's] body," a stomach bloated with poison (69). As "her face [becomes] more contorted and darker each moment," the prescription clerk forces the antidote "down her throat," and the grotesque displaces her beauty (71, 70).

As Frank walks home after the ambulance takes away a Rachel "with enough rat poison in her system to kill ten men," he cries, and though he "could not see the lights and shadows of the streets, [he] could see with a painful clarity the picture of Rachel, in a huge mirror, bending over [his] garbage can while the reflection of a unique beauty in her sinuous breasts burned in [his] brain and in [his] heart" ("R," 72). The "frightened child far from home" in the first paragraph of the story has become the focal point of a grotesque and framed tableau in the last. In the odd conflation of body parts—eyes, breasts, brain, heart—only the breasts are Rachel's, and the garbage can she is bent over does not lessen their effect.

What are we to make of the final paragraph? Should we see ourselves in Frank's middle-class sexualization of a "frightened child far from home"? Or should we sympathize with the memory of Rachel, forever bent over garbage? I argue that Caldwell wants us to realize that the only Rachel we see in the last paragraph is, quite literally, a mirrored projection of poverty that both repels and titillates. She is no more real than Frank's beginning-of-story definition of poverty as meaning one "wears the same dress" ("R," 60). Her poverty makes her beauty, in Frank's words, "unique": amatory yet haunting (72). Furthermore, the language used by Rachel throughout the short story (Rachel speaks only to tell Frank to "never try to find where [she lives]" and to insist that she must have a drink of water) is ignored by Caldwell's young narrator (60). The tension between a naive middle-class voyeur and a subject compromised by a systemic lack of voice is echoed in the story's not-so-balanced use of both the aesthetic, or beauty, and the grotesque.

With both Rachel and Pearl, Caldwell created an impoverished girl whose beauty positions her within the narrative as desirable; however, she is grotesquely silenced. In her discussion of Caldwell, Sylvia Jenkins Cook argues that the "uneasiness of most readers in the presence of a genuinely grotesque mode of vision and their consequent need to resolve paradoxes, resist confusion, and force incongruity into congruous categories is, of course, a measure of the successful operation of that mode."[61] What becomes fascinating, then, is the eighty years of critical silence regarding Pearl, the character I would argue most disturbingly presents—to borrow Sylvia Jenkins Cook's words—paradox, confusion, and incongruity. Pearl's curious absence from *Tobacco Road* dislocates the novel's center in a way that invites the reader to project her presence. In fact, Jack Kirkland's 1934 three-act adaptation of the novel does just that. As a play, Kirkland's *Tobacco Road* found unparalleled success with 3,182 Broadway performances in seven and a half Depression-era years.[62] The play became more comic the longer it ran, and though Caldwell approved the script, he was "perplexed by the excessive laughter" of the audience.[63]

Some of the differences in the play's adaptation of the novel streamline its narrative arc, such as bits of the novel's narration becoming dialogue so the audience has convenient access to plot points or character development. Before Lov enters the play, for example, we learn all the backstory necessary to understand the play's central conflicts: Pearl's tendency toward silence, Ada's one-time affair with Pearl's real father, and Ada's premarital advice to Pearl to run away. Some changes lessen the severity and grotesqueness of the novel, such as Lov trying to hug Pearl—"hold her for a minute"—the morning she runs away instead of "throw[ing] her down on the bed" to tie her up. Other changes, however, completely shift the plot of the play. First, Pearl's characterization changes dramatically. Kirkland ages her, noting in the stage directions that "[s]he looks at least sixteen, in spite of the fact that she is much less than that, and is almost as tall as Ada," as well as having Jeeter claim, "She's most a grown woman by now" while moving her dress to "the better to see her figure."[64] This is a sharp contrast to Caldwell's insistence on Pearl's smallness, much like Faulkner's characterization of Vardaman, who is small enough to be put "to bed in [a] trough" during the journey to Jackson (*AILD*, 117).[65] In the novel, Lov admits that Pearl is "still a little girl," even though "she was gaining in weight and height every day," but there is never a mention of her pubescent figure (*TR*, 4).

In addition to her presence onstage (Pearl runs home before running away to Augusta), the most notable of Kirkland's changes to Pearl is her language, a change paralleled in Ada's character. Both texts make clear that Pearl is like Ada, who also did not talk at the age of "twelve or thirteen." And in the novel, Caldwell writes as though Pearl has inherited a heritage of silence. In the play, however, Ada speaks aggressively, early, and often, a sharp contrast. Almost all her dialogue reveals her singular love of Pearl and desire for her to go to Augusta and not "stay here like your old Ma, raising a raft of children and no snuff to calm you when there ain't nothing to eat."[66]

Kirkland takes care to nurture this sentimental mother-daughter relationship. Ada is, in fact, the only character to whom Pearl speaks, sentences slightly more than the "barest of negatives and affirmatives" she is said to have once spoken to Ada before the events of the novel take place. In act 3 of the play, however, Pearl confesses to Ada her fear of going to Augusta and her desire to "stay here with you." Ada insists that Pearl could have "a hat to put on and shoes and dresses to wear like the gals in Augusta," to which Pearl replies, "I don't want none."[67] The play's middle-class viewer would likely read this moment with great sympathy: Who wouldn't want the beautiful Pearl to escape the rapacious Lov and the life of breeding Ada endured? By rewriting Caldwell's narrative to make Pearl come home before going to Augusta, Kirkland carefully employed sentimental tropes, "calibrating and adjusting the sensations of the [viewer] in finely tuned and predictable responses to what is viewed or read" to create right feeling.[68] The tensions between the impoverished and grotesque characters and the middle-class play-going audience require that difference be pronounced.

The grotesque, however, disrupts these moments of sentimentality. For example, Ada's final action of the play, to bite Jeeter's arm that is holding Pearl captive, frees Pearl to flee. The difference between Ada and the mothers in Kirkland's audience now exacerbates differences of class. In his 1997 *The American Stage and the Great Depression*, Mark Fearnow describes the cultural power of *Tobacco Road* as "downward conversion." "Throughout the play," he argues, "the dreaded scenes of poverty and dehumanization that haunted the people of the depression were invoked, and then pressed to the point of absurdity[, thus renaming them] as silliness and folly."[69] Though Fearnow's claim holds true when we consider the grotesque moments of the play, it neglects to consider the power of sympathy created by Kirkland's choice to give the audience an embodied yet vulnerable Pearl who speaks. The very real fear of a parent's inability to care for and protect their child during the Depression creates the desired sympathetic response. The bond of mother and daughter facilitates the coming together of difference (poor child character and middle-class playgoer), which gives the play its sentimental power. Right feeling triumphs with Pearl's escape.

Kirkland's sentimental resurrection of Pearl provides insight into the response of American culture to Pearl's absence in Caldwell's novel. I argue that the sheer popularity of the play affirms a reading of Pearl's original silence that fits comfortably into the audience's desire to find difference between the Lesters and themselves. Kirkland's *Tobacco Road* fleshes out the character of Pearl as a poor dependent child without the desire to leave her impoverished mother. And this, after all, allows the audience to rest assured that, if left alone, the Pearls of the South will stay on tobacco roads. They can feel sorry for Pearl's circumstances, but the grotesqueness of the Lesters makes such debilitating poverty seem very far from the real-life problems that will greet them when they return home after the play.

Caldwell's Pearl is much more complicated. At the end of the first paragraph of the play's stage directions, Kirkland sets the mood of the play with the following sentences: "Grim humor pervades all, stalking side by side with tragedy on the last short mile which leads to complete, eventual elimination. The pride and hope of a once aggressive group, pioneers in a great new world, thus meet ironic conclusion. The world moves on, *unmindful of their ghosts*."[70] To apply the metaphor, Caldwell's Pearl is a ghost and Kirkland's is not. Could this be Caldwell's rationale? Pearl's absence represents, on the one hand, a state of childhood innocence and purity, an aesthetic that the reader cannot fathom within the context of the Lester's grotesque poverty. This prompts the reader to acknowledge what narrative they project onto Pearl. Conversely, Pearl's absence allows Caldwell to make a very concrete claim, a subtle yet perceptible illustration of how the grotesque defines itself by banishing beauty.

Pearl never speaks. She is the heiress of Ada's heritage of silence, a silence broken only in the last decade by the "[h]unger [that] loosened her tongue" (*TR*, 2, 3). Jeeter does not "recommend [to Lov] the starving of Pearl, because he knew she would go somewhere to beg food, and would get it" (3). Thus, in her eight months of marriage to Lov, Pearl has not been without food. Perhaps this difference, the basic human need of sustenance, provides Pearl with the recourse to silence that her mother's starvation forced Ada to abandon. According to Fowler, speakers of anti-language are typically seen as "'deviant,' or 'criminal' or 'deficient.'" Pearl's lack of language in *Tobacco Road* is assuredly viewed by readers as a deficiency, by definition a lack or shortage. Yet her lack of language, because it is a *choice*, constitutes her silence as a "medium of negotiation."[71] After all, it is through her silence that she negotiates with Lov the parameters of their marriage: He provides sufficient food and shelter, and she "fix[es] herself up, woman-like," but refuses his requests for sex and conversation (169).

Discussing the ethical roles of literary critics, Nikita Dhawan's essay "Hegemonic Listening and Subversive Silences: Ethical-Political Imperatives" provides a useful ethics of representation that argues that silence "is a practice of confrontation, a 'counter-discourse'":

> It can function as a variation in the eternal repetition of discourses by causing a rupture in language, a subversion that turns language against itself. It is not just that one is silenced and thereby rendered invisible; rather, one can strategically choose to be silent by boycotting discourses, by refusing to participate in them. Ironically, dominant discourses require counter-discourses to continually reinforce and strengthen their hegemony. Silence is not necessarily a passive act of submission or repression. It can be a challenge to the monologue of dominant discourses that ruptures the power play between speakers and listeners, and creates conducive conditions for the "invisible," the "unsaid" to emerge.[72]

If we apply Dhawan's explication of the political power of silence to Fowler's work on anti-language, then we can conclude that Pearl "mean[s] differently" because she is not only poor but also a child in poverty. Anti-language is not just verbal play; it must also "facilitate an alternative social and conceptual reality for [its] speakers." Pearl's life of silence creates a reality in which she can, at least for now, survive. Caldwell's grotesque exaggeration of her silence is not a form of hegemonic control or a means of relegating the child to the margins. Instead, Pearl's silence is a way of drawing the reader's attention to the way they see and listen to a child in poverty. If we again reframe Dhawan's counter-discourse with Fowler's concepts of anti-language, then Pearl's silence makes plain "the limitations of readers' knowledge."[73]

While Faulkner allows the reader to see Vardaman's linguistic complexities, Caldwell only allows two paragraphs of access to Pearl's thoughts. A careful reading of her silence, however, opens possibilities for ethical reading. In his discussion of anti-language in literature, Fowler is careful to emphasize that access to the speaker's "alternative reality" is not the goal of anti-language. Instead, anti-language reveals "the antithetical logic of the relationship between an official and an unofficial voice: an unresolved, unmediated, antithesis which preserves a critical, dialogic openness in the novel's examination of its central ethical or social or psychological (or whatever) concerns."[74] In other words, Pearl's anti-language, her silence, operates as a mode of resistance largely because no one is listening to what she might have to say.

Pearl's silence is her means of survival, a subversive act of resistance.[75] While Lov claims that Pearl did not "[know] what he was talking about" when he told her that "cows were not any good until they had been freshened," it is clear that

Pearl understands her corporeal capital as a blond-haired, blue-eyed member of the Lester family (*TR*, 5, 4). After she runs away, for example, Lov tells Jeeter that she "always took a long time to fix herself up, woman-like" (169). Earlier in the novel in a moment akin to Frank seeing Rachel in the drugstore mirror, Lov measures Pearl's beauty by the way others see her. "For that matter," the narrator says, "no man who had ever had the opportunity of seeing Pearl had ever gone away without thinking the same thing," that "there was not a more beautiful girl anywhere in the world" (25). Pearl's beauty ensures her physical survival, but her silence preserves the body fed because of Lov's sexual desire. Pearl is a child from the lowest of class positions, and most of her choices are made for her. Jeeter's choice to give Pearl to Lov in a perverse reverse dowry is the most egregious example. Yet Caldwell's decision for Pearl to make three formidable choices signifies a fight for autonomy facilitated by a self-awareness that few expect of her.

Pearl's first choice is her aforementioned silence, the decision to "rarely open her mouth from the beginning of one day to the next" (*TR*, 2). Sylvia Jenkins Cook's observation that the Lesters are "a family of people so dominated by primitive instincts that even their most human faculty, that of language, has become no more than a chanting chorus of obsessions that are themselves at odds with the people's behavior" adds more legitimacy to Pearl's unity of silence and action. She is more self-aware than her parents and remaining siblings. Her second choice, to deny Lov the "benefits" of marriage, reinforces this claim (8). Ada cautions Pearl to "run away from [Lov] before she began bearing children," and Pearl both subtly ("always looking off into another direction when he came and stood in front of her" to see her pale blue eyes) and overtly ("fight[ing] back so fiercely whenever he attempted to catch her" that he needs Jeeter's help to catch her) resists his advances (30, 5, 6). Cook argues that what Lov "really wants is to have a more complete communion with the golden-haired child," not just sex.[76] While Cook's observation that Lov's desire to have conversations with Pearl is important and, I would add, complicates Caldwell's use of the grotesque in the novel, Cook's reading lessens the horror of Pearl's impending rape. It is, after all, when Lov "throw[s] her down on the bed [to] tie her up with some plow-lines to see if [he] could do it" that Pearl runs away, not when he watches her brush her hair or tries to make conversation (167). Running away, Pearl's third choice, reads as a stark contrast to the casualness with which many of her brothers and sisters left tobacco road, "as though they were only walking down to the coal chute to see the freight trains" (6). We certainly end up knowing a lot about the character who, for the entirety of the novel, never speaks and is never seen. Pearl's absence forces us to realize that we don't witness any of her other forms of communication.

Perhaps this is why, in a rare moment of omniscience, for only two paragraphs at the beginning of chapter 4, Caldwell's narrator gives us brief access to Pearl's thoughts. Caldwell's choice of *Tobacco Road*'s narrator is a key difference in the novel and his earlier short story "Rachel," which is narrated by a middle-class boy. "[I]n the tradition of realism and naturalism, a focus on the poor without a middle class narrator as mediator" allows this rare moment of insight into Pearl's motivations.[77] These two paragraphs give voice to Pearl's silence as well as her eventual choice to run away. The reader learns that she is afraid of "what would happen to her in the cotton mills, [for] she was too young to understand the things she heard about life there" (*TR*, 30–31). She is afraid of the dark and spends most nights crying and "trembling on her pallet on the floor" (31). This fear, an "unbearable feeling of strangulation," she "had never told any one" (31). Yet "after eight months in the house with Lov she had gradually grown braver" and thinks of running away to Augusta (31). Caldwell seems to suggest that Pearl's silence and sexual refusal of Lov enables Pearl to "[begin] to lose some of her fear" (31).

Perhaps the greatest insight we can glean from the second of these paragraphs is why Pearl runs away: "She had been to Augusta once with Jeeter and Ada, and had seen with her own eyes girls who were laughing and carefree. She did not know whether they worked in the cotton mills, but it made little difference to her. Down there on the tobacco road no one ever laughed. Down there girls had to chop cotton in the summer, pick it in the fall, and cut fire-wood in winter" (*TR*, 31). Pearl desires pleasure—to laugh. Jeeter seems to think that she ran away, like her sisters, because she wanted "stylish clothes," but the fact that she was not swayed by Lov's gifts of a weekly "pretty" (calico, snuff, or "green beads on a long string") suggests that those things were not her motivation (168, 3, 171). What she noticed about the girls in Augusta was not their clothing but their countenance. She understands that the laughing girls in Augusta most likely work in the mills, but she sees a great difference in mill work and work on tobacco road. For Pearl, life away from tobacco road has the possibility of laughter. For a novel known for its grotesque irony, it is of note that part of what Pearl seems intent on avoiding, the inevitable childbearing Ada warns her about, has been her sister Lizzie Belle's reality seven times already. Lizzie Belle was "the last one to leave home" to work in the cotton mills (66). Though Pearl actively resists a life of tobacco road poverty, certainly Caldwell suspects that circumstances similar to Lizzie Belle's await Pearl in Augusta.

In her essay "Poetry, Injury, and the Ethics of Reading," Elaine Scarry proposes that there are three ways that "literature has in fact helped to diminish acts of injuring": first, "its invitation to empathy" (not the act of generating compassion "but rather the capacity of literature to exercise and reinforce our recognition that there *are* other points of view in the world, and to make this recognition a powerful mental habit"); second, "its reliance on deliberative thought" or, in other words, to "think counterfactually, to think the notion that one does not oneself hold to be the case"; and third, "its beauty." For Scarry, beauty is again a tripartite construction. First, it has "attributes—such as symmetry, vivacity, unity—that anticipate those same but much more difficult to achieve attributes in the realm of justice"; second, it brings us pleasure but also draws our attention to our position away from the center, for "[f]eeling acute pleasure at finding oneself on the margins is a first step in working toward fairness"; and third, it reminds us of our "capacity [to create,] a prerequisite for justice." If beauty can have ethical power, the power to benefit "other, often unknown, persons" because we are reminded that "part of our interior remains capable of change," then Caldwell's observance that beauty has the power to be transformative reframes his use of the grotesque to disrupt.[78]

Forced at the beginning of the novel and chosen at its end, Pearl's absence is, in essence, Caldwell's ghost: banished beauty that stands outside and against the grotesque, that makes the grotesque all the more evident. Lov's crude self-restraint and his alternative, a startlingly civil discourse of discussing with Jeeter "whether it was advisable from the practical side, since Jeeter had had to contend with Ada for almost a lifetime," are, then, reactions to Pearl's beauty (*TR*, 5). Caldwell's insistence in both "Rachel" and *Tobacco Road* on the curious concomitance of beauty and the grotesque seems, at the very least, to suggest that beauty cannot be sustained within the context of poverty, that the grotesque supplants beauty because such poverty is unjust, imbalanced, and unnatural.

Are we to read Caldwell's pattern of silencing beauty, of covering the wound of poverty with the distractions of the grotesque in the ways that the long-running dramatic adaptation of the novel did, as a laughable erasure of suffering and silence? While Faulkner's concern is with the interiority of the child, Caldwell's purpose is displaying that which keeps us from even approaching the interiority of the poor child. Caldwell's inability to write the child's interiority shows us, according to Scarry's ethics of reading, that we must acknowledge the fact that beauty (that which is just, balanced, and natural) cannot exist side by side with the grotesque.

Because Caldwell so carefully presents beauty to (yet withholds beauty from) the reader—the mirrored tableau of Rachel and the way the reader must project a narrative onto Pearl's absence—he continually draws our attention to the ineptitude of our response to such suffering, for just as happened in the adapted play, confronting the grotesqueness of poverty becomes something we avoid, preferring instead laughter.

The fiction of Faulkner and Caldwell intentionally combats the belief that the autonomy of the poor Southern child is compromised by a systemic lack of voice by creating children who are both aware of their poverty and actively engaged in language that resists the injustice of their class position. The silences of these children create authentic fictions of the real. Collectively, their silence—for Vardaman the silence that comes with resignation and for Pearl the subversive silence of choice—makes audible not only the debilitating effects of the language formation of the poor but also and foremost the isolation of the child in poverty and their supposedly ineffectual means of resistance. Furthermore, the gradations in the rhetorical silences of these literary children demonstrate the difficulty of assigning language that begins to imagine the interiority, the complexity of a life in poverty. After all, Rachel's and Pearl's beauty is, to a large extent, wellness fostered by enough to eat.

CHAPTER TWO

Discourses of Play and Control

Ralph Ellison's essay "What These Children Are Like," a lecture given during a seminar titled Education for Culturally Different Youth in 1963 in Massachusetts, questions the application of the label "culturally deprived" to Black youth and instead asserts that they are "products of a different cultural complex." What unfolds within Ellison's essay functions as an introduction to the workings of anti-language within the language of Black youth. Contrary to the belief that "these kids have no capacity to manipulate the language," Ellison finds that the "question is how [one gets] this skill into the mainstream of the language." "How can we keep the discord flowing into the mainstream of the language without destroying it?" he asks. It must be forced to "sound and bend under the pressure of their need to express their sense of the real."[1]

Ellison attended this October seminar at the invitation of the federal government's Office of Science and Technology and to support the work of the Panel on Educational Research and Development. There is much to say about the seminar and, more broadly, educational reforms across the twentieth century that were designed in response to "kids who live in urban and rural slums, who go to poor schools and who, in the old days used to be known as the lower class, [and who] are not the middle class color," language those organizing the seminar used. For the purposes of this chapter, however, the early working titles for the event (from Seminar on Education for the Difficult 30 Percent to Seminar on Education for the Culturally Deprived Youth) and the final decision (Seminar on Education for Culturally Different Youth) give context to the prevailing narratives Ellison was countering in his remarks.[2]

Near the end of the lecture, Ellison claimed that Black idiom "exists precisely because Negroes need words which will communicate, which will designate the objects, the processes, the manners and subtleties" of Black culture.[3] Such discord is at the heart of anti-language, language that by definition exists "in an *antagonistic* relationship to the dominant culture."[4] Richard Wright, an early mentor of Ellison, took up this question of writing discord into mainstream language within his 1944 autobiography, *Black Boy*. As does Gavin Jones in his discussion of Wright's book, I want to confront the misconception of poverty's ability "to restrict the accrual of cultural capital and the attainment of tools that might enable its literary reputation." In his discussion of Wright's use of hunger as a focalizing trope that is both negative and positive, for example, Jones comes to the following conclusion: "The important point for Wright's theory of representation is that an individual can bear the scars of social suffering yet still have the capacity to depict this traumatic situation not because poverty is comprehended rationally but because its irrationality and damage, its bewilderment, are confronted and communicated."[5] My efforts differ from Jones's because I analyze Wright's language choices to convey such an understanding, an understanding ripe for anti-language.

Helpful here is Brooks Hefner's work to define a vernacular modernism, "a language of the streets" that "emphasizes the encounters between and across language marked by class, race, and ethnicity and normally considered out of the purview of elite literary language." Where Hefner rightfully "[highlights] the experimental power of working-class and ethnic language to transform literary representations," I argue that the concept of anti-language helps amplify the tensions between discourse communities.[6] For Fowler, "the author is constituted by the forms and the ideas of the discourses which (with their social conditions) [they have] experienced." "Creativity," he goes on to say, "is founded on the author's critical consciousness of these resources of discourse, and the practical skill to deploy language to a defamiliarizing effect."[7] This chapter explores the tensions between discourses of play and control as evidenced in the Depression-era writings of Richard Wright and Ralph Ellison. Wright's and Ellison's knowledge of the ways language is used to represent race and class and how it functions within particular genres is evident in both authors' ability to write within and against hegemonic discourses; furthermore, through motifs of play and control, they demonstrate that anti-language, language used "to a defamiliarizing effect," persists in the language of Black children in poverty and has rhetorical and political power.

Richard Wright's Anti-Language of Control

Wright's initial three chapters of *Black Boy* (1944), in which Richard is twelve or younger and his shifting family moves from place to place, best demonstrate his view of language as a space of control. The reader is first confronted with quick examples of Wright's proclivity to editorialize from the vantage point of his thirty-six-year-old understanding of the events of his childhood, standard within the genre of autobiography. For example, on the second page of the novel, Richard is four and has been asked by his mother to be quiet, as Granny is ill in the next room. Awaiting his mother's return, Richard "wandered listlessly about the room" and grew "resentful of being neglected."[8]

Wright's description of his resentment and neglect reflects his adult understanding of the larger context of his childhood, not this particular moment in his four-year-old experience, when he and his brother are bored but not hungry and when there are no adults nearby. Additionally, when recounting the afternoons he spent as a six-year-old in the neighborhood saloon intoxicated and repeating the "obscenities" he learned from the men who bought him drinks, Wright never includes any of his drunken language, referring only to "[seeing] more than I could understand and hear[ing] more than I could remember" (*BB*, 21–22).

My point is not to challenge the authenticity of Wright's autobiography, though some have.[9] Deborah Mutnick's *No Race, No Country: The Politics and Poetics of Richard Wright* (2025) provides a critical return to many longstanding assumptions about Wright. Helpful here is her work to nuance the autobiographical exactness of the early chapters of *Black Boy*. Wright's first biographer, Mutnick notes, detailed that Wright would have to "underplay [...] his own family's essentially middle-class status." Mutnick is careful, though, to contextualize that though Wright was not "as abjectly poor nor as educationally deprived as the protagonist of *Black Boy* is typically understood to be," the text is "close enough" to be considered autobiographical, and Wright, of course, had intimate knowledge of racial oppression, as well as his own and his father's family's economic hardships.[10] Thus, I am not interested in reading *Black Boy* for the purpose of interrogating the accuracy of the language he drafted as an adult for his younger self. (Such a project would be, by default, futile.) Instead, I find considering Wright's adult narrativization of his early childhood far more worthwhile. Wright is, of course, laying the groundwork for later themes in the autobiography, such as hunger and self-education, but I argue that we can also read as generative the tensions between his narrative choices to prioritize a rigidly normalized discourse for his younger self and the moments that such a discourse of control purposefully loosens.

Ruth Smith observes that in the early chapters a young Richard is often in a position from which "words slip uncontrollably from [his] mouth, or in which he fears losing control over his own tongue."[11] This tension, between Wright's efforts to control a narrative that is itself all about being unable to control, is most productively unreconcilable in the novel's first three chapters. The control that the genre of autobiography provides registers his commitment to using mainstream discourse that seems sharply different from language he tells the reader that he used as a child, language Gavin Jones notes is both emetic and imitative. However, there are moments in the text where Wright chooses to represent the language of the child in poverty with anti-language.

An early example of anti-language in these chapters includes the language of the street that twelve-year-old Richard learns to speak. In a modified and ironic call-and-response, the paragraphs of this catalog begin with quotes that, for the first time in the text, are written with idiom and end with a brief, often one-word sentence that, in essence, translates or makes clear the emotional context of the quote's delivery for a nonnative speaker. The call is given by unnamed Black children, and Wright's response reads like a playwright's stage directions: "Moving body agitatedly, stomping feet impatiently, and scurrying back to safe reality" (*BB*, 81). Wright's structure controls how the reader understands the young boys' slang immediately after it is spoken. He sets up the three-page hypothetical conversation among him and his friends as taking place after school let out while walking the street "until [he] would stumble upon one or more of the gang loitering at a corner, standing in a field, or sitting upon the steps of somebody's house" (78). Though the entire conversation builds from anxiety ("'You eat yet?' Uneasily trying to make conversation") to humor ("'You'd win the war with a new kind of poison gas!' A shouted climax"), the shift to more serious subjects happens organically ("'Maybe poison gas is something good to have.' The subject of white folks is associationally swept into the orbit of talk") (79). The subject of racial conflict recycles every time the conversation lulls to "[s]ilence," and its ensuing rapid progression is worth quoting at length:

> "Man, them white folks sure is mean." Complaining.
>
> "That's how come so many colored folks leaving the South." Informational.
>
> "And, man, they sure hate for you to leave." Pride of personal and racial worth implied.
>
> "Yeah. They wanna keep you here and work you to death."
>
> "The first white sonofabitch that bothers me is gonna get a hole knocked in his head!" Naive rebellion.
>
> "That ain't gonna do you no good. Hell, they'll catch you." Rejection of naive rebellion.
>
> "Ha-ha-ha . . . Yeah, goddammit, they really catch you, now." Appreciation of the thoroughness of white militancy.
>
> "Yeah, white folks set on their white asses day and night, but leta n——r do something, and they get every bloodhound that was ever born and put 'em on his trail." Bitter pride in realizing what it costs to defeat them.
>
> "Man, you reckon these white folks is ever gonna change?" Timid, questioning hope.

"Hell, no! They just born that way." Rejecting hope for fear that it could never come true.

"Shucks, man. I'm going north when I get grown." Rebelling against futile hope and embracing flight.

"A colored man's all right up north." Justifying flight.

"They say a white man hit a colored man up north and that colored man hit that white man, knocked him out cold, and nobody did a damn thing!" Urgent wish to believe in flight.

"Man for man up there." Begging to believe in justice.

Silence. (*BB*, 80)

In both content and construction, these three pages adroitly demonstrate the linguistic and cultural intelligence of Richard and his gang. From using "colored folks" to signify Black people leaving the South to the shift to the word "n——r" to signify a Black man pursued by bloodhounds to be lynched, the boys demonstrate an understanding of racial identity that shifts depending on the speaker, context, and purpose of the speech act. The anti-language of Richard's gang, as demonstrated in the passage above, is "constantly striving to maintain a counter-reality that is under pressure from the established world [. . . and] is constantly renewing itself—to sustain the vitality that it needs if it is to function at all."[12] By structuring the dialogue in this ironic call-and-response of child and child-now-adult, Wright demonstrates the boys' awareness of the functions of their speech, of "ideas [. . .] discovered, discarded, enlarged, torn apart, and accepted" in the public sphere of the street (*BB*, 81–82).[13]

While the very subversive act of speaking with such an anti-language seems to be mitigated by Wright's accompanying explanations of tone and purpose, Wright's explanations can be read as glossing, a technique that "draws attention to the limitations of readers' knowledge." "[P]lain and exaggeratedly simple," these glosses "[give] semantic information in terms which the [outsider] can understand."[14] It is as though Wright makes visible in the text a potential reader's ignorance. However, such moments of powerful and dislocating speech and preserved idiom only exist in *Black Boy* in carefully controlled situations.

A second rare example of the anti-language of the child in poverty comes from Richard's early exposures to racial tensions. In chapter 1 Wright signifies Richard's growing understanding by using quotation marks to demarcate the words "white" and "black." Though he "had seen white men and women upon the streets a thousand times," Wright explains, his "tardiness in learning to sense white people as 'white' people came from the fact that many of my relatives were 'white'-looking people" (*BB*, 23). It is only when Richard hears a story in the neighborhood of "a 'black' boy [. . .] severely beaten by a 'white' man" who was not the boy's father that he begins to stare at "white" people, "wondering what they were really like" (23–24). Thus begins his education in the anti-language of race: racially constructed meanings of words whose definitions shift placeholders when the racial identity of the speaker of the words changes, too.

The end of chapter 1 solidifies the connotations of the words "white" and "black" with and without quotation marks for Richard. Having run away from the orphan home in which he and his brother are placed while his mother, who is ill, searches for work, Richard is lost in an unfamiliar part of the city. "A 'white' policeman" whose "'white' face created a new fear in [him]" takes the child to the police station, where he "was surrounded by 'white' policemen [who] seemed to ignore [him]" (*BB*, 31). After Richard falls asleep, his "shoulder was shaken gently," and he wakes to find the "'white' face of another policeman," who "asked me questions in a quiet, confidential tone" (31). "[B]efore I knew it," Richard says, "he was not 'white' anymore" (32). For the rest of the book, only when race is construed in derogatory or explicitly socially constructed ways does Wright use quotations marks around "black" and "white." Fully immersed in the anti-language of racial difference, the child has learned "the secret, the thing, the reality I felt somewhere beneath all the words and silences" (47). And within these moments in the book's early chapters, Wright does not overexplain for his audience, which implies that they, too, already know what the child is just now learning. Instead, he draws attention to the irony of antonyms existing within the same word by the use of quotation marks.

The final example of anti-language comes in each of the first three chapters when Wright creates an anaphoric catalog that follows a vividly traumatic experience, often ending in an ellipsis that signifies a continuation of thought but a lack of representative language. In chapter 1, for example, Richard is beaten for setting the house on fire because he wondered how the white curtains would look when ablaze. "[B]eaten out of [his] senses" and afterward given medical orders to be kept in bed, as "[his] very life depended on it," Richard has hallucinatory dreams that change the way he, once well, sees the world (*BB*, 7). Twenty-three successive sentences begin with "There was" and go on to reveal "the moments of life [that] slowly revealed their coded meanings" (7). Several of the sentences carefully illustrate what the world looks like to a four-year-old child: "There was the experience of feeling death without dying that came from watching a chicken leap about blindly after its neck had been snapped by a quick twist of my father's wrist" or "There was the cloudy notion of hunger when I breathed the odor of new-cut, bleeding grass" (8–9). To describe cut grass as bleeding or to feel the emotional rush of death by watching a parent kill without pause with a hand at your eye level demonstrates the sensitivity of a child acutely aware of physical suffering from a young age. Yet several more of the sentences frame young Richard's observations with language decidedly different: "There was the vague sense of the infinite as I looked down upon the yellow, dreaming waters of the Mississippi River from the verdant bluffs of Natchez" (7–8).

Chapter 2's catalog follows the ironic moment when Richard's dog is "crushed to death beneath the wheels of a coal wagon" a mere week after Richard tried to sell her for one dollar and rejects an offer of ninety-seven cents. This catalog is more wholly in the language of the child and recounts "magic possibilities" that the "wet or dusty streets, indoors or out, the days and nights began to spell out" (*BB*, 71). It gives the reader access to the interiority of the child in poverty, a place of cause and effect that is not always rational. Within this twenty-five-sentence catalog are superstitions Richard is learning from the street and home, a strange code of logic and ethics that both punishes and demands good behavior for rewards: "If I kissed my elbow, I would turn into a girl"; "If I was good to my mother, I would grow old and rich"; "If I looked at the sun through a piece of smoked glass on Easter Sunday morning, I would see the sun shouting in praise of a Risen Lord" (71–72). As an adult, Wright looks back on all these conditional promises or punishments and sees that "[a]nything seemed possible, likely, feasible, because I wanted everything to be possible. . . . Because I had no power to make things happen outside of me in the objective world, I made things happen within. Because my environment was bare and bleak, I endowed it with unlimited potentialities, redeemed it for the sake of my own hungry and cloudy yearning" (72–73). This anti-language repurposed from religion, old wives' tales, and neighborhood lore is precisely as Wright describes it, a response engaged in making meaning out of whatever discourses are available. It is representative of a child whose actions result in responses that are often negative and violent and sometimes positive. This is a child for whom no one has yet offered a cohesive framework within which the child can sort or categorize.

In her analysis of the language Wright uses in his "literacy narrative" (and in response to other critics' pejorative readings of his "prose style"), Mutnick writes that Wright's prose "enact[s] the verbal potential of a child voiced by the adult poet he would become, expressing the spontaneous consciousness of what must have been mainly a felt sense in childhood."[15] It is important to note, however, that the places within his autobiography where Wright chose to shift to writing with the anti-language are only in the early chapters where he invites the reader into the youth of a Black child in poverty. Instead of a "felt sense," perhaps Wright's moments of anti-language represent not a "spontaneous consciousness" but rather one hard-fought in which the child works within language known and, at times, within the company of other young people to more accurately represent what he knows and is learning.

Yet Wright's language changes after these early chapters, and gone are the anaphoric catalogs that give range to possibilities even as they show them as futile. While the early chapters of *Black Boy* give way to brief moments attuned to the experimental language of the child in poverty, in the later chapters Wright largely maintains a firm commitment to a carefully editorialized version of the arduous process of growing up poor. The essence of this unstable if-then continuum, however, undergirds the hope Wright reluctantly pursues in the rest of the novel as he searches for the possibility promised in the North:

> I dreamed of going north and writing books, novels. The North symbolized to me all that I had not felt and seen; it had no relation whatever to what actually existed. Yet, by imagining a place where everything was possible, I kept hope alive in me. But where had I got this notion of doing something in the future, of going away from home and accomplishing something that would be recognized by others? I had, of course, read my Horatio Alger stories, my pulp stories, and I knew my Get-Rich-Quick Wallingford series from cover to cover, though I had sense enough not to hope to get rich; even to my naïve imagination that possibility was too remote. I knew that I lived in a country in which the aspirations of black people were limited, marked-off. Yet I felt that I had to go somewhere and do something to redeem my being alive. (*BB*, 168–69)

Once Wright is in Chicago, the Depression unfolds, and Wright's exploration of the political Left via involvement in a John Reed Club facilitates further writing, as well as initial support. ("We write articles about Negroes, but we never see any Negroes. We need your stuff," Wright is told [*BB*, 321].) Despite "endless pages [of] stream-of-consciousness Negro dialect" and in part because of the failed project of writing biographical sketches of Black Communists, Wright names his growing disillusionment with the disconnect between the ideology of the movement and its internal politics (284).

The language of the majority of his autobiography remains carefully guarded. The strongest example of this is a short paragraph in chapter 19 about his assigned relief work at the South Side Boys' Club. "They were a wild and homeless lot," he carefully writes, "culturally lost, spiritually disinherited, candidates for the clinics, morgues, prisons, reformatories, and the electric chair of the state's death house" (*BB*, 341). Pausing, in the very next sentence Wright says, "For hours I listened to their talk of planes, women, guns, politics, and crime. Their figures of speech were as forceful and colorful as any ever used by English-speaking people. I kept pencil and paper in my pocket to jot down their word-rhythms and reactions" (341). Finding structure and purpose in deviant and discordant language, Wright now observes from outside the if-then conversations with a decidedly firmer grasp of "their twisted dreams, their all-too-clear destinies" so close to the boy he just was (341).

Yet the metaphors and ironies within the language of the poor South Side boys are not recorded in the autobiography's dialogue; they are only discussed objectively. In *Writing Chicago: Modernism, Ethnography, and the Novel* (1993), Carla Cappetti argues that Wright's literary approach is informed by the Chicago school of sociology and its focus on the tensions inherent in the relationship between individual and society. This approach traces an individual's struggle against their "environment[, . . .] an inclusive term that indicates the group, the community, the culture, tradition, authority." Thus, she reads Wright's responses to, in particular, the language of "the street gang" as "the sociologist who interprets [the conversation] and distances himself in order to represent it."[16]

We see this tension also in Wright's more than two hundred articles for the Harlem Bureau of the leftist newspaper the *Daily Worker* during seven months of 1937 (seven years before he would publish *Black Boy*). Within these articles, the motif of hunger often includes explicit mention of children. A November 8 piece, for example, quotes Mrs. Adolphus Green, who, when asked to share the ages of her children, "declared timidly, 'I'm always asked to tell people how old my children are, they are so small. They simply don't get enough to eat.'" The last paragraph of an earlier August 4 article reads as follows: "THIS ISN'T FICTION; these are not scenes from the novels of Charles Dickens. The sidewalks of Harlem are real and hard; and black people on those sidewalks are truly starving." Midway through the piece, Wright uses "you" to try to mark his distance from his subjects, the young parents close to him in age.[17]

Wright's "you" both distances him from his journalistic subjects and is dependent on his presence in this powerful moment. This disconnect is further complicated by Wright's 1937 essay "Blueprint for Negro Writing," which appeared first in the journal *New Challenge*. In general, "Blueprint" criticizes Black writing in the past "for failing to focus on working-class Black struggles."[18] "Shall Negro writing," he asks, "be for the Negro masses, moulding the lives and consciousness of those masses toward new goals, or shall it continue begging the question of the Negroes' humanity?" Wright goes on to say that the Negro writer must possess "a deep, informed, and complex consciousness" in order to "depict Negro life in all of its manifold and intricate relationships" in such a way that lifts the "consciousness [of the race] higher." While "Blueprint" was critically reading the past to call forward "an intellectual space where a writer stands to view the struggles, hopes, and sufferings of his people," Wright's *Black Boy* seems, in Wright's narrative choices regarding the vernacular language of young people, to be caught in the trap he cautions against therein. Wright claims that "the Negroes' most powerful images of hope and despair still remain in the fluid state of daily speech," yet such speech is used sparingly in his autobiography.[19]

In "Blueprint" he also cautions against "a simple literary realism which seeks to depict the lives of these people devoid of wider social connotations" (another return to the Chicago school of sociology) and in doing so "do[es] a rank injustice to the Negro people." *Black Boy* illustrates that suffering from racism and poverty does not negate the potential for self-expression through written language, and his autobiography's own rare but complex moments of anti-language present language with the authority to persist in the midst of mainstream discourse. The language of the child in poverty, if allowed to come forth, demonstrates a "*complex simplicity*" Wright lauded in "Blueprint" within the works of other modernists, as it comes from a point of view that has "begun to feel the meaning of the history of their race as though they in one life time had lived it themselves throughout all the long centuries," even before full consciousness of such a history has emerged.[20]

While the motif of hunger governs the whole of *Black Boy* with an unrelenting hand, the metaphor of childhood operates more subtly in its margins as the text progresses. Early in the second half of the book, Wright names his process of "going through a second childhood" with the realization that "there were but few Negroes who knew the meaning of their lives, who could tell their story" (*BB*, 267). Wright states explicitly his desire to separate himself from such "unconscious suffering" (267). Then, in the last chapter after his final conflict with the Communist Party during a May Day parade, Wright stands still as the masses march around him: "But I did not feel belligerent. I had outgrown my childhood" (381). Childhood, in part 2, operates as a waypoint one progresses through to reach adulthood, an affect to be outgrown, controlled, and contained. Carefully allowing the reader glimpses of the antilanguage of the child in poverty, *Black Boy* chronicles the weight of acclimating to betrayal, what happens when possibility encounters unrelenting oppression. As his attention to the South Side Boys' Club demonstrates, Wright's insistence on controlling language throughout his autobiography is less an exercise in erasure that signifies authorial weakness and more an act of pseudocontrol that, in fact, registers the disruptiveness all around. The "then" to every "if" only further complicates that which precedes and weighs down that which follows.

Ralph Ellison's Repeated Returns to Children's Language of Play

For Ellison, conversely, the child's capacity brings forward new possibilities, and childhood is less a space to be outgrown and more a space to return to, largely because of what the child's language invites. Writing of his own childhood in Oklahoma City in *Shadow and Act*, Ellison notes that "quite a lot of our living was done in the imagination." Often using metaphors of play to describe the writing process, he notes that writers "begin their careers in play and puzzlement, in dreaming over the details of the world in which they become conscious of themselves."[21] When examining the chronology of Ellison's works, we see not only the influence of the children's rhymes he collected during his Federal Writers' Project (FWP) work but also the space of childhood as the focus of his early fiction.

Franklin D. Roosevelt's controversial New Deal programs were designed to get Americans back to work. One such program, the Works Progress Administration (WPA), included a group of public works projects framed around the arts such as the FWP and its sister projects in theater, art, and music.[22] Ellison joined the FWP in New York City in 1938 at the suggestion of Wright, who was a mentor to him, and in 1939 he began working in the Living Lore Unit.[23] Charged with collecting folklore in the streets of Harlem, the Living Lore Unit reflected the theories of Benjamin A. Botkin (named the project's national folklore editor in 1938), a shift that marked the FWP's turn to redefining folklore as the study of "living culture."[24] Botkin's insistence that folklore "constantly has to get back to the spoken word to be renewed" pushed against previous folklorists' understanding of the primacy of the past to argue for careful attention to the contexts in which "living speech" cataloged the lore born of a specific moment, including in urban contexts.[25]

Botkin's shift in emphasis within the study of folklore anticipated where the field was headed. His emphasis on revaluing the everyday mirrored trends in other social science fields in their approach to the study of play. Published in the same year that Ellison arrived in New York City, for example, sociologist Elizabeth F. Boettiger's *Children's Play Indoors and Out* delineates the ways adults are obligated to "supply the conditions, set the stage" for generative play for the white, middle-class children described but not explicitly stated as the focus of her research.[26] Boettiger's book is representative of the larger shift in research in the 1920s and 1930s from seeing play as "frivolous and useless" to perceiving it as a generative form of socialization into the work of adulthood.[27] Building on this shift, rhetorics of "progress" and functionality have dominated play studies across the twentieth century.[28] Yet contemporary play studies has turned away from seeing children's play as only a scaffolded placeholder on the way to the work of adulthood and instead has turned back toward childhood as a separate site of inquiry. Demarcating childhood as worthy of theorization insists on the capacity of children. Play, then, provides a frame for meaning making, as it requires children to critically read and interact with their community and, therefore, themselves. Thomas S. Henricks's 2015 *Play and the Human Condition*, for example, argues that play is a "sense-making activity" and that "[p]eople play in order to learn who they are, how they are situated, and what they can do." This "rebellion against the forms and forces of the world" is a process of self-realization that requires the player to be cognizant of what is, as well as what they hope to negotiate as an alternative.[29]

Play studies serves as an entry point for critically reading children's folklore gathered under the FWP. It invites us to analyze the ways in which these children actively made political and cultural meaning through their language choices during play in the scripts they took up, their revisions to those scripts, and their performance of those scripts for an adult audience. The archival record suggests that Ralph Ellison's method of recording children's folklore was not standard among FWP field-workers. When we read the children's folklore collected across the nation, however, we notice other patterns.[30] The most obvious pattern is that the same rhymes are frequently repeated, sometimes with slight variations that, even in their archival cataloging, have been attributed to regional contexts and differences in dialects. This framing parallels seminal mid-twentieth-century studies by Iona and Peter Opie, renowned folklorists of children's games, songs, and rhymes in Britain. It is imperative to note that the Opies often erased differences of class, race, and ability in their efforts to represent "the child population as a whole."[31] In the preface to *Lore and Language*, for example, we read the following:

> The study does not, however, except incidentally, include the lore current among children in the private, fee-charging establishments. And it does not, despite the sections on tortures and pranks after nightfall, set out to include the lore and language of the delinquent. We are concerned here merely with the fun-loving but father-fearing specimen who is typical of the vast majority. It seems necessary to say this because there continues to be such a spate of books about children who are socially deprived or mentally handicapped, or who are in trouble with the police, that a book about the ordinary child is rather extraordinary.[32]

The Opies' effort to establish a norm dismisses what they frame as opposite poles of childhood experience. One extreme is wealth, "children in the private, fee-charging establishments," though it is the second pole that receives the most attention for its lack and aberrancy: the "delinquent," the "socially deprived," and the "mentally handicapped."

Thus, in the Opies' supposedly normed sample, the commonality of the "ritual and phraseology" of children's lore was unexpected, yet they contributed "variations, even apparently creative ones," to "mishearing or misunderstanding." "[Occurring] more often by accident than design," they wrote, children's lore came from an "unselfconscious culture [. . .] unnoticed by the sophisticated world." This well-intended yet deficit thinking both celebrates and, in doing so, makes visible the lore of children while simultaneously trivializing children as agential language users: "Language is still new to them, and they find difficulty in expressing themselves."[33]

What becomes possible, though, if we read children's lore and rhymes while assuming a purposefulness to children's language? Furthermore, what happens when the language of children whose lived experiences differ from what is centered as "ordinary" is not excluded from the record but instead carefully listened to? My efforts to read children's language choices as "active practices" amid cultural scripts are attempts to answer Gubar's call for new methodologies that tend to possibilities of both-and, a "hermeneutics of recuperation" that prompts us, in these texts, to examine the performance of these rhymes, the revisions to and the enactment of the language therein. And this, of course, requires us to consider their use during and through play.[34]

Many childhood studies scholars have argued for the value of examining the material culture of children as a means of expanding the archive with which to study the lives of children, cultural constructions of childhood, and the ways children actively participate in creating culture. In *Racial Innocence: Performing American Childhood from Slavery to Civil Rights* (2011), for example,

Robin Bernstein argues that "[c]hildren do not passively receive culture. Rather, children expertly field the co-scripts of narratives and material culture and then collectively forge a third prompt: play itself. The three prompts then entangle to script future play, which continues to change as children collectively exercise agency."[35] Similarly, in her argument to tend to the "stuff they leave behind," Sánchez-Eppler notes that "looking at the things children make [...] shows how children's play is shaped by and expresses its social context."[36] While children's rhymes are admittedly different from material culture such as dolls or handmade playthings or journals, I build upon Bernstein and Sánchez-Eppler to argue that the rhymes gathered by FWP field-workers can also serve as an underexplored entry point, as they catalog scripts bound contextually to place and time as dutifully recorded by adults in the presence of children enacting these scripts on playgrounds, around sidewalks, and in yards. Ellison's ethnographic FWP work, then, offers additional insights, as his accompanying field notes offer rich context that was not often logged in the reports of other field-workers.

In Ellison's field notes, we see how agential and knowing children engage in a long-standing practice of dialect signifying meaning specific to the speaker's culture and context. A useful parallel is Katharine Capshaw Smith's close readings of the dialect poetry Paul Laurence Dunbar wrote for children in the Harlem Renaissance of the 1920s. Building on other scholars' work on play and the study of Black dialect specifically, Capshaw Smith writes that "play with language can comment on, and often imaginatively change, the nature of social structures and relations. Within the African American community, such play advances a serious subtext, for the structures of racism and inequity are likely targets of verbal inversions and subversions."[37] I argue that this same powerful linguistic play is present in the language of children recorded in Ellison's notes.

Ellison cataloged this language of play within children's rhymes in 1939 and 1940, years he spent working for the New York Writers' Project and, in part, interviewing children and visiting playgrounds around Harlem. Sara Rutkowski's *Literary Legacies of the Federal Writers' Project: Voices of the Depression in the American Postwar Era* (2017) reprints a handful of the jump-rope rhymes Ellison cataloged, which she describes as "meaningful within a folk group, and even as they change over time, their form is familiar and culturally binding."[38] I argue that the language employed in this "binding" form can be read as anti-language, language that "convey[s] a certain tension," to borrow again from Rutkowski's description of the rhymes.[39] As Halliday notes, anti-language creates an alternate reality that becomes a "*counter*-reality, set up *in opposition to* some established norm" in which "[i]t is not the *distance* between the two realities but the *tension* between them that is significant."[40]

Fowler found this tension also within the verbal play of the "rhymes and sayings of children's culture."[41] Anti-language, after all, "is constantly renewing itself—to sustain the vitality that it needs if it is to function at all," which we see in the variations of rhymes, variations often specific to the child's context.[42] It is important to note that the Opies demarcated extreme variations like this as intentional, nonstandard choices children make because of their lower-class position, though this isn't explicitly named and instead is implied in their analysis. In a section entitled "Secret Languages" within a chapter entitled "Some Curiosities," for example, the Opies mark back-slang as "slang, local dialect, a multiplicity of technical terms, word-twisting, codes, and sign language" as communication inaccessible to "outsiders" that "satisf[ies] an impulse common to all underdogs." While a reader could assume that the Opies see children, broadly, as underdogs, there is not-so-subtle language embedded in the short section that clearly marks this as the language of "some classes of children" even as the Opies acknowledge that even some "respectable children" have been observed using it.[43]

While the Opies even go as far as cautioning against such "curiosities" because of how "too much meaning can be (and very often is) read into the formulas of children's games and customs," Henricks's *Play and the Human Condition* brings together recent theories of play to remind us powerfully of the role play takes in navigating what is normed within a culture and its opposite: what might be.[44] Two specific ideas should be noted here. First, play helps make meaning that then moves one to action. As "a commentary on the lives of *communities*," Henricks argues, play "emphasizes the way people fit their activity to society's broader terms" or, conversely, "[seek] alternatives to established cultural patterns." This process "develops, maintains, and assesses action strategies." Second, play creates self-awareness, which requires cultural knowledge and incredible skill in navigating conflict. "Creativity," Henricks writes, "is a disputatious process; so is the maintenance of what is created. And getting anyone to participate wholeheartedly in such a fragile, perhaps trivial affair is a challenge of its own sort."[45] The language Ellison recorded of Black children at play represents a kind of cultural production not often heard, looked for, and listened to in the 1930s: a way of making meaning that signifies an understanding of the limitations of *and* joy within their cultural context, as well as the agency imbedded in their language choices.

The rhymes Ellison was collecting were intended for inclusion in a book about children's folklore by the New York Writers' Project. What remains of this unfinished and unpublished manuscript, *Children's Rhymes of New York City*, is housed in the Library of Congress. The folder in which this essay is housed is overflowing with scraps and paper-thin mimeographed pages of rhymes, a few with a cover sheet that catalogs the location, date, and other identifying information about their collection. Most rhymes do not have any notes attached to them: They have been cut into strips and stapled in horizontal rows—six or so to a page—on a sheet of typing paper. The folder also contains an opening essay celebrating the collecting of approximately a thousand rhymes from across New York City. Page 5 of the essay is a section entitled "Negro Folk Culture," purposefully separated from the rest of the essay, in which the folk rhymes of white and immigrant children are described, though they are not raced as such and instead presented as the unmarked default: "children."[46]

The language of this section is striking. Its overarching focus tends to be on the origins of the material, and the writer emphasizes that the "liveliest and most interesting of the rhymes are current among Negro children whose parents have moved to New York from the South." The writer admits that such rhymes show "innovation and invention," as they also demonstrate a "racial reaction to chauvinism and prejudice" present in the South and in New York. Yet the focus of the remaining two paragraphs is that "old English rhymes" are more prevalent here "than in any other group." The author partially attributes this to the "earlier and more benevolent days of the prebellum South, [when] Negro and white children played together, sharing their games and rhymes." The essay blithely ends—"In any case"—with a short paragraph noting the writer's pleasure in being able to include "so many" of the "rhymes and games of Negro children from an intrinsic, lively and often lovely section of American folk culture." Among this discomfiting nostalgia for an antebellum South in which Black and white children are at play sharing language—white to Black, of course, is suggested—we find the focus of the celebration to be the Black child's ability to turn old English rhymes so generously "share[d]" into something "lively" and "most interesting." The folder does not suggest how the rhymes were going to be cataloged in this never-published book. The closest the contents of the folder get to suggesting an organizational structure is this introductory essay, and if it was the template, then the rhymes Ellison collected would have been cataloged by their difference and celebrated for their vitality. The rhymes described in the rest of the eleven-page essay are categorized by their function (e.g., "rhymes used for rope jumping") and their use in school curriculum.[47]

Filed one container away are most of what remains of the rhymes Ellison collected.[48] As I have read and cataloged the rhymes, I have been struck by how children's anti-language in the rhymes establishes a common discourse separating insiders and outsiders, creates new narratives, and reclaims (or relexicalizes) language.

The most common patterns in the rhymes record a discourse intent on marking insiders and outsiders. Many of these rhymes are taunts, and some divide the child speakers from others in terms of racial or ethnic identity. The following rhyme is labeled as a taunt and was recorded several times in Ellison's papers (though identifying markers suggest that there are multiple copies of the same rhyme):

RED WHITE AND BLUE
YOUR OLD MAN IS A JEW
YOUR MOTHER IS AN IRISH POTATOE
JUST LIKE YOU.

(R.W.E.) Harlem Negro
130th and Lenox Ave.[49]

This is a variation of a common rhyme noted by some folklorists as being popular during World War I and the 1920s with Jewish and non-Jewish children (the use of either "my" or "your" signifies the user's identity).[50] The first line of the rhyme, the colors of the American flag, establish the rhyme's starting point, a kind of stock patriotism that makes the slurs that follow sharper against this symbolic background.[51] What follows in other recorded versions of the rhyme includes the same word used as an ethnic slur in the second phrase, "Jew," and then other ethnic slurs in the third phrase of the rhyme that are specific to the speaker's context (e.g., "Chinaman" or "Dago").[52] With the rhyme Ellison recorded, we see the child speaker's use of "Jew" and "Irish Potatoe [*sic*]" as slurs that demonstrate the child's understanding of racism and prejudice specific to their context. Of note in this rhyme is the anti-language that carefully marks the outsider allowing the unmarked insider to claim their power through using possessive pronouns.

In the same folder is Ellison's record of three rhymes of brothers who "operate a vegetable cart," William, age thirteen, and Eddie, age twelve (see figure 7). The last rhyme recorded on the page is as follows:

Cracker, Cracker
Ring the bell
Cracker, Cracker go to hell

In this rhyme, Ellison's ethnographic notes mark not only the origin of the rhyme, in this case when "the boys visited relatives at Charleston," but also its

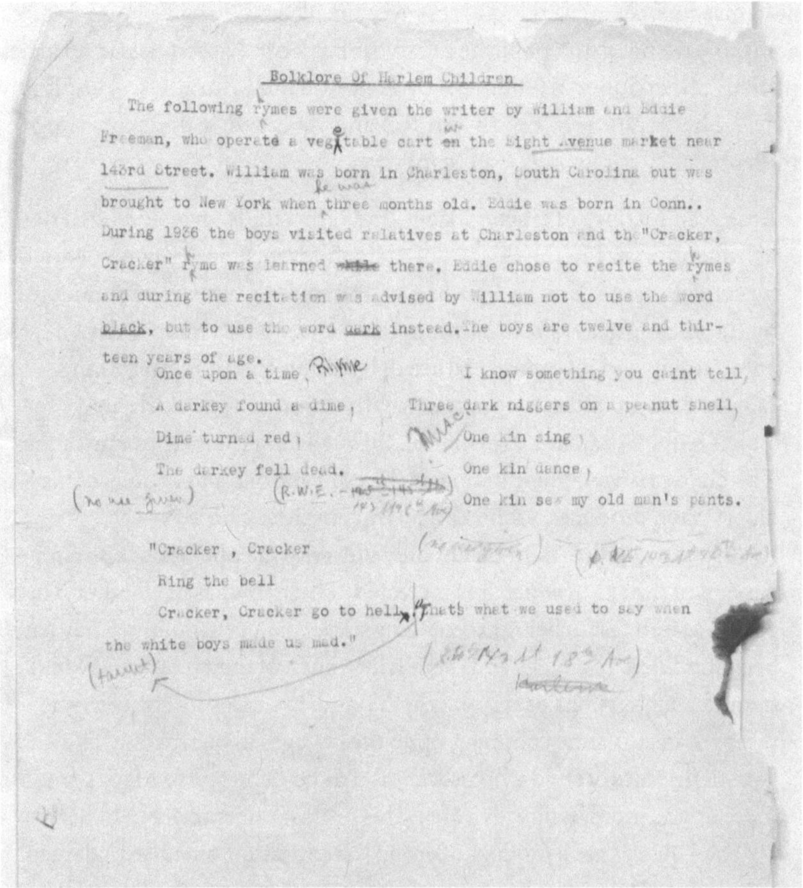

Folklore Of Harlem Children

The following rymes were given the writer by William and Eddie Freeman, who operate a vegtable cart on the Eight Avenue market near 143rd Street. William was born in Charleston, South Carolina but was brought to New York when three months old. Eddie was born in Conn.. During 1936 the boys visited relatives at Charleston and the "Cracker, Cracker" ryme was learned there. Eddie chose to recite the rymes and during the recitation was advised by William not to use the word black, but to use the word dark instead. The boys are twelve and thirteen years of age.

Once upon a time,
A darkey found a dime,
Dime turned red,
The darkey fell dead.

I know something you caint tell,
Three dark niggers on a peanut shell,
One kin sing,
One kin dance,
One kin see my old man's pants.

"Cracker, Cracker
Ring the bell
Cracker, Cracker go to hell, thats what we used to say when the white boys made us mad."

FIGURE 7 An annotated page from Ellison's interview with two brothers. "Folklore of Harlem Children," Negro Lore: Frank Byrd, Ralph Ellison, box A648, Folklore Project, New York City, Works Progress Administration, Federal Writers' Project, Library of Congress, Washington, D.C.

intent. "That's what we used to say when the white boys made us mad," Eddie is recorded as saying. "Cracker" was slang for whites in lower-class positions. The idiom "ring the bell" suggests the threat of an altercation, as to have one's bell rung is to be beaten in a fight or hit with such force that the fight ends. Here, too, we see children of Harlem using anti-language to mark boundaries of who is inside and who must remain outside (and what might happen if those boundaries are crossed).[53]

A second pattern in the rhymes uses anti-language to create new narratives within specific contexts. In Ellison's 1939 report, the second rhyme demarcates not only the child's understanding of places that are off-limits but also the consequences of seeking access to said places. "I won't go to Macy's" seems to have been first published the year before in *New Masses* in an article entitled "Street Songs of Children" by Fred Rolland, who also worked for the FWP.[54] The iteration of the rhyme Rolland recorded is different, and Rolland's prefatory paragraphs read as follows:

> American folklore of cities, villages, and farms finds vivid and often delightful utterance in the rhymes of their children. Those rhymes, enriched by contributions of an endless line of immigrants, have been remodeled by succeeding generations of youngsters, and we find them today an entertaining and revealing mixture of tradition and modernization. Language to a child is synonymous with action. These are rhymes which require dramatic explanation through game, dance, or burlesque. The child's naïve representation of the conventions and actions of his elders often produces a rollicking, if unconscious, satire.
>
> All poetry, to live, must be not only universal in content but also a repercussion of the age in which it was created. These rhymes of childhood have passed a stern test in being accepted by succeeding generations. They have been modified, of course, and therein lies much of their interest. We find innumerable versions of any one rhyme, and, in tracing its changes, we discover an authentic comment upon the changes in our society. The twentieth-century child who proclaims that he "won't go to Macy's any more, more, more" is already voicing his protest, superficial but indicative.
>
> These jingles are a product of group fraternization, amended, adapted, and accepted by collective approval. They come from sidewalks, back alleys, playgrounds, and playstreets, the folklore of the children of America.[55]

While parts of Rolland's approach engage in the typical deprecation of children's rhymes—"the child's naïve representation of the conventions and actions of elders"—he more powerfully lauds the "action" of a child's language and the collective construction of rhymes that provide "an authentic comment upon the changes in our society." Here the agential child chooses to repeat narratives that hold particular, agreed-upon meaning within their context, meaning that may only be conveyed in a particular moment in time and, therefore, not represented in a permanent record.

Working with a 1954 recording of the "Macy's" rhyme from Hell's Kitchen, Molly Rosner argues that it demonstrates that children "could identify where they 'belonged' in consumer society—and where they didn't" and that through the process of play "they reify and challenge the norms they're encountering."[56]

We see in Ellison's note that this was a ball-bouncing rhyme, which added emphasis to the key words in the rhyme. Most important, though, we see here the child's awareness and choice to repeat the rhyme and, in doing so, tell the story of what it means to be young and Black in Harlem. This abstract rhyme reifies a story these children knew to be true:

I WONT GO TO MACY'S ANY MORE, MORE, MORE!
THERE'S A BIG FAT POLICEMAN AT THE DOOR, DOOR, DOOR!
HE GRABBED ME BY THE COLLAR
AND HE MADE ME PAY A DOLLAR
AND I WONT GO TO MACY'S ANY MORE, MORE, MORE!

The rhymes Ellison recorded also show Harlem children's efforts to relexicalize language, a process "partial, not total," in which new words are used in ways that are "central to the activities of the subculture and that set it off most sharply from the established society."[57] While most FWP field-workers recorded only the rhymes of children and, occasionally, the information requested on the agency's cover sheet, Ellison's field notes remain the exception and, therefore, offer this insight into the ways the anti-language of these rhymes was ever in motion and crafted in response to both specific moments and broader contexts. For example, Ellison registered "one boy's attitude toward [Public School #89]," noting that "the first version [of the rhyme] was recorded before he knew his words were to be taken down, and the second, more respectable version, when he saw the pencil put to paper" (see figure 8).

1. REMEMBER THE EIGHT
REMEMBER THE NINE
REMEMBER THAT "CITY DUMP" 89.

2. REMEMBER THE EIGHT
REMEMBER THE NINE
REMEMBER THAT "WHITE HOUSE" 89.

Here we have a record of the child's language choices for the rhyme. The original—unstated—centers Public School #89 as the subject of the rhyme. The first recorded rhyme shows the child relexicalize (use different words for) the subject as the "city dump," an immediate shift that indicates the child's perception of the school. City dump, after all, signifies not only the child's distaste for school but also the child's framing of the school as in possession of the city, as a product of the larger social structure, which assigns value (or doesn't). Furthermore, the second recorded rhyme shows the child's

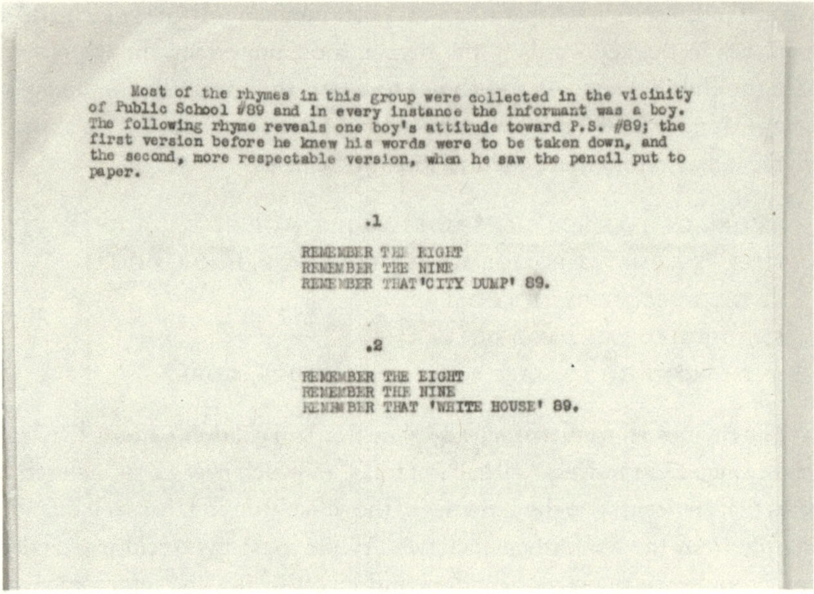

Most of the rhymes in this group were collected in the vicinity of Public School #89 and in every instance the informant was a boy. The following rhyme reveals one boy's attitude toward P.S. #89; the first version before he knew his words were to be taken down, and the second, more respectable version, when he saw the pencil put to paper.

.1

REMEMBER THE EIGHT
REMEMBER THE NINE
REMEMBER THAT 'CITY DUMP' 89.

.2

REMEMBER THE EIGHT
REMEMBER THE NINE
REMEMBER THAT 'WHITE HOUSE' 89.

FIGURE 8 Ellison's field notes about the "Public School #89" rhyme. Negro Lore: Frank Byrd, Ralph Ellison, box A648, Folklore Project, New York City, Works Progress Administration, Federal Writers' Project, Library of Congress, Washington, D.C.

awareness of an external audience, the expectation of how a child is supposed to revere school, and the dexterity of the child's language to immediately relexicalize—"white house"—to adhere to what the child sees as—to borrow Ellison's language—"respectable" language. The discursive power in the child's choice, however, is that the adjective "white" can also be read as denigrative, marking the school as a space of white control. The child's decision to make this more "respectable" revision for Ellison, then, the man with the pencil, can be read as the child's sarcasm and use of performative language that to the listener signifies one thing and in the discourse community of Harlem children will later mean something entirely different. We have no question which rhyme the child would use with PS #89 classmates.[58]

This example of improvisation and innovation of folk rhymes offers us the opportunity to see children in the process of defining their street, their neighborhood, their world. They speak in conversation with and against that which has come before, which is manifest in Ellison's attention to their language choices in both word and use. For Ellison, it seems, the child's capacity for imagination, for invention, for that which continually resurfaces old questions, seeks new answers, and brings forward new possibilities to what he called in various essays "method[s] of reordering the world" responds to the "moral and political problems which would not stay put underground."[59] Reading the language of these children in Harlem as anti-language suggests so. Ellison's later essays and interviews often center folklore as preserving universal experiences brought forward by "courageous expression [that] announced the Negro's willingness to trust his own experience, his own sensibilities as to the definition of reality."[60] Furthermore, in his body of work he continued to return to the language of children as a political force.

In 1940, 1941, and 1943, respectively, Ellison published the first three Buster and Riley stories, stories including children's rhymes. Scholarship does not dwell much on these stories. In 1988 Edith Schor read these early stories as rites of passage for Ellison, arguing that he "mastered" his craft; therefore, "[f]ittingly, [his] next stories have, as the protagonists, not boys but men." Furthermore, she argues that the rhymes don't develop the story itself and "[leave] nothing more for the boys, or the reader, to learn."[61] More recently, Barbara Foley's 2010 reading of "That I Had the Wings" does not pause on the role of childhood in these stories; instead, it catalogs the revisions to and annotations of the title that she found in Ellison's papers. With this catalog as her focus, she moves the story away from "more than a childhood reminiscence" into conversation with Ellison's concern over political events contemporary to his revisions.[62] Rutkowski reads the purpose of the rhymes as "protect[ing] [children]," as the "boys shield themselves from [the adult world] by rhyming and inventing games," which are "culturally binding" acts.[63] She uses words such as "claustrophobic" and "confinement" to describe the everyday realities of Black children in the 1930s. Tracy Floreani, in an essay focused on Oklahoma's influence on Ellison's writing, writes that "the Buster and Riley stories also reveal Ellison's lifelong interest in trying to capture precisely the rhythms of speech and lexicon of Oklahoma [. . .] as well as the naivete, humor, and folk culture that informed his own young sense of self."[64]

Reading against dismissals of these stories and assumptions that they represent childhood as but a phase to be outgrown, I insist that Ellison also sees joy in the childhoods presented in these stories. The anti-language in the Buster and Riley stories show Ellison's earliest insistence on the child's capacity for imagination and invention. Adults are ancillary here; their worries are threaded through but don't frame the story. Instead, we follow Buster and Riley down alleyways and through vacant lots, and the child is centered.

"That I Had the Wings" (1943) opens with Riley watching a young robin take its first flight from the nest and ends with his inability to teach young chickens to fly or, more accurately, to even catch them when Buster drops them from the top of the chicken coop, complete with hand-made parachutes tied with twine. His "sin" is witnessed by Aunt Kate, who prompts guilt: "It was always God, or the white folks. She always made him feel guilty, as though he had done something wrong he could never remember, for which he would never be forgiven. Like when white folks stared at you on the street."[65] For Riley, Aunt Kate's religious devotion is conflated with the power of "white folks," which is made evident for the reader in Riley's efforts to revise the language of his and Buster's rhymes (and Aunt Kate's hymns) throughout the middle of the story.

First, Riley recites this rhyme to Buster:

If I was the president
Of these United States
Said if I was the president
Of these United States
I'd eat good chocolate candy
An' swing on the White House gates—
Great—God-a-mighty, man—
I'd swing on them White House gates! ("TIH," 47)

After Aunt Kate scolds Riley for "takin' the Lawd's name in vain" and for not thinking about what would happen to his mother "if the white folks wuz to hear she wuz raisin' up a black chile whut's got no better sense than to talk 'bout bein' president" ("TIH," 47), she offers an alternative, a verse from a hymn:

Sing aaa-ho that
Ah had the wings of-vah dove
Ah'd fly to mah Jesus an'
Be at res' . . . ("TIH," 47–48)

Riley, however, refuses her invitation to join in and sing.

Instead, once the storm of Aunt Kate's wrath has passed, he offers Buster this revision, a rhyme that demonstrates this child's anti-language, his efforts to relexicalize, or reclaim, cultural narratives that promise flight to the divine to advocate for another kind of flight:

If I had the wings of a dove, Aunt Kate,
I'd eat up all the candy, Lawd,
An' tear down the White House gate. . . . ("TIH," 49)

Two specific revisions in language demonstrate this anti-language. First, in Aunt Kate's hymn, flight leads to the divine, to Jesus, to something away from the suffering of the present that provides rest. For Riley, the "wings of a dove" provide access to a different kind of power. Thus, the second relexicalization comes from Riley's first rhyme to his second. In the first, the goal is to "swing on the White House gates." We remember that part of Aunt Kate's scolding is thinking of the possibility of a Black child being president. Riley's response, then, in this second rhyme moves from not just eating the "good chocolate candy bars" and swinging on the White House gate but also eating "all the candy" and "tear[ing] down the White House gate." Again, this example of improvisation and innovation offers us the opportunity to see the child in the process of revising cultural narratives. Riley speaks in conversation with and against that which has come before, which is manifest in Ellison's attention to making visible the child's language choices.

Through repeated returns to the child, childhood, and the language of children, Ellison revisits, revises, and reclaims. Within his infamous unfinished novel, Ellison drafted the question "How does this child fit into his America?"[66] His answer? Not easily. What we see through Ellison's use of children's rhymes is the ways the Black child's anti-language—language that defines its own parameters against discourses of power and privilege—works to define, to relexicalize, to question dominant cultural narratives and norms.

IN WRIGHT'S *BLACK BOY*, childhood was a space to grow out of, full of language to be carefully controlled. Yet powerful anti-language haunts the margins of his writing about his childhood. For Ellison, childhood is a generative space of exploration, a space of return, a space of joy, and the child's language is an invitation to see differently. Similarly, though focused more broadly on texts by Black writers who worked for the Federal Writers' Project, J. J. Butts's summative paragraphs in *Dark Mirror: African Americans and the Federal Writers' Project* (2021) dwell on the irony that if "[h]eard correctly, these voices could have offered alternative understandings, local knowledge, a deep understanding of race, and, perhaps most importantly in the interplay of pattern and chaos, course corrections."[67] Wright's careful control and the rhymes Ellison collected require us, as readers, first to acknowledge children's capacity for and understanding of language and the ways in which it is used not only to reinscribe power within society but also to reclaim it. And then, as readers, the work becomes ours: If "heard correctly," the discord we find insists that we look around to see a society woefully out of balance and then return to listen differently to the anti-language of the child.

After all, as Riley says at the end of "That I Had the Wings," "We almost had 'em flyin'" (62).

CHAPTER THREE

The "Damaged" Child's Polyvalent Language

In the early years of the Depression, in the September 1930 issue of *New Masses,* Michael Gold cataloged the emergence of a new form of proletarian literature he called "proletarian realism." For Gold, in order for literature to "reflect the struggle of the workers in their fight for the world," it must "[deal] with the *real conflicts* of men and women who work for a living," for "the suffering of hungry, persecuted and heroic millions is enough of a theme for anyone." Literature must be written in "as few words as possible," he argued, for "workers live too close to reality to care about these literary show-offs [and] verbalist heroes."[1] Gold's project, defining the literature of the Left, has been taken up by many, and contemporary scholars generally agree with Gold's prescription, often categorizing proletarian literature as "realistic and naturalistic rather than with writers associated with symbolism and stream-of-consciousness narrative" common of modernist texts.[2] The writing that Gold, as editor, endorsed and published in *New Masses* responded to his call for literature stripped down, telegraphic, and straightforward—"swift action, clear form, the direct line, cinema in words"—by following the larger leftist tendency to focus primarily on the working-class adult body as a site of potential autonomy and power, as well as demonstrative of the damages of labor and inequality.[3] How, though, was suffering rendered when the bodies within texts written by proletarian writers were the bodies of the workers' children?

Gold's own prose offers an entry point to this question, although it blurs his own definitions of "proletarian realism." Published and reprinted eleven times in 1930 alone, *Jews Without Money* loosely follows Mikey's childhood on the Lower East Side between the ages of five and seven as told by the narrator, an adult Mikey looking back.[4] Though there is occasional dialogue, Gold almost wholly situates the events of Mikey's childhood using the past tense, the story's arc often framing for the reader the narrator's understanding of the past with the benefit of his present as an adult. Gold's attentive narrator takes care to show the powerful influence of poverty on young people and to narrativize the class consciousness that emerges. As Mikey shares after telling a story of both being beaten by his mother for making a prostitute cry and "learn[ing] all those bad, nasty things in street," for example, he reflects that "[i]t was my world[....] We *had* to live in it, and learn what it chose to teach us."[5] The tension between "what [the street] chose to teach" and the child's learning of such lessons drives the novel. Plenty of 1930s proletarian novels and poetry illustrate powerfully the fact that children's bodies suffer because they are casualties of a capitalist system. These novels also often intricately associate the child within a setting and talk about them from a distinct third-person point of view or in ways that place childhood in the past, as in Gold's fictional memoir.[6] Therefore, I'm interested in how much of proletarian realism places a directive set of explanations around the act of experiencing the text or, in other words, the act of reading the child.

This chapter first explores representations of working-class children and children in poverty in Farm Security Administration (FSA) photographs, Popular Front art, and proletarian texts written by women. Then I ask, What shifts when, from within the collapse, children are allowed to speak or to narrate? What happens when space is made for the child within the text so that childhood is presented to the reader as a place to learn from children, not just a placeholder on the way to adulthood and gaining class consciousness?

Texts that attend differently to and make space for the voice of the child force the reader to bend, to kneel, to look at the world from a different point of view. This narrative shift demonstrates the effects of poverty on the language of the child, and by demanding more investment from the reader, it engenders a meaningful response. In other words, while proletarian literature makes clear the damages of poverty on the body of the child, I argue that the texts that attend to the complicated modernist dialectic of the child's language, such as Tillie Olsen's *Yonnondio,* also ask how life can be sustained amid such damage.

Reading the Child in Proletarian Realism

A successful commercial photographer for wealthy families in the 1920s, Dorothea Lange looked elsewhere for work after her business suffered during the Depression.[7] She was hired to work for the California Emergency Relief Administration in 1935, which quickly led to her most enduring work, photographs of depressed rural spaces for the documentary photography project of the FSA.[8] For Entin, however, Lange's work (*Migrant Mother*, specifically) is characteristic of the way the bodies of the poor were often presented in 1930s fiction and photography, "vacillat[ing] between an aesthetic of sentiment and an aesthetic of scrutiny." These parallel modes, he argues, "represent strategies of social control through embodiment. In both, the poor are reduced to their bodies, which become material manifestations of their subjectivities, which are in turn made transparently legible to narrator, reader, and viewer. In this sense, both sympathy and scrutiny are modes of ideological management, ways of rhetorically containing potentially strange or threatening figures."[9] Entin also references Sally Stein, an art historian who argues that Lange's "photography deemphasized the social and environmental context in order to focus on the body alone as site of social formation and deformation."[10]

The work of historian Linda Gordon pushes back against such claims such as Stein's, arguing that Lange's careful attention to writing her own detailed captions (because "without words [. . .] photographs could be universalized") demonstrates a photographer whose "concern with context was an integral part of her art," a photographer who disliked the way *Migrant Mother* was "wrenched out of [its] context." In 1939 Lange started to add names to her captions, something Gordon speculates could have been the result either of the end of her time with the FSA and its rules or of the close relationships she had established with the migrant workers she was photographing in Oregon. To record names was to violate "the academic standards for interviews with research subjects," and the FSA explicitly prohibited the taking down of subjects' names. Gordon's discussion of Lange's later 1930s work in Oregon includes several photographs whose captions consist of an entire paragraph or even several single-spaced typed pages.[11] It is revealing, then, to examine an early FSA photograph and caption from Lange's time in 1936 in Elm Grove, Oklahoma, through both Entin's and Gordon's arguments.

The fierceness of the young girl in *Damaged Child* bears a striking contrast to other children pictured in Lange's Depression photographs (see figure 9). While children often looked directly at her camera's lens, this photograph includes a directness of composition and an unadorned style that separate it from other photographs. The child stands in front of what appears to be piecemeal sheets of repurposed corrugated aluminum. We see the child from the waist up: Her arms are bent casually, one hand is hidden in her shift, and the other hand, though partially cropped, seems to be tugging at the cloth. The seams of the metal intersect behind her head, the horizontal and vertical lines drawing the viewer's eyes to the child's. The crescent neckline of her shift mimics the shape of her face, drawing up the viewer's eye and making the parallel lines of her taut mouth, her rigid brows, and the horizontal seam of the metal all the more fixed. The child's shadowed eyes unapologetically return the camera's stare, almost as if they dare the viewer to look not at the mended shift or the pieced wall but at the child Lange's caption identifies as "damaged."

To read following Entin (and Stein) might suggest that the contrast of the child's pale skin with the dark metal frames her suffering without fully contextualizing it, without offering a suggestion of why she is standing here and

FIGURE 9 Lange's photograph bears the title *Damaged Child, Shacktown, Elm Grove, Oklahoma* in the archive at the Oakland Museum of California. Farm Security Administration, Office of War Information Photograph Collection, *Child Living in Oklahoma Shacktown*, LOC 2017763116, Prints and Photographs Division, Library of Congress, Washington, D.C.

who is watching over her and what she might eat tomorrow. Doing so creates an "aesthetic of sentiment" that elicits right feelings of sympathy in the viewer, feelings that too easily end in worry over the child's visible collarbone and thin arms—"material manifestations of [her] subjectivit[y]"—and never manifest into "specific political demands" particular to a determined social and environmental context.[12]

To read following Gordon is to pay close attention to Lange's caption, *Damaged Child, Shacktown, Elm Grove, Oklahoma*. Lange's choice to identify this child—not the right strap of her shift or the shack in front of which she stands—as damaged is at the core of the work of reading the classed child. What qualifies this child as damaged in 1936? Her thin arms and visible collarbone? Her androgynous haircut? Her gaze, which unapologetically returns the camera's stare? What is it, this photograph asks, that we expect of the child in poverty?

I contend that this photograph resists the duality of control that Entin suggests. Yes, to a middle-class viewer the child is a "potentially strange or threatening [figure]," but there is more at stake here than middle-class discomfort. The child who looks back so fiercely and without ever seeming to blink requires of the viewer the acknowledgment that the child is looking back just as much as being looked at. There is very little, if any, angle in the trajectory of subject and camera lens in this photograph, while so many of Lange's photographs are the result of the camera angled down toward a child and thus present the child from an adult point of view. The leveled optical field of this photograph demands that we acknowledge the child's point of view, or at least stoop to it temporarily. Furthermore, this child, it seems, knows that she is the recipient of the viewer's sentiment and scrutiny. Lange's caption, however, provides for the viewer a framework through which to see the child, a narrative act that counters Gordon's praise of the ethical work of Lange's captions. It is the caption, not the contextless photograph, that most "rhetorically contains" this child.[13]

An emphasis on the child's body as a source of sentiment and scrutiny manifests itself differently in the central narrative of the Popular Front. As Mickenberg argues, the Left in general "had consistently paid attention to children," yet with the broadening interests of the movement represented by the Popular Front, the focus shifted from the "suffering [of children] under capitalism" toward interests of "children's psychological as well as physical well-being." The practices and philosophies of "[r]aising children" became "a political act" for those with enough time to read child-rearing columns and manuals.[14] This was a sharp contrast to the earlier party discourse summarized in "The Proletarian Child" by Michael Gold. "The environment of poverty," he wrote, "and the compulsions of poverty, will always be more powerful than any school system in its effects on children."[15] In other words, for the poor child, hunger created "a very different set of concerns from [those of] middle-class children."[16] Art from the *New Masses* emphasizes Gold's corporeal narrative in its occasional depictions of proletarian children. (Most of the time, leftist art featured muscle-bound adult bodies at work.) The "Art Issue" from October 1, 1935, provides a striking contrast of both grotesque and sentimental representations of children in a single page (see figure 10).

FIGURE 10 Page 27 from the October 1, 1935, issue of *New Masses*, one of fifteen pages of art from the special issue, "Art Issue," *New Masses*, October 1, 1935, https://www.marxists.org/history/usa/pubs/new-masses/1935/v17no1-oct-01-1935-NM.pdf.

At the top of the page is Georges Schreiber's *Family Affair*.[17] A cross in the background, the bowed posture of the mourners, and the single flower in the child's hand suggest a graveside scene. Gradations of gray shadows make heavy the mourners' backs and faces, rendering their distinguishable facial characteristics suggestions, not definite brushstrokes. Most shadowed is the young widow, whose modest veil further darkens her face. By contrast, her child, towheaded and simply dressed, is oddly without shadow, as though a light illumines only him and his white flower. In fact, even his mother's fingers on his shoulder are only lightly sketched, not darkened as the rest of her hand not touching the boy is. Schreiber's choice to present the child with only the slightest of shadows on his face suggests him as the painting's focal point, an innocent victim whose father was taken from him too soon. While he and his mother are without coats (which other mourners in the scene are wearing), his illumined body also draws the eye of the viewer to his smallness and vulnerability in an effort to elicit a sentimental response: What took this child's father from him? How will his mother provide for him? How long until this child's body becomes shadowed too?

The round cheek of the fatherless boy becomes the painfully gaunt cheeks of the sisters in George Biddle's *Starvation* at the bottom of the page. In what seems to be a tent or some sort of impermanent dwelling, these sisters, one naked and the other barely clothed, weakly hold on to their mother. Eerily prophetic, Biddle's painting is almost identical to Lange's *Migrant Mother*, though Lange took her photograph and published it five months later. Just like Biddle's mother, Lange's mother also holds her hand to her mouth with worry, looks away from the viewer, and partially serves as a hiding place for two anxious children. The differences of Biddle's painting, however, are more pronounced: The viewer must navigate the faces of the suffering children; furthermore, the living hands above the ground grasp with what strength they have—the mother's dress, her finger, her shoulder—while the hands below are awkwardly bent and empty. The most obvious difference between the two, though, is the exposed grave immediately below Biddle's suffering Madonna in which three corpses lie, even in death without rest. To suggest so overtly the impending reality of these bodies is to force upon the viewer the consequence of starvation. Yet what draws a sentimental response first—the hungry children, their sinewy bodies, and their mother's worry—quickly becomes a grotesque repulsion of stiffened, angular, decaying bodies.

The children of page 27 are presented to the viewer as damaged. In some ways, Schreiber's child is rendered more ominously: The shadows of working-class suffering wait for the boy with the white flower in his small hand.

Biddle's children, however, are so obviously damaged by their poverty: Reduced to literal skin and bones, the dead and the living are not so different. These pieces of revolutionary art are "material manifestations of [subjects'] subjectivities"; however, instead of designations of reproof, these embodied examples of suffering "[return] ultimately to the body as the site that bears the marks, the damage, of being poor," fitting for a movement born on behalf of bodies at work.[18]

Thomas S. Willison's introduction to this October issue, "Revolutionary Art Today," begins by defining revolutionary art as the attempt to render what novelists and poets naturally do, "be attentive to the minutest variations of internal life," but they do so not through the abstract, as art had previously done, but in the very real bodies and settings of working-class life. For Willison, the "momentous or moving reality, which is the reality of class struggle and the decay of capitalism," is "too complex and many-sided to be photographed in cold blood." Revolutionary art must be "capable of widening and deepening the scope of the meanings in a representation" in order to both represent and be accessible to the masses: "The revolutionary cartoon and mural exhibit this continuity of art to the highest degree; in their most realistic aspect they are much less realistic than the corresponding easel-pictures and often recall the creations of abstract art; but they are, in consequence, far more compact or extensive, pointed or thorough, in their realism." The colorless fingertips of Schreiber's young widow or Biddle's grotesque corpses mirroring their still-living selves illustrate the moments that Willison called "much less realistic" yet more "pointed [. . .] in their realism."[19] (This definition of realism is similar to Allred's idea of modernism as a "radicalization of literary realism, in which the relationship between the real and representation becomes a primary object of contemplation.")[20] It is as though these artists created bodies as syntax, bodies that not only endure narratives of suffering but also articulate it through their status as damaged.

This same emphasis on the suffering body of the child is championed in many proletarian texts written by women during the Depression, primarily prior to the Popular Front. Though they often are not the center of the plot or its narrator, working-class children are consistently offered up as the most egregious, the most affective casualties of capitalist systems through forthright presentations of their damaged bodies. In other words, these writers deliberately avoid the excesses of the sentimental tropes and schemes so common to the presentation of children in popular texts and photographs of the Great Depression to insist on a candid account of the suffering of children; ironically, this detached style of narration creates the very goal of the sentimental genre, right feeling. We do not need a narrator to tell us that it is unnatural for "the young ones [to grow] thinner."[21] By drawing attention to the most vulnerable, female writers propose that these small bodies are just as important to the Left as the bodies of the adult workers, the quintessential symbol of the proletariat.

Grace Lumpkin's plot-driven *To Make My Bread* (1932), for example, follows the McClure family as they move from rural Appalachia to work in a mill town. The book follows the standard plot outlined in Foley's definition of the proletarian bildungsroman, a novel in which "the protagonist's espousal of—or at least growth toward—revolutionary class consciousness embodies in microcosm that change that is occurring, and must continue to occur on a larger scale, in the working class."[22] For the first forty chapters of the book the main characters, John and Bonnie, are children. From the beginning of the novel, they are hungry: "The pains were grasshoppers jumping from one blade of grass to another. They hopped from one place to another in his belly and each time they lit a sharp pain struck [John]. Bonnie felt the pains. She sat in a corner with her arms pressed tightly over her belly. She was trying to hold the grasshoppers from jumping."[23] John's and Bonnie's awareness of their suffering negates the impossible desire of their mother, Emma McClure, for them to not know that "trouble and sorrow are ahead of [them]" (*TMMB*, 85).

Once the family is in the mill town, the reader quickly learns the futility of Emma's desperate desire to "make money if she tried hard enough" (195). As she works as a spool hand, a very young Bonnie works at home caring for a neighbor's baby, whose mother "had no time to let it finish nursing" on her lunch break (197). This cycle is repeated with Bonnie's children in chapter 48 when "she left the children at home with five-year-old Emma," her daughter (317). Lumpkin's heavy-handed repetition of the name Emma frames poverty as cyclical. Time and again in the novel, Lumpkin's narrator pauses to remind the reader of the homogeneity of the bodies of working-class children: "wan and stunted," with "the mark of the mill," having "grown no larger [. . .] at ten or eleven" (270, 324, 344). In each cycle of the family's struggle, the children's bodies are offered to the reader as proof of the impossibility of normal growth and health despite their mothers' sacrificial efforts. They are permanently damaged and coded as such for the reader.[24]

In Leane Zugsmith's 1938 short story "Room in This World," the child becomes a part of protest, a literal embodiment of sentimental propaganda. The story is told from the mother's point of view in narration laden with introductory clauses that halt and hesitate as she verbally tiptoes around her husband, Ab, who has been let go after nine years as a building watchman. Because no one is listening to his demands for reemployment, Ab decides to mimic that which he has read about in the newspapers when "a fellow and his whole family [. . .] go out with signs, asking for his job back."[25] Unable to leave the five-month-old baby, Pauline helps Ab make signs for the children who accompany him on the family's (his?) first picket. Zugsmith gives careful attention to the making of the picket signs. "If the sign's for the kids it had oughta say something about 'my Pa' and so on," Ab directs Pauline. "'Please get my Pa back his job.' How's that?" he asks (48). Ab and Pauline intentionally assign language to their children, language designed to evoke right feeling and a desired sentimental response. Jappy and Frances quite literally are given texts for their bodies to carry: Pauline carefully sews the texts to the children's jackets. Jappy, three years old, wants to carry his Popeye doll, a "wooden figure from which all the paint had streaked" and for whom his mother also makes a sign (49). "Might do good," Pauline thinks, "them seeing a little kid with a doll" (49). More realistically, however, it was probably Jappy's smallness, "almost asleep on his feet," and his eight-year-old sister's trembling thin legs that caused "the expression on the new super's face" (50).

Just as Frances and Jappy are given texts to carry, the majority of children in proletarian novels and stories in the 1930s are given language by a third-person narrator. There are, however, a few moments within these texts when the author catalogs the child's acquisition of language. In *To Make My Bread*, for example, John wonders about the meaning of the word "ambition." Instead of asking his older brother, who said the word, John "repeated the word to himself and laid it up to remember at another time when he could find out the meaning from someone else," according to the narrator (*TMMB*, 122). Ultimately, proletarian fiction written by women focuses more on the damaged body of the child than the child's language, language acquisition, or self-expression. Janet Zandy notes that "class marks not only our tongues, but also our bodies."[26] These women writers imply that the presentation of the corporeal suffering of children is more than enough to create the desired emotional response in the reader by taking care to use language that catalogs the suffering of poor, young bodies.

The Anti-Language of Mazie Holbrook

In a less literal approach to realism, Tillie Olsen's *Yonnondio*, begun in 1932 and unpublished until 1974, also makes clear the corporeal burden of poverty, refusing oversimplified stereotypes of the rural and urban poor to insist that the people in poverty work every moment of their lives. It is often noted that over half of the opening chapter of *Yonnondio* is Olsen's short story "The Iron Throat," which was published in the April/May 1934 issue of the *Partisan Review: A Bi-Monthly of Revolutionary Literature Published by the John Reed Club of New York* under Olsen's maiden name, Tillie Lerner. Constance Coiner's reference to "The Iron Throat" illustrates the pattern among literary scholars' reference to the text, as she quotes the influential 1934 review by Robert Cantwell, which praised the story as "a work of early genius," yet she does not discuss the story beyond this concise narrative of publication and critical reception.[27] This way of reading "The Iron Throat" places the short story's value in its biographical waypoint. This aligns with other waypoints in Olsen lore, notably, the "hoped for ending" often referenced by scholars: A nineteen-year-old Olsen planned a novel "in which the children grow up and become writers, jazz musicians, and Communist organizers" as they come of age during the Depression.[28]

What if, instead of reading "The Iron Throat" biographically, we consider the text as it was published, as a self-contained short story? "The Iron Throat" begins with an atypical attention to the child's acquisition of language and how class shapes that acquisition. The story begins with Mazie awakening to harsh noise, the whistle of the coal mines "tearing at her." The sentence concludes with this independent clause: "The sound meant, in one way, terror."[29] While in *Yonnondio* this clause would become "breathing a terror," in Olsen's original short story we see how the sounds of labor, in this case, the mine whistle, are central to the curriculum of this young child.[30] This aligns with leftist thinking of the Depression era. For example, Arthur Wallace Calhoun wrote in his 1930 essay "The Child Mind as a Social Product" that

> [e]ven in its self-activity, the developing child mind can do little but copy patterns furnished by the social environment. The child is no spider equipped with the means of spinning endless distinctive webs out of the inward parts. Language, the sole avenue to a human mentality, is absolutely and entirely a gift from the social environment, and as languages differ in genius and structure so will the minds fashioned by their use differ in spirit and function. No child even acquires the culture of his bodily forebearers unless he is privileged to drink it in, not with his mother's milk, but with his mother tongue.[31]

Olsen, however, might have taken issue with Calhoun's arachnid metaphor, for as "The Iron Throat" continues, she chronicles how Mazie indeed "spin[s] endless distinctive webs" from the dissonant discourse around her. For example, before falling back to sleep, Mazie lies listening to her parents' conversation and overhears a new word, "edjiccation" ("IT," 4). Obtaining a definition for it is the second question Mazie asks her mother after waking to a crying baby, which Mazie warms to her body before diapering him with an old flour sack. Mazie's first question is "What's there to eat?," a question of availability, not preference, for the six-and-a-half-year-old child (4). Corinna Lee reads Mazie's monologue as demonstrating her "naivete toward the greater ideological and cultural meaning of these signifiers (social and economic capital, ecological damage)."[32] However, these early paragraphs can also be read as Olsen's insistence on the role language plays in developing class consciousness, a continuous process that, in this child, has already begun to emerge in her exploration of language.

Olsen continues to make clear how difficult Mazie's pursuit of language is amid such physical suffering. After Anna sends the children outside that morning and they lie on "the one patch of green" in the yard, Olsen allows Mazie an entire paragraph to ponder the words and phrases she knows: "She pushed her mind against things half known, not known," beginning with her name ("IT," 5). From there she first catalogs two skills, one physical (diapering a baby) and one linguistic (telling ghost stories), before leading into a loose and associative stream-of-consciousness monologue of those words and phrases. Her whole world, we realize by her catalog, is shaped by the mine, the "bowels of the earth under" her, or the fact that after "the whistle blows [. . .] payday comes" (5). The sensitivity of the child, from her knowledge of payday to the use of a simile to describe the wind in her hair, "soft like the baby laughing," is presented without sentiment as the fragments of Mazie's thoughts wrestle with ways to use the "things [she] am a knowen" to explain what she "am not knowen": "Men and daddy goin in like the day, and comin out black. Earth black, and pops face and hands black, and he spits from his mouth black. Night comes and it is black. Coal is black. It makes a fire. The sun is makin a fire on me now, but it is not black. Some color I'm not a knowen it is [. . .] but I'll have that learnin someday" (5). Primary colors, words structuring children's early learning in school, are absent from Mazie's vocabulary. Coal, after all, is black.

Mazie also understands the physicality of words. When beginning to think about the mine, for example, "a phrase trembled into her mind" ("IT," 5). Yet by the end of the paragraph, her sentences are nothing more than noun phrases trailing off into ellipses; Mazie does not know how to make sense of returning a dead miner, their neighbor's son, to "the bowels of the earth" when the "ghosts down in the mine" were the ones to start the fire that killed him (5). This paragraph demonstrates both Mazie's hunger for and her conscious acquisition of language, an anti-language comprised of a vocabulary of labor and death housed in the unyielding crucible of the mines.

The rest of the story exposes the reader to that which will try to take Mazie's language away as a child, as a female, and as one who is poor. Desiring her father's "recognition of her place, her desire, her emotions," Mazie follows him into town, anxious because she feels "all the world is a-cryen" ("IT," 8). Jim reassures her, cautioning her, "Don't worry your head about those things. Wait'll you grow up" (8). But Mazie has more questions. She asks her father why they "aint livin like [the boss man]," with running water, an indoor toilet, and white tablecloths. The central word of his answer—"he's a coal *operator*"—is misconstrued by Mazie as "operation" (9, emphasis added). The way Olsen presents this misunderstanding demonstrates not only Mazie's six-and-a-half-year-old literal logic but also her keen self-consciousness: "'Oh,' another wall of things not understood gone up. Something made the difference. A big word. Like what happened to Miss' Tikas when she was cut up. But how could he cut up a mine, his knife would have to be awful big" (9). As she waits for him outside the saloon, Mazie watches one side of the culm bank burn. Starved for color, she describes it as "[l]ike what happens to the back of your eyes when you close 'em after seein the sun" (9). Mazie shivers in the cold in the last paragraph of the story, the wind blowing "fine bits of the dust" onto her face, "remind[ing] her of the rough hand of her father when he caressed her, hurting her, but not knowing it, hurting with a pleasant hurt" (9).[33]

Anna remains a secondary character in "The Iron Throat," even referred to several times as "Mrs. Holbrook." (Olsen changes "Mrs." to "Anna" in *Yonnondio*.) It is Jim and Mazie, "the miner and the miner's daughter," as R. W. Steadman described them in his 1939 "Critique of Proletarian Literature" for the *North American Review*, on whom the story centers. Steadman's further description of the story states that it is "[t]hrough the delicate reveries and fragile heartbreak of a child, [that] a whole world of fear and tenderness and hopelessness is revealed."[34] In the aforementioned 1934 review in the *New Republic*, Cantwell wrote that "[i]n the fragments of Tilly [*sic*] Lerner's novel, in *The Partisan Review*, the imagery, the metaphors distilled out of common speech, are startling in their brilliance."[35] And it is through Mazie, a child, that the reader most accesses these metaphors "distilled out of common speech."

How, then, might reading forward from "The Iron Throat" inform our return to *Yonnondio*, first published forty years later?[36] I argue that Olsen's short story establishes her commitment to chronicling the language acquisition of the child in poverty, as well as the capacity of the child's language, which is often evident in the anti-language she drafts. While diverse 1930s texts demonstrate the damages of poverty, Olsen also asks how life can be sustained amid such damage, exploring the language that emerges from a life of violence and profound discontinuity.

Just as in the short story, the language of the novel itself is discontinuous, slipping from and into different points of view and wandering into various perspectives, especially when considering the novel's young protagonist, Mazie, and her mother, Anna. With few exceptions, Mazie is read by scholars only in conjunction with Anna. For Elizabeth Jameson, the relationship represents a "continued reproduction of working-class womanhood, a cycle of mothering, housework, wage work, and sexual vulnerability that distinguished working-class women and men, girls and boys."[37] Laura Hapke's reading of the tenuous mother-daughter relationship is far more bleak: "Anna tyrannizes over [and] robs Mazie of her childhood," thus conflating "self and (m)other."[38] Paula Rabinowitz's reading counters, finding Mazie and Anna "protect[ing each] other at crucial moments," which provides Mazie with the knowledge, welcomed or not, of "what 'being poor and a mother' mean for the working-class female."[39] Such paired discussions naturally evolve from a novel whose primary female characters' voices are, at times, indistinguishable near the end of the text. However, such readings rely too heavily on an explanation of Mazie that rarely moves beyond seeing the female child as her mother's generational shadow. I contend that Mazie's autonomy and her subjectivity remain important to Olsen as she catalogs, explicitly in "The Iron Throat" and continuing in *Yonnondio,* the process by which a poor child learns of suffering and then develops the language to articulate it, a process inextricably linked with the body.

Olsen's journals reinforce her commitments to representing "the horror of being a working-class child" (see figure 11).[40] Few scholars, however, focus explicitly on the children in the novel. Denning, one such exception to this trend in Olsen scholarship, reads *Yonnondio*'s power in making visible this horror in his chapter on proletarian ghetto pastorals in *The Cultural Front.*[41] Chris Robé's 2008 "Saint Mazie: A Socialist-Feminist Understanding of Film in Tillie Olsen's 'Yonnondio: From the Thirties,'" takes a different approach, focusing on the concept of imagination (in conversation with an earlier essay by Anthony Dawahare). Robé argues that "[t]he children possess a certain amount of imaginative freedom from having their thoughts less constrained within the limited societal roles of worker, mother, and father than adults do. Although the children are constantly being shaped by the ideological forces of home, industry, and school that work to dull their senses and confine their thoughts, their imaginations still can resist such strict regimentation."[42]

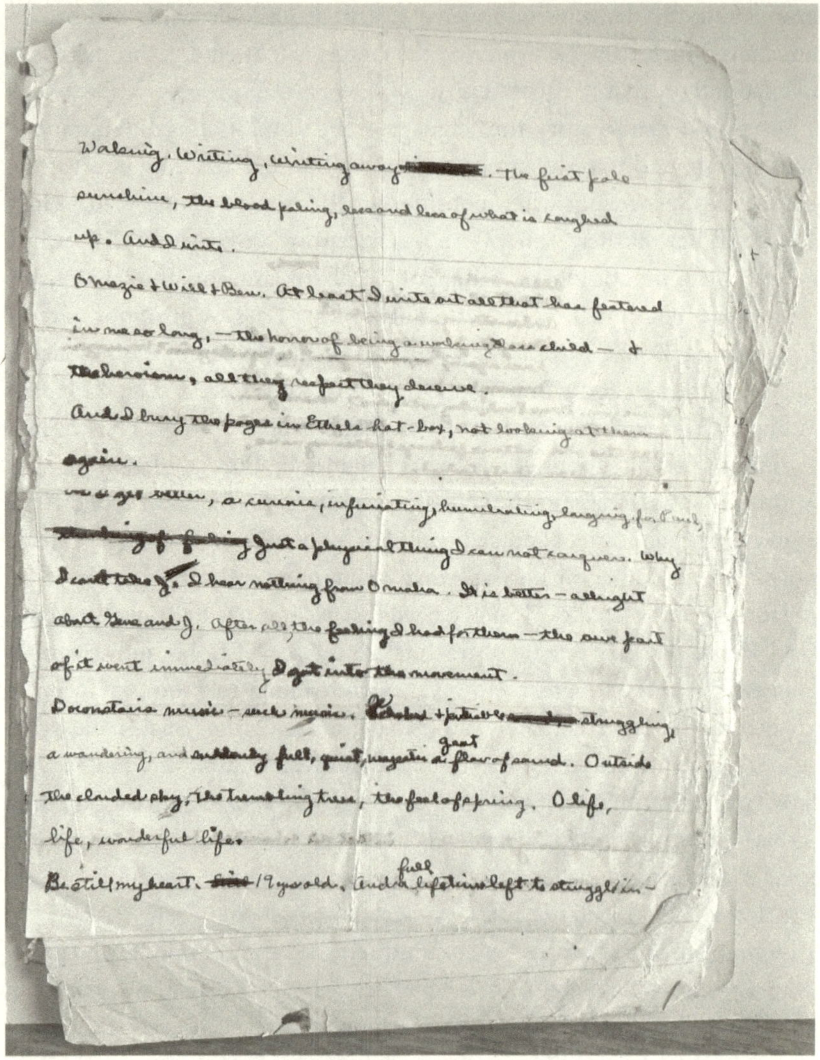
Walking. Writing, writing away [redacted]. The first pale
sunshine, the blood paling, less and less of what is coughed
up. And I write.
O Mazie + Will + Ben. At least I write out all that has festered
in me so long, — the horror of being a working class child — &
the heroism, all the respect they deserve.
And I bury the pages in Ethel's hat-box, not looking at them
again.
[illegible] I get better, a curious, infuriating, humiliating, longing for [illegible],
[illegible] Just a physical thing I can not conquer. Why
I can't take J. I hear nothing from Omaha. It is better — all right
about Gene and J. After all the feeling I had for them — the sure part
of it went immediately I got into the movement.
Downstairs music — such music. [illegible] + patient + [illegible] struggling,
a wandering, and suddenly full, quiet, majestic a great flow of sound. Outside
the clouded sky, the trembling trees, the feel of spring. O life,
life, wonderful life.
Be still my heart. [illegible] 19 yrs old. And a full lifetime left to struggle in —

FIGURE 11 A page from Tillie Olsen's journal. "Yonnondio, makings," collection M667, series 1, box 15, folder 28, Tillie Olsen Papers, Special Collections and University Archives, Stanford University. Copyright © 1974 by Tillie Olsen. Reprinted by permission of The Frances Goldin Literary Agency.

"Imagination," however, as used here, is unnuanced, amorphous, vague, and nebulous. It adheres to a framing of age that clearly demarcates childhood as separate and removed from an adult way of thinking and, somehow, less affected by constraining social roles, which are of course shaped by class. I argue that Olsen is interested in the specific ways that children, through language, move within and against such expectations and the systems that govern them.

We see this in the new material Olsen added to "The Iron Throat" in chapter 1 of *Yonnondio*. While enthralled by the colors, Mazie is attacked by a mentally ill drunk and almost thrown into the mine shaft, an offering to the voices this man hears tell him "[t]he mine was hungry for a child" (*Y*, 11). Once rescued and home, attuned to the suffering of her family, Mazie tries desperately to situate the experience within language, "against things half known [and] not known" (3). For example, during her assault near the mine, language is both a physical burden ("screams tore at [her] throat, caged there") and afterward an emotional release ("[w]ords came, drunken[:] Fear. 'Momma. Poppa'" [11, 12]). The tension between the unspeakable, that for which there is no language, and what must be spoken remains Mazie's burden throughout the novel. It is in chapter 4, however, that she begins to understand not only why the Holbrooks suffer but also the unjustness of their suffering, an understanding that Olsen insists is both linguistic and somatic. For the child there can be no gain of knowledge—or, in other words, language—that does not also register within her body.

ACROSS THE ARC OF the novel, Olsen then attends to the child's process of language formation, a process shaped by systems that the child must learn to navigate and name. Once Mazie begins to grow in her awareness of these systems, so too does her use of anti-language. Mazie's formal introduction to language comes that fall with her first enrollment in school. Eight but unable to read, she and Will are placed in the same first-grade class (*Y*, 34). Quickly moved up a grade after "the crooked white worms of words on the second-grade blackboard magically transform[ed] into words known and said," they are fascinated most by the "far countries [and] strange peoples" of the upper grades' lessons, not the "primer already breathlessly raced through with only silly sentences as a reward" (34). If language is without purpose, the Holbrook children do not feign interest. The lesson learned parallel to their grade placement, however, is their poverty. "For the first time," Olsen tells the reader, "Mazie was acutely conscious of her scuffed shoes, rag-bag clothes, quilt coat" (35).

When such knowledge becomes "intolerable," Mazie returns to a text from their gentle neighbor, Old Man Caldwell, a nonsense poem (*Y*, 35). Instead of mimicking his lighthearted delivery, Mazie's adaptation of the poem is delivered in "a deep mysterious voice" that "ripen[s] into tragedy" in stanza 2:

O Were I a Lum Ti Tum Tum
In the land of the alivoo fig
I'd play on the strum ti tum tum
To the tune of the thinguma jig.

And if in the Lum Ti Tums battle I fall
A thingamys all that I crave
Oh bury me deep in the whatcha may call
And plant thingumbobs over my grave. (*Y*, 35, emphasis original)

Mazie's response to great sadness is the comfort of nonsense verse. For Mara Faulkner, the "playful mystery" of the rhymes "affords Mazie a refuge from poverty."[43] I would argue the inverse, that within the nonsense words and the intentional shift in tone that her recitation takes resides an anti-language that denies the frivolity of language without meaning within a childhood of poverty. Though the poem seems to include nonsense words, it begins with lament and longing—"O Were I a Lum Ti Tum Tum"—and proposes an alternative reality of happiness for the speaker if only she were "[i]n the land of the alivoo fig." Then, in the second stanza, the speaker longs for what she most desires, "thingumbobs" to be planted "over [her] grave" if in the "battle [she] fall[s]."

For Fowler, "the element of verbal play links anti-language with the special rhymes and sayings of children's culture."[44] Yet Olsen's careful construction of Mazie's language here demonstrates a seriousness, a commitment to purpose that complicates commonplace associations of play and lightheartedness often attributed to children's verse, rhymes, and games (as discussed in chapter 2). Mazie's appropriation of Caldwell's poem, achieved by changing the tone of its delivery, neither "lifts her out of poverty" nor provides a "refuge from poverty," as Mara Faulkner argues.[45] Instead, Mazie's anti-language both longs for an alternative narrative arc and hopes against the futility, the fantastical impossibility of its existence. Admittedly, Olsen's narrator does tell the reader that "reciting [the poem], the sadness would ebb [and] the autumn world became blue and gold again" (*Y*, 35). But one must remember that every reprieve Mazie finds within nature is accompanied by "the sad hurt[, which] would gather into her again" (33). It is as though Mazie's "deep mysterious [recitation] voice" is akin to the "muffled sonorous sound" described within the epigraph at the start of the novel (which comes from a Walt Whitman poem of the same title); "a wailing word [. . .] borne through the air for a moment," it becomes "blank and gone and still and utterly lost" if there is no audience to acknowledge its existence.

CALDWELL'S SYSTEM OF language contrasts with the system Mazie first encounters in school. In their first conversation, Caldwell joins her, lying on the ground to also look up at the stars. Mazie first spins a narrative explaining the stars: "Splinters offn the moon I've heard it said. But more likely they're lamps in houses up there, or flowers growin in the night" (*Y*, 32). Caldwell's response ("Stars are suns") and the questions such an answer prompts in Mazie ("Then what is the sun, a fire?") combine to form the first time an adult has answered her questions with accessible language and enough detail to satiate her curiosity (33). Olsen carefully notes that Caldwell honors Mazie's initial explanation of the stars in the way he frames his history lesson about the Greeks, who had also "found in [the stars' names and] shapes images of what was on earth below" (33). Caldwell builds on what Mazie already knows, honoring her language as having purpose. Mazie's desire for knowledge—"a great hurt and wanting" (33)—is palpable, even painful. Caldwell's summation of this truth at the end of this section of the chapter both honors Mazie's intellect and summarizes the entirety of the novel: "Children have marvelous minds. I hate to see what life does to 'em" (34).

For the nine pages that Old Man Caldwell graces Olsen's text, Mazie has an ever-ready outlet of reprieve, a system in which her language finds space and is encouraged to explore and to inquire. Thus, that autumn, when "a hunger and fear pushed" her out of doors and away from home, Mazie finds herself at his house (*Y*, 37). Caldwell's daughter, Bess, calls her in to see the dying man. His broken sentences of advice ("Build on the knowing with the wondering"; "No, there is more—to rebel against what will not let life be") are interrupted by Olsen's narrator, who offers to the reader a small paragraph of Caldwell's existential lament, having turned from a "life of softness and ease" to a "stern life [of] people hard, bitter, and strong," although he feels he "brought them nothing" (38). Were it not for this scene, Caldwell would seem a gentle upper-class interloper above reproach in Olsen's attempt at proletarian realism, a grandfatherly figure whose wisdom engages the intellect of the child. Yet his inability to articulate that which he "[does] . . . *not* . . . *know*" instead signifies "words meaningless and strange, meaningless when one tries to understand, but meaningful for a fleeting second" (38, emphasis original).

That "fleeting second" becomes Mazie's pursuit in the remainder of the novel, a yoking of "each step pain" among shadows that "clutched at her" and the memory of "kind still hands of sound," the memory of language that somehow sustains (38, 37).

Lisa Orr argues that Caldwell's final advice for Mazie to remember that "the roots you need, are where you are now" is a reminder to "remain loyal to her class[,] the source of her political usefulness." Such a reading (framed by Olsen's original narrative *intent* for the novel, not its actual pages) proposes that the "fact that Mazie has been damaged [. . .] makes her the better activist."[46] Instead of unethically assigning damage as the measure of one's political worth, perhaps the way in which Caldwell articulates his words to Mazie, his physical struggle to express language, serves as a model for Mazie to emulate. His deathbed "words were incomprehensible. They parched [her] fear, but thirstily she still watched his eyes" (*Y*, 37). Olsen's use of "thirsty" as an adverb signifies that Mazie is, quite simply, "hungry for more than food," a description Olsen later used to describe the Depression era.[47] Reading this moment in the context of the hoped-for ending of the novel ignores that which the child learns to emulate to survive in the present. The future is too uncertain and too far away and, in the case of *Yonnondio*, "unlimn'd."

THE CONCLUDING SCENE OF chapter 4 not only provides one of the most poignant examples of Mazie's understanding of the corporeality of language but also serves as the climax to the first half of the book, the moment in which Mazie assigns language to that which she feels and thus moves to concretize her own system of meaning. For Rabinowitz, "[l]anguage resides within [Mazie's] body."[48] Suffering, of course, resides there too. By the end of the fourth chapter, the two—language and suffering—are, for Mazie, firmly ensconced in the body. In March Mazie anxiously awaits Anna's impending labor. Mazie, looking at Anna's swollen belly, "could feel words swollen big within her, words coming out with pain, bloody, all clothed in red" (*Y*, 43). Earlier, in the first ten pages of the novel, the narrator had explained Mazie's emotion of fear using a similar metaphor: "It came to Mazie like dark juices of undefined pain, pouring into her, filling the heart in her breast till it felt big, like the world. Fear came that her heart would push itself out, roll out like a ball. She clutched the baby closer to her, tight, tight, to hold the swollen thing inside" (7). The difference in chapter 4, however, is that emotion is now being codified as language, actual words "swollen big within her" (43) that are painful to birth. The four concluding chapters of the book demonstrate Mazie's understanding of how surreal and nuanced moments of active language acquisition through verbal play, exploration, and creation dissipate as her new environment pushes her to abandon a world of language to accept a world of corporeal suffering, a world of "tired words that slip out in monosyllables and are as if never spoken" (47).

Within this realization that there is no system in which language ameliorates suffering, what was accessible to the reader is gone; instead, the language of chapter 5 often breaks down, representing but not clarifying the family's suffering. Olsen's narrator returns in the middle of chapter 5, for example, with heavy-handed sarcasm that linguistically represents the ironies the Holbrooks are too tired to articulate in ways that exaggerate the ridiculousness of such claims within the lives of the poor. Using another exercise in dialectical semantics, which Fowler names as a basic characteristic of anti-language, the narrator erases the spaces between words, capitalizes common nouns to assert their paradoxical authority, and links with hyphens clichés whose pronouns are not representative of the whole. The narrator's anti-language inverts intended meaning with these slight typographical alterations: "ifyoureallywanttoworkyoucanalwaysfindajob" and "something about pursuitofhappiness" (*Y*, 62); the "God Job" and the "Sins of the Fathers [. . .] Visited on the Sons" (63–64); the children "pulpy with charity starches" who "chant the lesson after the teacher: we-are-the-richest-country-in-the-worr-uld" (64). What Fowler would call "verbal intimacy," "the solidarity of shared class languages," is parodied here in ways Olsen's class-conscious narrator modifies these empty signifiers.[49]

Aligning the style and structure of Olsen's novel closer to Leon Trotsky's *Literature and Revolution* (1924) than to Gold's proletarian realism, Coiner's analysis of *Yonnondio* focuses on the narrative intrusions and their "guidelines for readers, directing us as we proceed through the novel how to read—and how not to read—structures we are accustomed to finding in aesthetic works and exemplifying how those structures can be used to subvert the dominant culture from which they have been appropriated." These disruptions, she argues, echo Bakhtin's notion of heteroglossia, language that disrupts a dominant, singular meaning: "The myriad of heteroglossic voices of the marginalized constitute a social and political force against the tyranny of dominant discursive modes in any language community." Coiner's use of heteroglossia demonstrates the inclusionary power of these voices and their interrelationships. And *Yonnondio*'s multiple narrators, then, "maximize the possibility of heteroglossia."[50] I would argue that reading for anti-language focuses our attention on how the voice disrupts and the particulars of the subversion. This is where anti-language gains power: from a speaker's awareness of the norm and revision of it, too.

Crucially, Coiner also surfaces the difference of the role of the reader in Olsen's writing. "[I]n the act of reading," she writes, we "engage in an active, complex, and creative process not unlike that of writing."[51] We must engage with hegemonic linguistic formulations, protocols, and practices. How does Olsen's text position us to respond? In short, Coiner rightfully finds disruption in the work of the narrator's heteroglossia; I find it also in the children and how Olsen details the process by which the child uses language to make meaning from chaos and invites the reader to do so, too. For example, Olsen returns the burden of narration to the family for the chapter's climax, a grotesque retelling of Mazie's earlier assault at the mine that shuffles the roles assigned to each member of the family after Anna faints from complete exhaustion of mind and body. Olsen spares Mazie from narrating the horror of waking Anna but not the events that unfold when Jim returns drunk and rapes Anna. While Mazie's head is under the blankets, language of which she is unsure again loops in her consciousness as if repetition alone will bring clarity or, at least, assurance: "No use to tell him, not a bit of use, stiffly repeated itself and marched round and round her head. No use, no use" (*Y*, 75). As she listens to Anna's ignored protests ("the words, the words leaping"), Mazie once again assumes the role of mother, attempting to protect her brothers from hearing until her father comes for her help (75).

Here Mazie takes control, her language choices relexicalizing Anna's current condition: "Momma went dead again, Poppa" (*Y*, 75). After Jim kneads Anna's womb to stop the bleeding of the miscarriage and leaves for the doctor, Mazie is left alone with her mother's still body and must quiet Bess, who needs to nurse. While waiting, Mazie talks continuously, her language an intentional effort to again repurpose the narrative arc of Caldwell's nonsense poem in an attempt to quiet Bess and divert them both from "the naked thigh, the coarse hair, all the blood" (76). Yet gone are nonsense words; the Lum Ti Tum Tums become Bess and Mazie, and the "land of the alivoo fig" is anywhere that is not near Omaha: "I'll hold ya and love ya, Bess, I'll tell ya a story, see, I'll diaper you and I'll tell you a story, onct upon a time the night was quiet, and the river, a cool river, Bess, was goin along, goin along, talkin to itself so happy, and it said maybe Bess would like to come and Mazie too and it dont go by no cities, Bess" (76). Their responses to the trauma, Anna's incoherent fragments and Mazie's petitions for Bess's silence, are blended without attention to grammar or attribution of speech in a paragraph whose cadence is guided by the pauses of Bess's cries or Anna's shrieks. Often the sounds of all three crowd into a single sentence. Halliday claims that "the speakers of anti-language are constantly striving to maintain a counter-reality that is under pressure from the established world." "Constantly renewing itself," this type of anti-language manifests itself in the feminine collective of sound Olsen orchestrates in this paragraph.[52] To an outsider, such as the doctor whose parenthetical comments of judgment pepper the following page ("Damn fools, they ought to sterilize the whole lot of them after the second kid"), such sound represents chaos; to the Holbrook mother and daughter, it is the sound of language struggling to articulate suffering and shocked to realize "so much blood was in a body" (76).

Anne Pancake argues that *Yonnondio,* as a proletarian bildungsroman, does not present "progress in a specific direction"; therefore, it rightfully disrupts the upward mobility narrative of the American Dream. However, she also insists that Mazie's consciousness remains static: "[B]ound by her class position, [Mazie] can at best maintain the economic, intellectual, and emotional plane on which she begins. If Mazie changes at all, the direction is regressive." Mazie's love of school, Pancake goes on to say, "is extinguished by age eight," a further indication of her "regression." This classist metric discounts the knowledge Mazie has gained. Pancake's central argument, that the proletarian bildungsroman is not a progression that guarantees "permanent economic inequalities as transient differences to be rectified," is astute, but to characterize Mazie's maturation as regressive dismisses the capacity of the child.[53] Furthermore, it negates the structure of Olsen's prose and the work it requires of us as readers: We must learn how to read the language of the child in poverty.

Of course, Mazie *is* disconcertingly closer to silence here. Yet because *Yonnondio*'s modernist experimental language and narrative miscellany give the reader access to a less literal style of realism, examining the development of Mazie's polyvalent anti-language—a dialectic bound to the corporeal—illustrates the way language emerges from a life of violence and profound discontinuity, the way a single voice can speak against inherent power structures even as the speaker is becoming more fully aware of their existence. In chapters 7 and 8, then, Olsen returns to the motif of education at work in the novel since the first chapter to ask how life is to be situated amid such damage. Or, in other words, to ask what provides reprieve from suffering such as this.

AS EARLY AS PAGE 3 and prompted by Mazie's inquiry, Anna defines "edjication" as meaning "your hands stay white and you read books and work in an office" (*Y*, 3). Yet later, when the family is living in the city and the children again have access to school, school becomes for Mazie the place that most sharply identifies her class differences, not the place that provides access to white hands, books, and an office. Olsen renders Mazie's hatred of their new school in abnormal presentations of language that reflect her resistance. When we read her language of resistance as dialectical semantics, we are invited to read differently the typographical features such as nonessential capitalization, the removal of spaces between words, and aural presentations of spelling and sound (149). Mazie hears the teacher's welcome, for example, "MazieandWillHolbrookhavecomefromthecountrywheretheygrowthe-cornandwheatandallourmilkcomesfromsayhellotoMazieandWillchildren," as a generic, strung-together identifier of difference and from that point on wears the label of outsider with defiance (49). As she stands in front of the class, "faces mad and tired and scared and hungry and dead and their eyes like they want to eat you up," Mazie turns to the words on the blackboard for comfort: "Na-tion-al-it-ies" (50), represented on the page as though Mazie is sounding out each syllable. She also works her way through the accompanying list piecemeal, attempting to create associations that will help her make sense of the strangeness of the experience and the myriad of faces that do not look like hers. Similarly, Mazie tries to make sense of the newness of the racial and ethnic diversity of her new classmates by wondering if "the mine was here in the city too" and if her Black classmates also "had to live in the mine" (50).

That night, unable to communicate, Mazie attempts to disassociate, especially from Anna's postpartum depression and new pregnancy (*Y*, 58). As the Holbrooks visit old family friends, Mazie's language, once so full of metaphor, is incomplete. In response to the songs the adults sing, songs of "longing, a want undefined, for something lost, for something never known," Mazie's similes end in ellipses: "Oh, singin is like . . . Mazie, broken, searched for the word, feeling tears stand behind her eyelids. Singing is like . . . But no right words would form" (53). The text shifts away from Mazie to Anna's point of view for the rest of the novel only to return to Mazie's thoughts for short paragraphs or half pages. For Mazie, life in a city of meatpacking houses is "a voiceless dream to be endured," a phrase Olsen uses twice, verbatim, in less than twenty pages to describe Mazie's everyday life (59, 73). Shifting the emphasis of the novel to Anna allows Olsen to push back against national myths of class mobility, as Anna's narrative of upward mobility rests on the promises of education yet becomes empty clichés that neither she nor her children find merit in by the novel's end. After receiving a failing school report from Mazie, for example, Anna half-heartedly scolds an empty room and tells the nonverbal baby that "learnin's the only hope a body's got in this world" (67).

In the heat that suffocates the end of the novel, a rare moment of objective narration reveals the irony that children such as Anna's, "already stratified as dummies in school [and] condemned as unfit for the worlds of learning, art, imagination, invention," spend the summer months doing that for which they are supposed to be unfit—"learning, art, imagination, invention"—between the daily tasks of survival (*Y*, 103). Nevertheless, for Anna, books remain "marvels," "(*places your body aint ever been, cant ever get to go; inside people's heads; things you wouldn't never know*); keys, too, in that door to a better life on which opportunity would knock" (107, emphasis original). The only library to which Anna and her children have access is a "squat dirty converted store front (good enough for packingtown, they said) shelved with opiates and trash and marvels (from which most of the children are already turned in outraged self-respect, for it is not through books, the printed word, or so it seemed, that they had been judged poor learners, dumb dumb dumb? Told: what is in us has nothing to do with you)" (107). Poignant here is Olsen's unusual syntax, which half-heartedly buries the library's ironies between parentheses. Within the second set of parentheses, for example, Anna's hopes of "that door to a better life" is voluntarily shut by "packingtown" children in response to both their perceived illiteracies and the imagined discourse of the books themselves, books that judge, make fun, and speak, as the "us" of the last sentence signifies the books' articulation of class difference.

Within the Olsen Papers at Stanford University, there is evidence of how often Olsen returned in her drafting to the disconnect between the ways language functions in conventional systems of literacy, such as schooling and libraries. The two examples included here (see figures 12 and 13) were not included in the novel or in Olsen's 1989 edition of *Yonnondio*, which features three "fragments" of what happens next to the Holbrooks after the novel ends. Both "makings," as Olsen called these surviving scraps and drafts, appear to be draftings of the children's experiences in the packingtown school that take place between the aforementioned first day of school in chapter 5 and the beginning of the following summer break, which begins the final chapter of *Yonnondio*. These experiences take place in winter in the context of the "wind knived playground" (which both makings mention), in which children in poverty "bear too much, the laceration, the continual laceration in the school" (see figure 13). Within one typed page, hand annotated as from 1934, Olsen drafts toward her general claim ("the lessons so foolish, so futile lessons, what would they teach these children of poverty—what could these lessons give them that was not known"), which makes plain why packingtown children "so hate book learning, to get out a reade[r] from the library, a typical one, and all the bunk in it, all the so transparent lies."[54] The other page (see figure 12) offers an example of the "futile lessons":

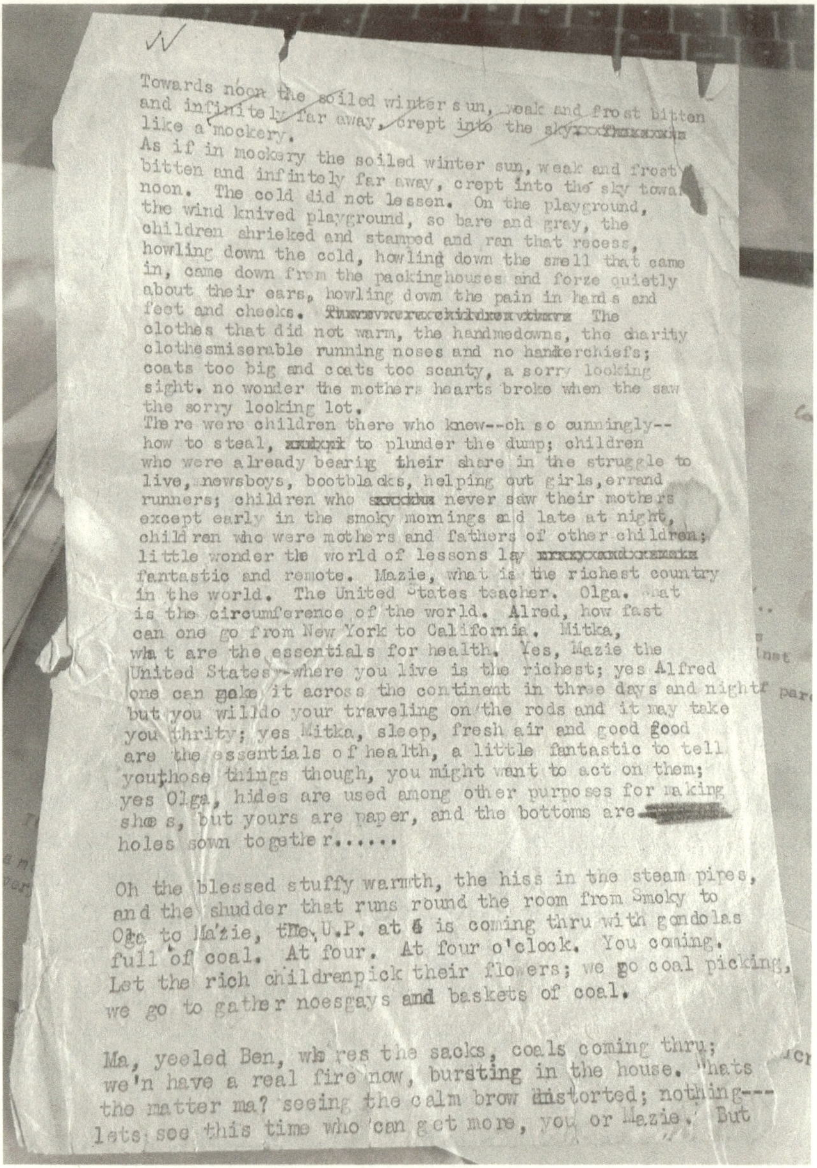

Towards noon the soiled winter sun, weak and frost bitten
and infinitely far away, crept into the sky
like a mockery.
As if in mockery the soiled winter sun, weak and frost
bitten and infintoly far away, crept into the sky towa
noon. The cold did not lessen. On the playground,
the wind knived playground, so bare and gray, the
children shrieked and stamped and ran that recess,
howling down the cold, howling down the smell that came
in, came down from the packinghouses and forze quietly
about their ears, howling down the pain in hands and
feet and cheeks. The
clothes that did not warm, the handmedowns, the charity
clothesmiserable running noses and no handkerchiefs;
coats too big and coats too scanty, a sorry looking
sight. no wonder the mothers hearts broke when the saw
the sorry looking lot.
There were children there who knew--oh so cunningly--
how to steal, to plunder the dump; children
who were already bearig their share in the struggle to
live, newsboys, bootblacks, helping out girls, errand
runners; children who never saw their mothers
except early in the smoky mornings and late at night,
children who were mothers and fathers of other children;
little wonder the world of lessons lay
fantastic and remote. Mazie, what is the richest country
in the world. The United States teacher. Olga. hat
is the circumference of the world. Alred, how fast
can one go from New York to California. Mitka,
what are the essentials for health. Yes, Mazie the
United States--where you live is the richest; yes Alfred
one can make it across the continent in three days and nights
but you willdo your traveling on the rods and it may take
you thrity; yes Mitka, sleep, fresh air and good food
are the essentials of health, a little fantastic to tell
youthose things though, you might want to act on them;
yes Olga, hides are used among other purposes for making
shoes, but yours are paper, and the bottoms are
holes sown together......

Oh the blessed stuffy warmth, the hiss in the steam pipes,
and the shudder that runs round the room from Smoky to
Olga to Mazie, the U.P. at 4 is coming thru with gondolas
full of coal. At four. At four o'clock. You coming.
Let the rich childrenpick their flowers; we go coal picking,
we go to gather noesgays and baskets of coal.

Ma, yeeled Ben, wheres the sacks, coals coming thru;
we'n have a real fire now, bursting in the house. Whats
the matter ma? seeing the calm brow distorted; nothing---
lets see this time who can get more, you or Mazie. But

FIGURE 12 A page of makings from Olsen's papers. "Towards noon," "Yonnondio, makings," collection M667, series 1, box 4, folder 5, Tillie Olsen Papers, Special Collections and University Archives, Stanford University. Copyright © 1974 by Tillie Olsen. Reprinted by permission of The Frances Goldin Literary Agency.

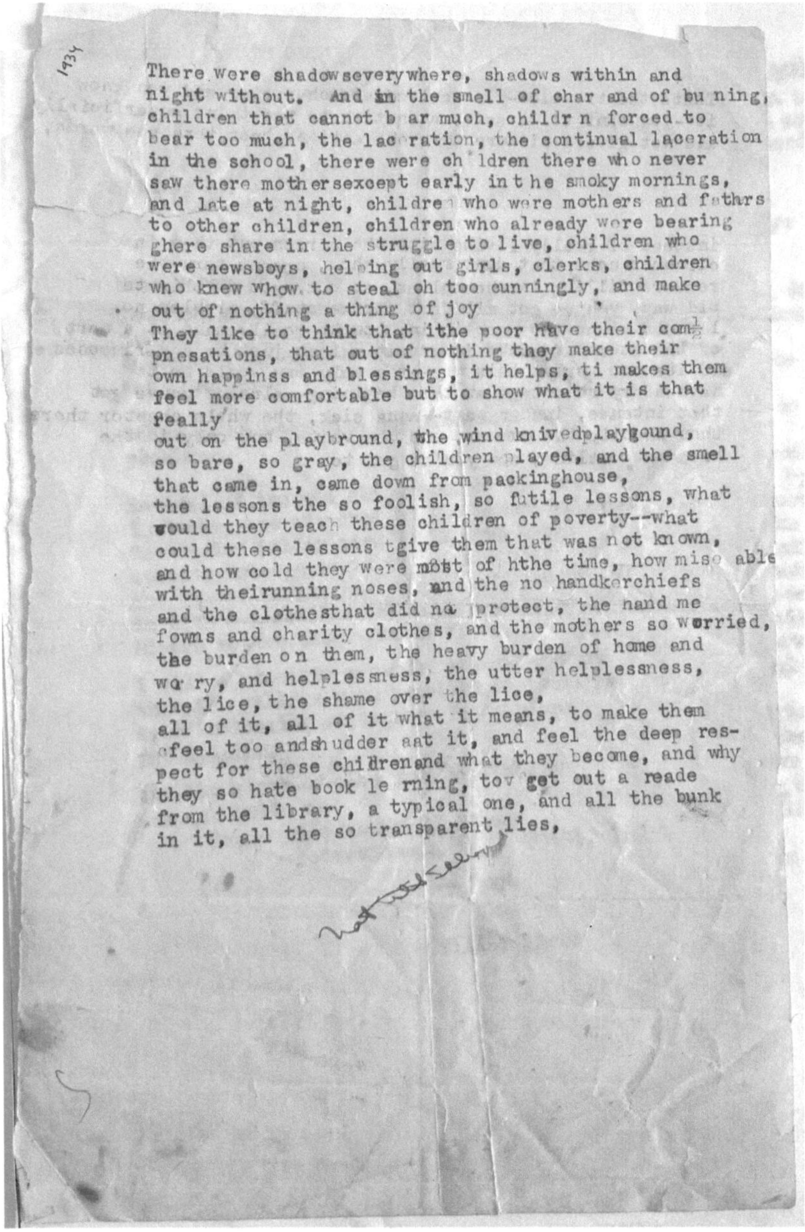

1934

There were shadowseverywhere, shadows within and
night without. And in the smell of char and of bu ning,
children that cannot b ar much, childr n forced to
bear too much, the lac ration, the continual laceration
in the school, there were ch ldren there who never
saw there mothersexcept early int he smoky mornings,
and late at night, childre who were mothers and fathrs
to other children, children who already were bearing
ghere share in the struggle to live, children who
were newsboys, hel ing out girls, clerks, children
who knew whow to steal oh too cunningly, and make
out of nothing a thing of joy
They like to think that ithe poor have their com½
pnesations, that out of nothing they make their
own happinss and blessings, it helps, ti makes them
feel more comfortable but to show what it is that
feally
out on the playbround, the wind knivedplaygound,
so bare, so gray, the children played, and the smell
that came in, came down from packinghouse,
the lessons the so foolish, so futile lessons, what
would they teach these children of poverty--what
could these lessons tgive them that was not known,
and how cold they were most of hthe time, how miso able
with theirunning noses, and the no handkerchiefs
and the clothesthat did no protect, the hand me
fowns and charity clothes, and the mothers so worried,
the burden on them, the heavy burden of home and
wo ry, and helplessness, the utter helplessness,
the lice, the shame over the lice,
all of it, all of it what it means, to make them
feel too andshudder aat it, and feel the deep res-
pect for these chidrenand what they become, and why
they so hate book le rning, tov get out a reade
from the library, a typical one, and all the bunk
in it, all the so transparent lies,

FIGURE 13 A page of makings from Olsen's papers. "There were shadows," "Yonnondio, makings," collection M667, series 1, box 4, folder 5, Tillie Olsen Papers, Special Collections and University Archives, Stanford University. Copyright © 1974 by Tillie Olsen. Reprinted by permission of The Frances Goldin Literary Agency.

> There were children there who knew—oh how so cunningly—how to steal, to plunder the dump; children who were already bearing their share in the struggle to live, newsboys, bootblacks, helping out girls, errand runners; children who never saw their mothers except early in the smoky mornings and late at night, children who were mothers and fathers of other children; little wonder the world of lessons lay fantastic and remote. Mazie, what is the richest country in the world. The United States teacher. Olga, what is the circumference of the world. Al[f]red, how fast can one go from New York to California. Mitka, what are the essentials for health. Yes, Mazie the United States—where you live is the richest; yes Alfred one can make it across the continent in three days and nights but you willdo [*sic*] your traveling on the ro[a]ds and it may take you thirty; yes Mitka, sleep, fresh air and good food are the essentials of health, a little fantastic to tell you those things though, you might want to act on them; yes Olga, hides are used among other purposes for making shoes, but yours are paper, and the bottoms are holes sown together. . . . . .[55]

The order Olsen drafted these pages is unknown, though their filing in the archive indicates that they were drafted in the 1930s. I include these makings here not to suggest that they should have been included in the novel but to demonstrate Olsen working through her commitment to critically reading these systems through the ironies inherent in being a poor or working-class child within them. It is also of note that what she decided to include in *Yonnondio* about school, represented in three pages within chapter 5, shows the anti-language of these children, an act of resistance.

Olsen's return to these broken systems in *Yonnondio* and in these archival makings sets up the last chapter of the novel, in which she explores how Mazie's capacity for anti-language works within and actively against these systems. Because the Holbrook children, just like their impoverished playmates, have come to believe that "what is in [books] has nothing to do with [them]," they invest their energies in the labor of play (*Y*, 107). In doing so, they find their own texts: slang and clichés they adopt from film that were not intended for inclusion in the curriculum of a sentimental childhood, as well as parodies of nursery rhymes from the far corners of their urban playground. Olsen's curious repetition of the word "text" within this two-page span begins with twelve-year-old Jinella, Mazie's playmate, who chooses the narrative of the movies as her "text" as she plays in her tent at the dump among discarded high-heeled shoes and jewelry made of fish lures and machinery parts: "Take me to the roadhouse, I want to make whoopee. Hotcha. Never never never.

O my gigolo, my gigolo. A moment of ecstasy, a lifetime of regret" (109). Jinella's sexualized texts are sordid perversions of the "onceuponatime and theylivedhappilyeverafter fairy tales which the librarian had selected for Mazie" (107). At home, Ben's "terrible texts" also borrow their rhyme and meter from tales for children (109). The final rhyme is especially foreboding:

> *Mother, Mother, I am sick.*
> *Call the doctor quick, quick, quick.*
> *Doctor, Doctor, will I die?*
> *Yes. You will. And so shall I.* (*Y*, 110, emphasis original)

Mazie's response when she hears Ben is, in a motherly gesture, to "[gather her younger siblings] to her" and request of their father stories of "when [he was] little" (*Y*, 110). But their father is too tired ("the day at Cudahy's has thieved Pop's text"), and he sleeps instead (110). Similarly, for Anna, whose "apron front [is] still wet from doing dishes, it is too late for texts," and the children are left without an alternative narrative (110). Neither the library nor the parents have the resources to engage the children in a different discourse or offer them a different text.[56]

Chapter 8 completes for the second half of the novel Olsen's four-chapter pattern of struggle, silence, redemption, and hope. July finds the children out of school and engaged in a feverish combination of work and play: "Children [. . .] plan, measure, figure, design, invent, construct, costume themselves, stage dramas; endlessly—between tasks, errands, smaller children to be looked after, jobs, dailinesses—live in passionate absorbed activity, in rapt make-believe" (*Y*, 103). Yet Mazie struggles to live in this dual world of play and work. The remainder of the chapter shifts to the dog days of summer and moves back and forth between the labor (play) of children at the dump, their mothers at home, and adults at the packing house at which Jim now works, painting each as a separate but familiar hell. Mazie moves through the end of the chapter angrily. Her frustrations manifest themselves in a series of questions she demands of Anna after being made to help with the canning: "Why is it always me that has to help? How come Will gets to play?"; "Why couldn't *I* get borned a boy?"; "Why dont I have no place?" (122–23). It is of note that Olsen gives such language to a child. Mazie, almost nine, articulates that which Anna can only think. Though Anna questions who will care for the children if not her, it is only in the depths of her postpartum depression that she allows herself the luxury of thoughts as rebellious as Mazie's: "And a separation, a distance—something broken and new and tremulous—had been born in her, lying by herself those long unaccustomed hours free of task" (89, 93).

Mazie already knows this—the language that can come when the body is at rest—which explains her growing rage as the novel progresses. The futility of Mazie's linguistic struggle against becoming the "bounded body" of her mother culminates in Mazie's physical collapse. If there were not another child whose understanding of suffering has found language, then Mazie's hopelessness here would seem irreparable.

AS THE NOVEL CLOSES, Olsen draws our attention to what the child has learned about language and its ability to resist, to rename, and to relexicalize. She makes plain the necessity of a recipient for a text, inviting us as readers to take up a model of ethically responding to the classed child by, in part, responding to the new knowledge produced by the child. It is important to note that Olsen does not return Mazie to conventional literacy here. Though the 1989 *Yonnondio* edition postscript sections and archival makings mention explicitly Mazie's turn to books, they are without mention of an event, text, or any sort of catalyst: "Mazie reading away, reading away. Suddenly, books all"; "Mazie reading even while doing dishes"; "wit [*sic*] the kids & the laundry & her pride over Mazies sudden & perplexing brilliance."[57] By not including Mazie's move to conventional literacy in the first edition of the novel, Olsen insists that the child's growing class consciousness can be internal, a series of moments and experiences when the child uses language to explore and to push against her world.

This is why the novel's last pages also offer Erina, Olsen's grotesque representation of the knowledge that burdens Mazie. Erina is the only person to whom Mazie longs to speak figuratively again and from whom she longs to listen to language still living, still resisting. The second mention of Erina in the text is when Mazie, Annamae, and Ellie are "scrabbling" and "grubb[ing]" in the dump for "findins" (*Y*, 118, 117, 116). Providing "a large number of alternatives for the important concepts of the counter-culture, either synonyms or finely differentiated variants," Mazie and her friends overlexicalize the labor of finding and bringing home from the dump objects both useful and aesthetically pleasing, which signifies the importance they assign to their labor of play.[58] Olsen crafts this anti-language as the setting into which Erina, an epileptic child of ten or so "with her bones sticking out like great knobs," begs the girls for pennies for ice cream to ease the hurt she tells Mazie resides "inside" (118, 119). Mazie fears the ill child as well, the "pus [that] oozed from her eyes [and the] weed stickers—maybe lice—in her hair," but she doesn't flee from her, largely because of the dream she had the night before, a dream in which "her body [was] becoming Erina's body" (119).

Within a moment created by the anti-language of these children, Olsen requires the reader to navigate their parallel but dissimilar discourse as each child makes meaning through language. While Mazie grubs, the girls' talk and Erina's sentences form a strange mixture of religious clichés and careful observations of the world at her feet. For Rabinowitz, "Erina repeats the sermons and invectives hurled at her, turning them into personal jeremiads that she in turn hurls back at the world."[59] I would add that Erina's astute observations of the natural world function as metaphors for her suffering, and it is this, her understanding and articulation of suffering, that makes Mazie "[want] to hear Erina talk—but not have to look at her" (*Y*, 120). For example, "a sick-happy feeling to be with Erina, to listen to Erina" rises in Mazie as Erina cautions her to "watch for the little ants[. . . .] Dont hurt their houses. They have to hurry and work so hard and carry heavy things and I sees them carry each other sometime" (119–20). This mention of a compassion that eases the labor of another causes Mazie to realize that what she "had thought was dirt on [Erina's] cheek was bad bruises," and in response to this new knowledge, Mazie "gently" tells Erina to rest while she finds something cold for her to eat (120).

Where the other girls saw the grotesque, Mazie sees suffering. Erina still repulses her, yet Mazie is drawn to the way Erina assigns to her suffering language that resists. Furthermore, Mazie thinks that Erina will listen to her attempts to articulate suffering, or that which might relieve it. What Mazie wanted to tell Erina, that "last night she dreamed she swung the Big Dipper round and round and drank the night with the stars in it," Mazie scolds herself for thinking of in Erina's absence (*Y*, 121). Mazie's stars of ice represent an anti-language desperate to represent a counter-reality that she, still a child, needs. But she knows too much. She knows that "stars are fire" and that ice is not available to her; she knows the burden Old Man Caldwell could not quite articulate but wanted her so desperately to know. Mazie physically responds to this frustration, throwing a "corncob from the gutter" at the woman who looks at her while holding a "handkerchief to her nose, real delicate" (121). When Mazie returns home, she demands of her mother questions Anna cannot comprehend. Mazie then faints and sleeps so long that Anna is worried.

But when Mazie wakes, for one paragraph the language of the "place between the outhouse and the garbage dump" briefly returns, and she "pushed her mind hard against things half known, not known" (*Y*, 3):

> Somehow on the couch in the kitchen beside Ben, head to his feet, feet to his head. The sun is slanting its long last rays through the window. An

> iridescence floats on her hand, rainbows the wall, shifts in scales of hue here and there in the room. What is it, what is it? The hanging prism? One of the rays, touching it, has cracked open; burst; unfolded the radiance. The other rays still slant unbroken—straight shafts of light, clear threads of glass. Are the rainbows, the floating pools, the radiance folded into each one of them too? Where kept? How hidden? The wonder dazes her head and she turns her hand to hold the stammering light, unlock its magic, but she grasps shadows, and the iridescence glides onto Ben's unconscious face.
>
> Not knowing an every-hued radiance floats on her hair, her mother stands at the sink; her knife seems flying. Fruit flies rise and settle and rise.
>
> Lovingly: "Momma." (*Y*, 130–31)

The color Mazie craves draws her to her mother. While it seems impossible for the reader to dismiss the worry that Mazie's verbal rage might quickly dispel into Anna's silent inner monologue, for now Mazie is drawn to the plurality of the light's rays, even though she is unable to hold "the stammering light" (*Y*, 130). For now "Ben shifts around to lie in Mazie's arms" and asks her to "splain to me about bad dreams" (131). For now Mazie's anti-language is needed. For now there is another child who needs her to make meaning out of suffering.

As Ben waits for Mazie's narrative, with "astonished joy [Bess] clashes the [fruit jar] lid down" (*Y*, 132). In a rhythm akin to chapter 8's repetitive imperatives of the workers ("*Steamed boiled broiled fried cooked. Geared, meshed*") and Anna ("Skim, stir; sprinkle Bess; pit, peel and cut; sponge; skim, stir"), Bess begins to create sound: "Bang, slam, whack. Release, grab, slam, bang, bang" (125, 128, 132, emphasis original). The difference between Bess's onomatopoeic language and the commands that drive Anna and the packing house workers is threefold. First, it is organic, "[c]enturies of human drive [at] work in her"; second, it brings her great joy, a "human ecstasy of achievement"; and third, it communicates hope: "The fetid fevered air rings with Anna's, Mazie's, Ben's laughter; Bess's toothless, triumphant crow" (132). Here Bess's rhythms of labor provide the family with a reprieve. Her sounds can also be read as early moves toward language. Scholars often read Bess's play in this chapter as hopeful. I argue, however, that it also shows Olsen's interest in the child's acquisition of language.[60]

Bess's labor—labor that provides a reprieve and, thus, sustains—manifests similarly in Mazie's compassion for Erina's suffering, which also demonstrates an understanding of how to see the other as other. By situating that moment within a grotesque representation of bodily suffering exacerbated by poverty, Olsen mimics a middle-class reader's discomfort with poverty. Mazie, we remember, "wanted to hear Erina talk—but not have to look at her" (*Y*, 120). As Rabinowitz notes, "children stand metaphorically for these depression sites," and they thus "[enable] a new look at what [is] beneath view."[61] Mazie demonstrates the ability to respond to someone in a lesser place and to recover her worth. This moment of ethical recuperation is not the revolutionary resolution Gold's proletarian realism called for; instead, it is a small reprieve.

This reprieve, however, forces the reader to consider a question Judith Butler frames in her essay on the role of the humanities in the public sphere: "Whose lives are grievable"?[62] "I want to say," she begins,

> that sometimes people seem to be endowed with a certain value, that is, their lives are regarded as valuable and they assume a certain form and bearing under that regard. Great efforts are made to protect and defend those lives, and yet in other instances, lives are regarded as disposable or are so stripped of value that when they are imperiled, injured, or lost, they assume a social ontology that is partially constituted by that regard. Hence, they are not cause for worry; their potential loss is no occasion to mourn. Someone who never existed has been nullified, so nothing has happened. The "grievable" postulates a future conditional, a perspective from the future; indeed, to be grievable is a precondition of being valuable in the present.[63]

Because "the ungrievable bear the mark of those who will never be mourned because they were never understood to be living," Butler's premise suggests an obligation to attend to the ways in which those in an anti-society live in the margins.[64] In response to children creating their own sense of space, their own language, and their own texts, Mazie demonstrates how to escape—if only temporarily—the suffering body. Mazie, quite simply, finds Erina's suffering grievable.

Certainly no proletarian artist or writer would have answered a question such as Butler's without mention of the child. *Yonnondio*, however, evokes an ethical response because Olsen teaches us how to listen to that which we might otherwise reject, ignore, or not even hear: the ability of multisided and polyvalent discourse to register the stresses underwritten by economic structures. The anti-language of this vulnerable other prompts the reader to process overlapping registers not as chaotic or nonsensical but as the child's efforts to shape order from clutter and to engage others in the problems of their world, a world marked by loss and damage. The labor required of the reader is not intended to be comparable to the labor of survival of the child within the narrative (and such a conflation would be unethical in its centering of the reader). Instead, this labor requires a reader to become aware of the incredible capacity of the child's language to make meaning by forcing the reader to be aware of what it might look like to read ethically, to see the child and their language as grievable.

Mazie's education teaches her that language is a text, something constructed by, first, a speaker like her parents (Anna's "too late for texts" after dishes or "the day at Cudahy's has thieved Pop's text" [*Y*, 110]); second, a larger system (like the text "the librarian had selected for Mazie"; the gendered and sexual text the boys construct for her, "*Evrybody* [*sic*] *sees your pie*"; or the text of the packing house town, "tired words that slip out in monosyllables and are as if never spoken" [107, 108, 47, emphasis in the original]); or, third, herself ("A phrase trembled into her mind, 'Bowels of the earth'" [4]). Mazie also realizes that language is a text shaped by environment, such as the mine metaphors ("And a lamp like poppa's comes out, but in the sky") she uses throughout the novel (4). Yet as Mazie learns that her language is a text that can question, "Why dont I have no place?" (123), she also realizes that language is a text that begins to languish where there is no one to receive it, the lesson she learns from her mother. The novel itself ends with a cautionary caveat on the fate of texts without a reader:

> Reader, it was not to have ended here, but it is nearly forty years since this book had to be set aside, never to come to completion.
>
> These pages you have read are all that is deemed publishable of it. Only fragments, rough drafts, outlines, scraps remain—to tell what might have been, and never will be now.
>
> *Yonnondio! Yonnondio!—unlimn'd they disappear.* (*Y*, 133, emphasis original)

By making the autobiography of the novel its conclusion, Olsen begs her reader to hear the texts of the poor and the working class, texts that—unless limned—become "blank and gone and still, and utterly lost," texts that become ungrievable lives (Walt Whitman, as quoted on *Y*, ix). She does so by bending and kneeling to look at this depression site through the anti-language of the child in poverty. Reading forward from "The Iron Throat" and in Olsen's archived makings, we see multiple returns to how the language of the child demonstrates a growing class consciousness because of the child's efforts to navigate systems of language and meaning.

CHAPTER FOUR

Reading (in) Class

Children in the 1930s in the aforementioned Young Pioneers, a U.S.-based Communist youth club, were strongly encouraged to subscribe, read, and write to and for the magazine *New Pioneer*. The back cover of each monthly issue was an original full-page comic. Serialized only across the first few issues, the comics thereafter stood alone, consistently reinforcing recurring themes across the magazine and distilling the mission of the organization into episodic bits as if to entice a new reader to turn over and open the issue or to help a returning reader quickly advertise the magazine to their neighbors and classmates.

Steve Prohaska's back cover of the March 1933 issue, for example, tells the story of a girl named Mary and her strategic rebellion at school (see figure 14).[1] Her teacher, unnamed, confiscates her *New Pioneer* magazine because it "isn't fit for a young girl like you to read" and gives it to the principal, who eagerly tells Mary that she "burned it." In a panel positioning Mary and the principal nearly at eye level (in the next panel we do see that the principal is seated), Mary demands that the principal "pay for it." She does, and Mary happily makes change. The penultimate panel shows the class all quietly reading the next day, the *New Pioneer* magazines that Mary and her friends have sold to their classmates tucked inside textbooks and thus completely out of sight of the teacher. Mary deftly works within and against the system of the school and its teachers, which Prohaska illustrates with rigidly lined faces, sharp exclamation points, and anonymizing rows of desks. The final panel of the comic rewards a young reader with the revelation that "Mary's adventure actually happened to Edith—Age 10 of Great Falls, Mont." For any reader, adult or child, the overt critique of school is readily apparent; so, too, is the idea that Mary and Edith had every right to read this magazine and to use their language to speak back to those in power and to tell others of this experience.

Centering and celebrating the agency and capacity of young people—especially those sympathetic to or in the working class—resonates as a theme across Young Pioneer publications. Martha Campion's introduction to the 1934 pamphlet *Who Are the Young Pioneers?*, for example, includes these paragraphs:

> Many people say "Oh, kids! What can kids do?" Well, these stories show that "kids" can do a lot.

FIGURE 14 The back cover of the March 1933 issue of *New Pioneer*. *New Pioneer* 2, no. 11 (March 1933), box 35, Radical Pamphlets, Center for Southwest Research, University of New Mexico.

> Others say "Oh, children shouldn't bother about serious things! Children should just play and be happy."
>
> We think you should play and be happy, too; but we think most of you want to do and can do something more than that.
>
> We think most of you have brains and want to use them. We think you know how to think for yourselves, too, in spite of the fact that in the schools and newspapers and movies they try to make you think the way that they want you to.
>
> We think you should know about serious things and talk about them. And we know that you have enough sense to understand them and enough spunk to do something about them.[2]

This orientation was in stark contrast to the broader cultural belief that "children should be shielded from the political realm and from the hard realities of society and economics."[3]

THIS CHAPTER CONTINUES MY exploration of the language of children in poverty during the Depression era and language created in literature for young characters in this and other precarious class positions. While it might seem banal to note that the seminal texts grounding previous chapters in this manuscript were written by adults for adults, doing so surfaces a different question, one that I would argue expands our capacity as readers to engage ethically with representations of the language of young people considered the classed other: *What changes, if anything, when the intended reader is instead a child?*

A comprehensive analysis of children's literature in the Depression era is beyond the scope of this project.[4] However, I would like to pause to look closely at three groups of texts within 1930s literature for young people that help us take up this question differently. In mainstream literature of the period for children, we primarily see authors choose language that replicates pervasive cultural narratives about class. In these fictional works, such as commercial novels and school readers, anti-language emerges with far less frequency than in the more experimental modernist texts discussed in earlier chapters. Leftists writing for children also worked to instill in young people a very precise kind of class consciousness, and language was proffered more explicitly for specific children to try on and, in their rehearsal, share with other children. Yet the language offered was rarely anti-language. Thus, across genres, these adult authors made choices about what to include or not on behalf of their anticipated young reader and, in doing so, made a claim about what was best or necessary for a child reader of a particular class position. This chapter considers what meaning young people from different class positions were invited to make as readers of these texts, as well as what resistance was modeled (or not) and, therefore, implicitly or explicitly sanctioned by adult writers of three very different kinds of texts.[5]

Reading to Recruit and Reclaim the Classed Other

Some of the most overtly political texts written for children were an extension of the growth of the Left in the early decades of twentieth-century American culture before the rise of the Popular Front. There was great concern that these proletarian texts for children be "uncorrupted by commercial imperatives or public school politics," and the number of texts produced was really quite small.[6] This small body of proletarian literature for young people "explicitly challenged the dominant social order," including arguing for racial justice and against models of traditional schooling that only further replicated the class structures of capitalism.[7]

I'm most interested in the aforementioned youth magazine, *New Pioneer,* which first began in May 1931.[8] This was the official publication of the children's organization (ages seven to seventeen) that began in 1923 and then was "rebranded" as the Young Pioneers of America in 1925.[9] A direct response to the growing conservative youth organization the Boy Scouts and their troop structure and camping programs and akin to Lenin's youth organization of the same name, the Young Pioneers was largely comprised of the children or siblings of Communist Party members, even as a stated goal of the organization was to recruit working-class children whose parents were not members.[10] *New Pioneer* was written with such recruitment in mind.

Within the periodical and other publications from New Pioneer Publishing Company of New York, young readers saw unified, explicit claims about the qualities Young Pioneers should possess as "political thinkers and actors in their own right," itself an agential framing of what childhood should be.[11] Martha Campion, one of many editors of *New Pioneer* and author of the 1934 pamphlet *Who Are the Young Pioneers?,* wrote that "[t]he YOUNG PIONEERS explore the system of society and government under which we live. They see how people live, and understand more and more how the people who own the country cheat the people who do all the work. Then they spread this truth to other people. The Pioneers today fight on the side of the workers in the great struggle that is always going on between the workers and the bosses."[12] Given the organization's permanence across the 1920s and the acceleration of national economic hardship across the early years of the 1930s, the earliest issues of the *New Pioneer* offer the chance to read the organization's response to the growing Depression and its effect on young people.[13]

The editorial of the first issue of the *New Pioneer* in 1931 demonstrates this concern for young readers (see figure 15).[14] One sentence, deep within the second paragraph, can be read as specific to the Depression: "I bet many of you fellows and girls work after school or maybe all day long, because your parents are out of work or underpaid." Again in paragraph 3 there is brief mention of "children of unemployed workers." These are not the topic sentences of the paragraphs in which they appear; instead, they are supporting details in the editorial's framing of the primary conflict impacting the lives of children, that between the "[b]osses and workers." The long-standing issues of the organization—ending child labor, organizing to effect change, providing public services ("free lunches [. . .], playgrounds, parks, gyms, pools"), and promoting youth exercising their voices—are centered. Economic hardship, after all, was not new for "American workers and farmers' children."[15]

Each issue of the magazine included stories as well as recurring columns, such as the conversational "Science and Nature for Johnny Rebel," which was full of "questions asked by every person who is alive"; how-to articles, such as "How to Make Furniture from Boxes," or, in later issues, tutorials for various sports or camping skills; "LAFFS," jokes and puns often submitted by children; and "American History Retold in Pictures," which is described in the June 1931 issue as "lots more interesting than the history you've been taught in school."[16] Across the early years of the magazine there is evidence that children not only returned to these core issues but also mirrored the language offered in adult-written stories and columns, most notably in the "Dear Comrade Editor," which was a two-page spread full of short letters from young readers of the magazine. As they had been encouraged to do, many children wrote in reporting the membership numbers of their local troop or their efforts to sell subscriptions to *New Pioneer*. And consistently there were letters demonstrating Young Pioneers' commitments to racial equality: Morris Motzkin, age twelve, of Malden, Massachusetts, wrote in about his new "Pioneer Troop of workers' children, black and white alike," in the March 1934 issue.[17]

From the beginning, children wrote in to give voice to the worsening conditions specific to their context and most often paired those brief narratives of injustice with specific action they were taking, often in their Young Pioneer troop. Alice, Antonie, and Irene from Liberty, West Virginia, for example, wrote in about the "cut in their [fathers'] wages" leading to "starvation conditions which are forced upon us by the bosses," while Elmer Hyppa from

HELLO FELLERS! HELLO GIRLS!

HERE I AM, boys and girls, your new magazine! How do you like me in my cover of colors? Boy! Do you know I am the best and only magazine ever printed for American workers and farmers' children?

Go on and read me! You'll find stories. You'll find sports. You'll find all kinds of pictures. There's news and stories about children in other lands. You won't have to look far to find how to make and build things, either. I might as well tell you right now, there's just two kinds of people. Bosses and workers. And I stand four-square for workers and the workingclass children. We have to fight together with our parents for the things we want and that belong to us. And say! I bet many of you fellows and girls work after school or maybe all day long, because your parents are out of work or underpaid. Well, you and I both are against child labor. Let's get together and make the bosses cash in out of their profits to maintain children who now must work.

Show me around to your friends. Tell them how I help to lead the fight for free lunches for children of unemployed workers. Tell them I'm for free playgrounds, parks, gyms, pools—and more of 'em. Tell them I'm helping prepare for International Children's Campaign, May first to fourteenth. We boys and girls have to stick together all over the world. And by Jiminy! Don't you forget what's going to happen on May thirtieth. That's the First National Youth Day. It comes right on Decoration Day, when the whole boss class is preparing to remember the last war, and we all know that another war is coming. But, we'll all shout right at the bosses that we're going to get all the workingclass children organized against the coming war.

You must make many friends for me, comrade, I belong to you. And the more boys and girls that adopt me as their own, the harder will it be for the bosses to stop me.

Listen! Something tells me you can help me a lot better. How about sitting down now and writing up some story about your school, or about a sport game. Send in pictures and photos. You should do everything to put me on the map as the best boys and girls magazine. Sharpen up your pencil and send in all your stories or pictures.

PIONEER

50 EAST 13th STREET o o NEW YORK, N. Y.

A MAGAZINE FOR WORKERS' AND FARMERS' CHILDREN

EDITORIAL BOARD—Myra Page, V. Jerome, J. Preval, Burt Grant, Hugo Gellert, William Gropper, Harry Potamkin, I. Trauber.

CONTRIBUTING EDITORS—Mary Adams, Phil Bard, Max Bedacht, Bishop William Brown, Jacob Burck, Julia Davis, Marion Davis, Robert Dunn, William Z. Foster, Lydia Gibson, Mike Gold, Maxim Gorky, D. Grossfeld, Grace Hutchins, Harry Kaplan, Melvin Levy, Grace Lumpkin, Paul O'Higgins, John Dos Passos, Abel Plenn, Esther Shemitz, Dr. Slatkin, Otto Soglow, Sadie Van Veen, Joseph Vogel, Ryan Walker, Waly, Wex, John Worth.

Subscription 50 cents a year in U. S. and colonies and Mexico. Single copy 5 cents. Second class mailing rights pending.

VOLUME 1 NUMBER 1

FIGURE 15 The editorial of the May 1931 issue of *New Pioneer*. *New Pioneer* 1, no. 1 (May 1931): 2, box 35, Radical Pamphlets, Center for Southwest Research, University of New Mexico.

Buckley, Washington, wrote in to say that his family was "not getting very much for our [farm] products but the capitalists are making good profits."[18] Alice, Antonie, and Irene also wrote of their willingness "to go on a strike" for free lunches and clothes at school, and Elmer included $1.95 with his letter and a "greeting list" on behalf of his fellow troop members. As the Depression deepened, there were more and more letters that offered evidence of the hardships families and students were experiencing and far fewer letters that spoke of the hikes of a particular troop or letters only naming a Young Pioneer's success in gathering subscriptions.

In the act of choosing to write for this column, a young writer must have known the conventions of this section of the magazine, as well as the broader scripts of the organization. Historian Mary Jo Maynes's discussion of historical children's agency is helpful here, as she argues that "everyday activities embody historical agency." In particular, she takes as her focus personal narratives, which "show how individuals strategize and act, not alone, but rather always embedded in social situations, in institutions, and in history."[19] Reading Young Pioneers' letters to "Comrade Editor" as personal narratives, then, offers us the opportunity to examine the meaning-making choices within their language by reading them as indicative of both the personal and the institution in which they chose membership.

While in some issues "Comrade Editor" offered specific prompts for opportunities to win a magazine subscription, prompts were not common. It is significant, then, that there were children's letters that included no expected mentions of Young Pioneer motifs, such as troops, subscriptions, and strikes, all of which signify a belief in the possibilities within their movement to address these problems. Some letter writers in the "Dear Comrade Editor" pages only wrote of the injustices they were experiencing. James Pearson Jr., from White Earth, North Dakota, for example, wrote about the Red Cross aid families like his were receiving. "The Hoover government figures that our calves are worth more than us children," he wrote. "They allow our parents to borrow $3 a month per head to feed them but that 30 cents a month is enough for a child."[20] Other letter writers included short vignettes about injustices they had witnessed, such as Eugene Lang and Benjamin Epstein in November and December 1931, respectively (see figures 16 and 17).[21] While the language of these two letters suggests that the letter writers themselves were not experiencing this level of poverty, other letter writers, such as James Pearson Jr., spoke plainly of their lack of basic needs. At times, the title "Comrade Editor" gave to a child's letter suggested action, though sometimes titles were merely descriptive. Al Goldenberg from Brooklyn, for example, wrote about seeing "two kids run after a truck, break open a box of fruit and pull out some fruit. When the truck drove away I asked one of them why he did it. He told me it was the only way to get eats. I could not talk to them any more because they began to run after another truck."[22] Comrade Editor's provided title—"LOOK THEM UP, AL—THEY SHOULD BE PIONEERS!"—invited Al to action. Regardless, these vignettes offer evidence of what the young writer had anticipated was worthy of printing, which represents their choices to work within and against the normed language of this particular discourse community and its class-laden scripts.

There were other child-authored texts in the magazine where young writers played within these Young Pioneer scripts and, at times, used anti-language to do so. Most often, this anti-language emerges in children's adaptations of popular culture texts such as songs and nursery rhymes. Contemporary adaptation studies scholars invite us to think about how adaptation is "an interactive, relational process" in which the creator of the adaptation makes meaning from "engag[ing] in processes of rewriting and revision," a product of their own understandings.[23] I see these Young Pioneers' adaptations, then, as requiring knowledge of the ways popular culture texts were widely understood, as well as an ability to revise these texts to align with both Young Pioneer ideology and the child's lived experience. Billy Marcus from San Francisco, California, for example, "thought over a song" and offered in his "Dear Editor Comrade" letter to "sing it, here goes":

My country 'tis of thee,
Land of misery,
Of thee I sing.
Land where our fathers starve,
Land where small children cry,
For need of bread and milk,
Land of misery.[24]

Billy abandoned the song's rhyme scheme and creatively altered the cadence of several lines' rhythm in favor of precise imagery that recasts America as a land not of liberty but of "misery." The first verse of the version of "My Country 'Tis of Thee" most well known to American schoolchildren in the 1930s contains allusions to the Revolutionary War and the Pilgrims.[25] For Billy, a more accurate representation of the nation's progress is whether or not its citizenry, including "small children," is fed.

The *New Pioneer* also published young writers' poetry in space remaining at the end of articles or within other columns.[26] Several of these poems

Chi:dren Eat Garbage

One day when I was downtown with my Dad, I saw a couple of men and a little child about seven years old walking down the alley. I wondered what they were going to do, but then I saw them looking in the garbage can. The men had a sack into which they were putting melons and other garbage. The little boy picked up a cantaloupe and broke it open and ate it although it was rotten and moldy.

Eugene Lang, age 10 years,
Denver, Colo.

FIGURE 16 Eugene Lang's 1931 letter to "Dear Comrade." *New Pioneer* 1, no. 7 (November 1931): 18, box 35, Radical Pamphlets, Center for Southwest Research, University of New Mexico.

were adaptations of widely known nursery rhymes. Nursery rhymes, as texts crafted explicitly for children and built from purposeful repetition, are also often purveyors of heavy-handed moral lessons. Scholars across disciplines consider nursery rhymes part of children's folklore (see earlier discussions of children's rhymes and folklore in chapters 2 and 3). In his discussion of the power relationships in children's folklore, Felicia McMahon and Brian Sutton-Smith identify patterns, including the "strategic ways that children create the folklore that subverts adults and empowers children." One such pattern is antithesis, "an expressive behavior that presupposes an oppositional tension and demystifies the dominant culture through parody." While McMahon and Sutton-Smith are quick to note the

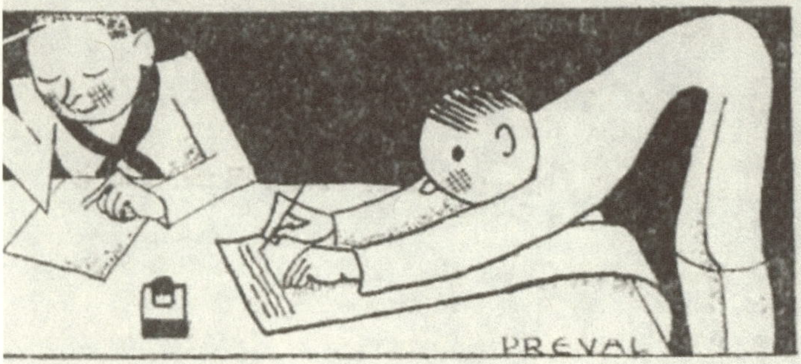

Fight Against This

Not long ago a bunch of families were evicted and they took tents and settled down along the river front of the Missouri. One of the families hasn't even got a tent so they took the body of a car and fixed it up and live in it. That is all right in the summer time but what's going to happen in the winter?

Benjamin Epstein, 10 years old,
Sioux City, Iowa.

FIGURE 17 Benjamin Epstein's 1931 letter to "Dear Comrade." *New Pioneer* 1, no. 8 (December 1931): 21, box 35, Radical Pamphlets, Center for Southwest Research, University of New Mexico.

need for caution when considering "under which conditions children's folklore becomes subversive," I would argue that the overt political commitments of the *New Pioneer* provide substantiation aplenty.[27] For a child reader of the *New Pioneer* to adapt a nursery rhyme and submit it for publication demonstrates their awareness of the rhyme's power and a willingness to negotiate, through language and in public, something different.[28] Adaptation, then, I argue, can be one way young people develop and use anti-language.

In October 1932, seven-year-old Arthur Josephson of Trenton, New Jersey, published "Capitalism's Finish," an amalgamation of two nursery rhymes, "Humpty Dumpty" and "London Bridge Is Falling Down":

Capitalism's Finish
Capitalism sat on a wall—
Capitalism had a great fall—
All capitalism's soldiers, priests, and men
Could not put capitalism together again.

Capitalism falling down—falling down—
My fellow workers,
Here come the Pioneers
To clear it away, and
Then the Workers will
Have their day.[29]

Accounting for the possibility that an adult editor titled Arthur's rhymes or that they were submitted not as a set but as standalone pieces, it remains true that both are about falling, and both nursery rhymes would have been familiar to *New Pioneer* readers. If the verses were read together as printed, then the child's argument more fully aligns with the scripts within the *New Pioneer* magazine of critiquing how "[t]he workers and the workers' children, are all slaves to the rich bosses that rule this country" and the need to elevate the working class.[30] Arthur's adaptation begins with "Humpty Dumpty," in which capitalism is personified. Reading forward, the qualities of the original subject of the rhyme—a fragile, unwisely elevated, and unfixable egg—make clear Arthur's argument about the instability and precarity of such an economic system. In his adaptation of "London Bridge Is Falling Down," Arthur's anti-language deviates significantly from the commonly known nursery rhyme. The first line of the stanza is familiar to the reader and makes plain the catastrophe that is in motion, the fall of capitalism. The remaining five lines, however, belong to the working class. Arthur's anti-language of adaptation names the Young Pioneers as those who will "clear it away" so that the adult "Workers will / Have their day." Capitalism will destroy itself, Arthur's rhyme argues. And it will be young people who lead the way to a world in which the worker is centered.

A similar argument can be found in Isadore Carvin's untitled adaptation of "Jack Be Nimble," which was printed in a small subsection of "Pioneer Poems" entitled "Mother Goose Retold" in the January 1932 issue. Tightly aligned with the rhyme scheme of the well-known nursery rhyme, Isadore's tidy adaptation recasts Jack's story as one not of luck but of agency:

Jack be nimble,
Jack be quick,
Jack join the Pioneers
And the bosses we will lick.[31]

Traditionally, this rhyme was about good luck (if the person jumped over a candlestick without extinguishing it, good luck would follow them for a year).[32] Isadore still calls upon Jack to be nimble, and his quickness in joining the Pioneers makes possible collective action.

It is Isadore's (and Billy's and Arthur's) own linguistic nimbleness that offers a subversive invitation, through adaptation, for their fellow comrades. Although adaptation is, of course, not confined to modernist texts, returning to Eysteinsson's discussion of the ways in which modernist texts force an engagement between the reader and the text helps us see how these young radicals' use of anti-language in adaptation fosters an "aesthetics of interruption" that invites the reader to participate through play and repetition.[33]

Reading as the Classed Other

Adult names within the pages of *New Pioneer* (e.g., Bernarda Bryson's March 1934 illustrations in the article "Bread Line" and William Siegel's work as art editor, as seen in the drawings for the February 1933 article "Our First Mayor") are also found in the attributions of the catalog of the New Reading Materials Program, children's books for use in schools and published as the Popular Front gained strength in the latter half of the 1930s.[34] Between 1937 and 1942, the Board of Education of the city of New York worked in conjunction with the New York City WPA to produce locally written and produced readers for first- and second-generation immigrants within the city school district in response to the problem of "illiteracy."[35] The motivations for this work was both assimilationist and revolutionary. Long embedded in the mission of American schools has been the work of assimilation, particularly through language acquisition that explicitly privileges language systems that reinforce narratives of whiteness and class privilege. At the same time, as Victoria Grieve's article "The Visual Production of Citizenship: Children's Literature of the Works Progress Administration, 1937–1942" (2013) demonstrates, this project was framed by new and progressive approaches in educational research out of Teachers College at Columbia University.[36] This project also aligns with broader cultural shifts in the perception of working-class children "from a component of the labor force to a subject of education."[37] In a March 15, 1936, front-page article about the New Reading Materials Program in the *New York Times*, the New York City children, who were the target audience of these books, are described as "youngsters inured to hard knocks" who might be persuaded to read these books as "they know [these stories are] from real life."[38]

In Lane Van Hook's 1936 fourteen-page book, *Taro Taki*, for example, the title character is eight and has immigrated from Japan. Homesick, he sits on a bench in Central Park to look at the cherry blossoms while his school friends play nearby. A "large" and blue-eyed American soldier sits next to him, and after carefully prompting and then listening to Taro's story of home, the unnamed soldier describes his time in Japan, which both affirms the child's memories of his home country and provides the space for the soldier to tell the child about the 1912 origin of the Central Park cherry blossoms, a story of honoring the Japanese people as "strong and brave" and able to "see the beauty in growing things."[39] *Taro Taki* begins and ends with Taro playing with boys with distinctly common American names—Tom, John, and Dick—who gently respond to Taro's homesickness and patiently invite him to return to their collective play.

Midway through the reader, Van Hook pauses the story to give attention to the process of Taro's language acquisition and, notably, his desire to speak English. This short paragraph provides perhaps the most overt illustration of the purpose of the city of New York's New Reading Materials Program: "Slowly Taro talked. Carefully, very carefully, he chose the words. He found the English language hard to use. But he wanted to talk to the man about his own garden in Japan."[40] The American soldier does not correct Taro's narrative, as this is not an overt or heavy-handed language lesson. Moreover, there is no need for correction, as Van Hook renders Taro's sentences as perfectly grammatical, composed mostly in a simple subject-predicate pattern indicative of the ways elementary schoolchildren were invited to learn the structures of the English language.

The readers consistently lauded education even when the stories blended realistic settings with allegorical elements. *Riquitin and the Old Men* traces a child's journey to a city in Puerto Rico to become "a student in the big school in that wonderful town in the valley," for he had "learned all there was to be learned in the school at home." As he tries to find the city, he meets three generations of unbelievably old men who—as is casually mentioned—make hats to "be sent to a place called New York" and worn by men "on a street called Broadway." These old men try to talk him out of the journey based on their childhood experience long ago, for "it was a very, very hard climb when we came home again." By the book's conclusion, the oldest of the men joins Riquitin at school, convinced that "[i]f you knew to how to read [. . .] even if you never saw" wonderful things such as electricity and cars and roads, "you would know all about" them.[41]

My interest in the 144 readers preserved in Columbia University's Rare Book and Manuscript Library gave me the rare chance to learn from a collection of texts intentionally written for an explicitly named group of young people whose class position often precluded or at least complicated their access more broadly to books.[42] What changes when a majority of the intended readers are working-class children or children in poverty? Embedded throughout the readers, which mirror Depression-era literature and popular culture, are class anxieties, even when the texts are not explicitly focused on class.[43] Many of the readers that more explicitly take up family stories of economic hardship show first-generation families or children. *The Bull Who Would Not Fight* centers Rafael, whose father—"a plain workingman," a toymaker—still lives in Mexico. Rafael lives with his aunt Carmen, and there is no mention of Rafael's mother. When his class at school studies Mexico, Rafael's knowledge of bullfighting and toreadors is first solicited and then refuted by his teacher, who insists on the cruelty of bullfighting, as "[American] ideas are different." Nevertheless, she invites him, "without getting excited," to tell what happens in the "game of bullfighting." When he begins to enact the moves of a toreador, everyone laughs. Rafael's classmates later bait him into a humiliating backyard pantomime of a bullfight in which they insist that he be the bull, complete with his handkerchief for a tail. The text makes visible to the reader Rafael's anger: "Rafael looked so fierce. His black eyes flashed and so did his white teeth"; "Rafael shook with anger." It is of note that this is the only "fight" we see in *The Bull Who Would Not Fight*, a cruel and dehumanizing interaction that finds Rafael left alone with "[h]ot tears of anger [running] down his face," "angry with the other boys but [. . .] even angrier at himself."[44]

At home, his aunt scolds him for fighting again and punishes him by not letting him play with the wooden toys, toreadors and a bull that his father made and that arrived in the mail that day. In his dream that night, Rafael dreams he is in Mexico with his father and that a bull refuses to fight. The anthropomorphized bull tells Rafael that a brave man "fights only when he has a very good reason." The reader's theme is explicitly stated. While Rafael's aunt tells him "more [times] than [he] could count" that it is "wrong to fight," the bull's qualifying phrase complicates her command by making it possible that there might indeed be justifiable reasons to fight. Midway through the story we are told that "[w]hen Rafael was especially glad or sad he talked in Spanish."[45] Similarly, it is of note that this qualifying phrase comes not from Rafael's schoolteacher, whose assimilationist scoldings earlier in the story diminished and devalued the child's knowledge, but instead from an anthropomorphized bull in Mexico that appears in his dream. Rafael's moments of resistance come from his first language and first culture. There is ample evidence to support a reading of *The Bull Who Would Not Fight* that offers a more nuanced understanding of what assimilation requires and how within its parameters there are spaces of resistance.

The framing of Rafael's father as hardworking and as fully present as possible is another subversive pattern in these readers, as the fathers of working-class or impoverished families are overwhelmingly depicted in positive ways that counter many early twentieth-century stereotypes of immigrant families and align with New Deal and Popular Front narratives about working-class fathers. In *Tommy and Tugboat George*, Tommy's tugboat captain father—once school is out for the summer, of course—brings Tommy aboard to learn how essential tugboats are for all ships, even "the finest ship in all the world."[46] It is not surprising that families in the readers who are presented as either middle or upper class (or were prior to the hardships of the Depression) are raced white, and we do not often learn of the father's occupation.[47] Across classes, if a family does not have a father present, there is always a justifiable reason given. Just as Rafael's father sends a "post card that always came on Fridays" as he works in his small toy shop, any absent fathers in nontraditional families are plainly accounted for in ways that preserve the dignity of these families.[48]

Furthermore, several readers also draw attention to the rights and value of workers. In *Oh, but a Gander Can't Talk, Part II*, a gander demands (and receives) "a salary just as you would pay a person" for his labor.[49] Osler Dunn's *Bobby and Bones* directly counters the idea of farm and ranch laborers as of less worth because their work means they are "dirty" and depicts their strong, weathered bodies in stark woodcuts (see figure 18).[50] There are still, however, clear demarcations between social classes. This is most evident in Cecil Boulton's *Verses of All Sizes and Shapes*. Interspersed between whimsical poems recounting flying kites or wishing for a friend that are illustrated with fair-haired and well-dressed children, five of the twenty-two poems celebrate the labor of working-class men, and one poem even tells of a working-class female hairdresser named Jennie (see figure 19).[51] These six poems honor workers' labors even as they also express complete mystery about where these workers come from:

When the streets
  Are white with snow,
From out of nowhere
  Comes Big Joe.[52]

Workers' surnames, when given, are ethnically marked—Tom McBride and Tom O'Flynn.

Because the readers include narratives of citizenship and Americanness that are linked tightly to narratives of class mobility, they provide us with a better understanding of the common assumptions about what kinds of language help a person gain access to such a class position. What entry points of resistance did the readers provide? There are two readers in particular that present powerful explorations of the tensions between the New Reading Materials Program's careful attention to what the young people described as "illiterate" might find familiar or interesting and the nationalist and assimilationist narratives discussed here with an emphasis on class and language. In particular, Norma Keating's *Mr. Chu* offers a remarkable story of relationality between an impoverished child and an elderly man, and a short story entitled "Dimps" presents the anti-language of a child tramp within an unlikely genre.

"Dimps" is included in the third of the five *Read and Laugh* books by George Barnet, books that, true to their title's promise, present a range of stories with nondescript settings framed and illustrated as lighthearted fare. The child protagonists in several of the stories are "poor little boy[s]" "looking for work," though we learn no more about their lives or homes as the stories unfold.[53] Through a clever bit of wit, helped along by their pluck or sometimes by the result of an innocent misunderstanding, each protagonist finds a favorable outcome by the story's end. Class politics in the *Read and Laugh* stories rely more heavily on stereotypes than do many of the other readers. The thief in "Detective Dan," for example, turns out to be a servant in a rich household, and Mr. Sobersides in "Two Giants" constantly demeans and ridicules the servants he employs.

The narrative arc of "Dimps," a ten-page story near the end of book 3, is an exception to these patterns. Presented first to the young reader as "a merry lad," Dimps is always "laughing, smiling, or whistling."[54] Yet in the second paragraph, we learn an exposition that serves as a sharp contrast to this merriness: "Nobody knew where he lived. But that was not strange for he did not live anywhere. He had no home. He would tramp around the country, day in and day out. He would sleep where he could and eat when he could. But no

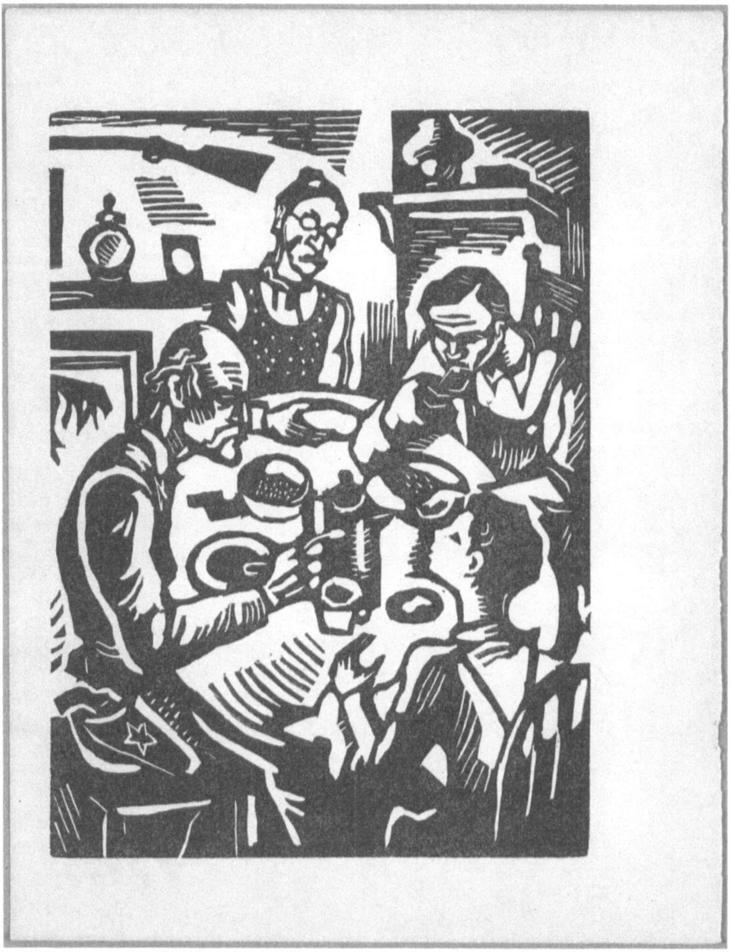

FIGURE 18 An example of William Sigel's woodcuts in *Bobby and Bones*, by Osler Dunn, page 8.

matter what happened he always tried to be merry" ("D," 17). We enter the story as Dimps enters a "strange town" he has never been in before (18). As people begin "hurrying home for dinner," Dimps, hungry, sits on some steps and whistles. "'Well,' he said to himself, 'if I can't eat, I can whistle'" (19). He is quickly scolded by an old man, the owner of the steps, so Dimps moves to the curb with "his feet in the street" (20). In perhaps the most overt act of resistance in the entire New Reading Materials Program corpus, Dimps then tells the old man, "You can't stop me here" (20).

This act of resistance (or persistence?) seems to soften the old man, who moves closer and asks why Dimps feels he must whistle. Dimps's

THE SAND HOG

He toils at night
When others sleep,
Digging a tunnel
Dark and deep,
Under the river
Black and wide.
They call him a sand hog—
Tom McBride.

26

FIGURE 19 Page 22 of Cecil Boulton's pencil and watercolor art in *Verses of All Shapes and Sizes.*

answer—"I whistle because I am sad"—is not only contrary to the opening paragraphs of the story but also repeated by the old man to all the people from the town who begin to gather and gawk along with the admonition that Dimps's rationale for whistling clearly means he is "crazy" ("D," 20, 21). A policeman is called because of the "crazy man down the street," a linguistic shift that marks Dimps as different from and older than the "lad" he was at the beginning of the story and the "lad" he will return to being at its end (22, 17, 27). The accompanying illustration shows the policeman towering over Dimps. The policeman

FIGURE 20 A two-page spread, illustrated by Cecil Bolton, in "Dimps" by George Barnet, in *Read and Laugh Stories, Book Three*, 22–23.

holds his club firmly in his right hand and reaches toward Dimps's right shoulder with his left hand. The ears of the two dogs foregrounded in the illustration are lowered, and several of the people in the crowd look concerned. Dimps is still sitting, his back to the reader. His response to the policeman's question, "What is the matter here?," addresses only one portion of the context of the now crowded street: "Nothing is the matter with me" (23; see figure 20).

Dimps's answer leaves unsaid the rest of the situation, a "great big crowd" of adults gathered around a child who is illustrated with ragged clothes and unkempt hair whom they have decided is a "crazy man" and whom the reader knows is hungry ("D," 21, 22). The next page, however, begins with an illustration in which Dimps resists physically by standing to address the policeman, their eyes parallel (see figure 21). Through Dimps's language choices in this conversation with the policeman, Dimps's resistance continues verbally in a call-and-response pattern in which the child's verbal gymnastics elicit pleasure from the crowd, laughter, and payment in pennies:

> "What are you sitting there and whistling for?" asked the policeman.
>
> "Because I am sad," said Dimps.
>
> "And what are you sad about?" the policeman wanted to know.
>
> "Because I am hungry and have no money," said Dimps.
>
> "Then why don't you go to work and make some money?" asked the policeman.

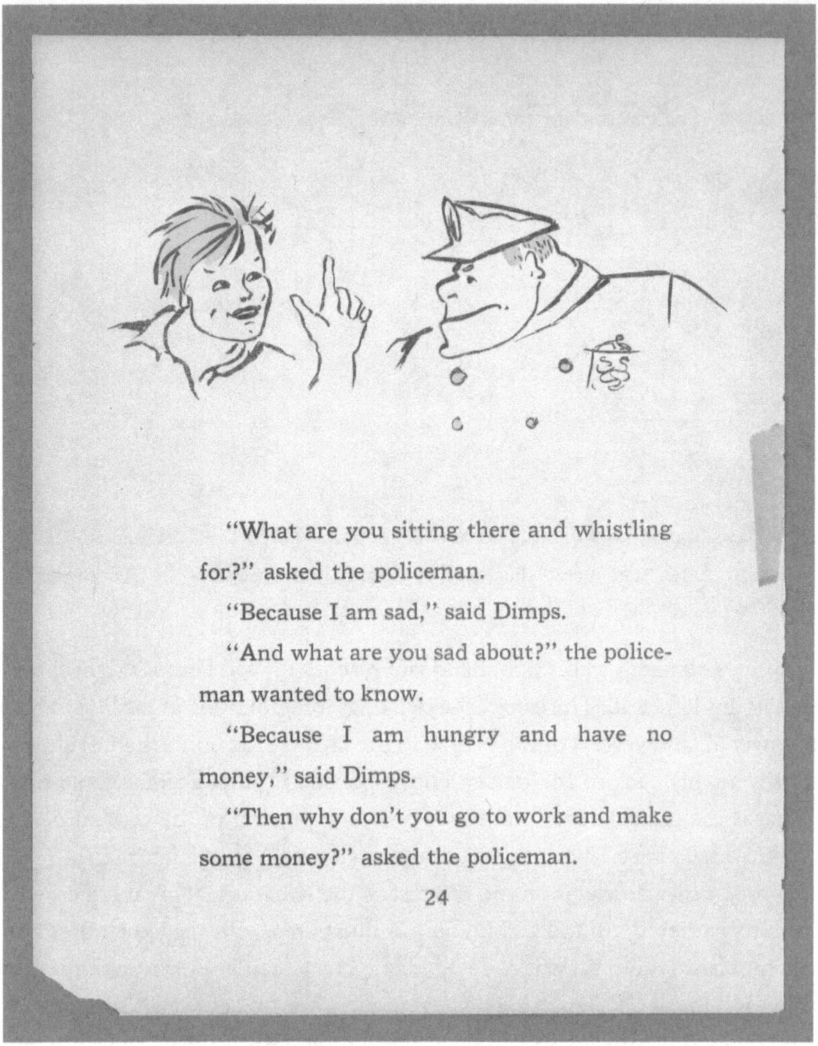

"What are you sitting there and whistling for?" asked the policeman.

"Because I am sad," said Dimps.

"And what are you sad about?" the policeman wanted to know.

"Because I am hungry and have no money," said Dimps.

"Then why don't you go to work and make some money?" asked the policeman.

24

FIGURE 21 The illustration from page 24 from "Dimps," by George Barnet, in *Read and Laugh Stories, Book Three.*

"Because when I work, it makes me sad," said Dimps. "And when I am sad I have to sit down and whistle. And how can one work and sit down and whistle at the same time?"

At this everyone in the crowd laughed and laughed. Even the policeman smiled. Then someone threw a penny to Dimps. And the crowd felt so happy that everyone there started to throw pennies.

Dimps picked the pennies up and soon had more than enough for his dinner. ("D," 24–25)

The crowd "[waits] outside [the lunchroom] and watch[es] him eat," as does the reader through the illustration ("D," 26). Full, Dimps begins to whistle again, angering the policeman, who hasn't followed Dimps's logic: "When I am hungry, I whistle because I am sad. And when I have had a good dinner, I whistle because I am merry" (26).

Dimps's verbal play leaves the policeman "scratch[ing] his head" and the townsfolk thrilled. They claim that he's "not crazy at all, but just a very merry lad" ("D," 26, 27). Dimps is described no longer as an adult but again as a child. His anti-language is taken at face value by the town, and he walks away with a full belly and pennies to spare. By upending the policeman's discursive power, Dimps demonstrates through his language not only an awareness of such power structures through "modes of resistance" but also the discursive savviness to navigate the policeman's language toward a desired end.[55]

Wit saves the day in the *Read and Laugh* stories whose protagonists are impoverished young boys. "Dimps" is no exception to this narrative pattern. But this story is the only one in which a child in poverty does not learn a lesson dispensed by paternalistic adults or a paternalistic narrator. Dimps brilliantly speaks and intentionally moves within systems designed to exclude him. It is his expectations that govern the story's outcome, not the expectations of adults or of a bullish policeman.

In the end, Dimps's anti-language is found within a collection of stories entitled *Read and Laugh*, and he is thus framed not to be taken seriously. Can there also, though, be power in his resistance? By the end of their stories, the other impoverished young boys in *Read and Laugh* have guaranteed work, or we are told that each child has grown up to have a successful career. Dimps, on the other hand, leaves town full and with a few extra pennies. We leave him in the present. His hunger will return. We have no reason to believe that an adult is waiting in the next town to help care for him. What, then, is a child reader to infer about the classed other in *Read and Laugh*?

One final reader in the New Reading Materials Program offers a different model of response, not to a child's anti-language but to a kind of relationality that invites a young reader to enter differently a likely familiar story of struggle. Norma Keating's *Mr. Chu* (1938) begins with an extended introduction to the title character, who "live[s] above his shop in Chinatown" and whose subtle dialect she preserves, a rarity for the readers.[56] On his face "[t]here were more happy wrinkles than sad ones," and we meet him while he is playing the moon (a traditional Chinese stringed instrument) and waiting for Johnny, a red-haired, blue-eyed orphan, to arrive (*MC*, 2). Keating invites her young reader to know Johnny through subtle details: He arrives to Mr. Chu's at six or seven each night, which we must infer is when he is done working at Mr. Lee's store; Mr. Lee has given Johnny "a place to sleep" behind his store, but Johnny has no permanent home; Mr. Chu and Johnny explore the city together in winter, staying warm in building elevators or subway trains, and in summer, listening to music in the park (3). We are also told that Johnny is so small that he "could not reach the bell" outside Mr. Chu's door (5).

The storyline of the reader invites us to enter their rhythmic evening ritual.[57] Mr. Chu makes dinner as Johnny sets the table, and the omniscient narrator describes the Chinese dishes from which they eat and that they then wash and return to the cupboard, deftly weaving in brief references to stories of the Chinese philosophers Mr. Chu recounts to Johnny. Johnny politely requests Mr. Chu to play his moon, and they gently bicker about which song Mr. Chu will play, with Johnny requesting "any Chinese music" but Mr. Chu choosing the folksong "Old Kentucky Home" (*MC*, 17).[58] The evening concludes with Johnny falling asleep at the table as he listens (see figure 22). Keating's attention to the details and the onomatopoeic sounds of their rituals—"Twang, twang, twang, went the strings of the moon" as Johnny slept; "'M—m—m—,' breathed Johnny" (17, 18)—are sketched into Bernarda Bryson's illustrations, too (20). The resolution of the story finds Mr. Chu, his "happy wrinkles gr[owing] happier and happier," covering an exhausted Johnny with a blanket and talking aloud about his plans: "Johnny better stay here all the time" (21, 19).

Just like "Dimps," *Mr. Chu* does not mention Johnny going to school, nor does Keating invite a young reader to take up a tidy lesson about hard work. There is no mention that Mr. Chu wants Johnny to stay with him to begin working in his shop (though the possibility certainly exists). Johnny has not earned care in *Mr. Chu* but rather is cared for because he has need. The familiarity and ease with which Johnny and Mr. Chu prepare, eat, and tidy up after their dinner, explore their city, and gently banter about what music Mr. Chu will play suggest that their relationship is mutually beneficial, and Keating's prose and Bryson's illustrations offer evidence that being together brings each of them joy. While the majority of the New Reading Materials Program readers present whole (or, if absent, carefully accounted for) families, *Mr. Chu* offers a young reader a different kind of family, a family grounded in a cultural tradition not framed or qualified or modified by the nationalist narratives so present in many of the readers. Johnny chooses to come each night, and Mr. Chu chooses to have Johnny stay. Each honors the other's choice.

FIGURE 22 Bernarda Bryson's illustration on page 16 of Johnny asleep in *Mr. Chu*, by Norma Keating.

Reading about the Classed Other

Commercial texts emerging near the end of the Depression era targeted a readership significantly different from that of the New York readers: children whose families could purchase books. Mickenberg's capacious *Learning from the Left* meticulously catalogs the effects of left-wing politics on mid-twentieth-century American culture through children's literature. In particular, she traces the influence of the Popular Front, which emerged in the middle of the 1930s, in reframing leftist sentiments as "'twentieth-century Americanism,' or as rooted in native revolutionary traditions" that also found a foothold in parallel shifts in children's literature. Opportunities to use books for young people for the purposes of "political socialization" developed alongside growing understandings of a "more democratic vision of adult-child relations [that accompanied] a waning belief in childhood innocence and more children's books that grappled with real-world issues." As the nation neared the end of the Depression and anti-Fascist national sentiments rose in response to the Second World War, realism emerged as a trend in literature for young people and "reflected a growing belief that children were autonomous beings, independent-minded, concerned with social justice, and entitled to know something about the way the world works."[59]

Yet while children's novels from the 1940s began to depict more young characters in poverty and from the working class, they largely continued to reinforce hegemonic middle-class ideals. In Eleanor Estes's *The Hundred Dresses* (1944), for example, the poorest child, an immigrant named Wanda Petronski who "always wore a faded blue dress that didn't hang right" though it was "shabby but clean," like her house, serves as the catalyst for other children's moral growth (both those precariously in the working class and those firmly in the middle class) as they learn to never "stand by and say nothing again" when others were cruel because someone was "funny looking or because they had strange names." Notably, though, while Wanda rarely speaks, Estes represents her dialect ("I got a hundred dresses home"), and Wanda's father chooses to move his children to the city away from the prejudice of the town.[60] Doris Gates's *Blue Willow* (1940) catalogs a family who, having lost their ranch in Texas five years earlier, returns to the middle class through virtuous hard work. There are many radical moments within the novel: headstrong ten-year-old Jenny is the child of migrant workers, and her dear friend is a child of migrants from Mexico; Jenny's teacher at the camp school values each child's unique knowledge, inviting the children to share "which part of the country they had thought the most interesting in their time traveling around."[61] Nevertheless, the plot again and again serves to demonstrate the family's status as worthy poor. In *Strawberry Girl* (1945), a book developed with the aid of the Federal Writers' Project Florida guidebook, the author, Lois Lenski, takes care to present to the reader what she calls in the foreword "the flavorsome speech" of the "Florida Crackers" who shared with her "incidents [. . .] too dramatic for [her] purpose [that] had to be softened."[62] The novel traces assorted conflicts between two families, the Boyers, whose ten-year-old daughter, Birdie, has to reassure classmates at school that she is a "Cracker," and the Slaters, who continue to experience hardship until their patriarch is "converted" and begins to follow the model of hard work seen in the Boyer family. While the Boyers appear barefooted in illustrations and their language offers some regional dialect, Lenski takes care to demarcate their family as different. Their insatiable work ethic—despite very realistic setbacks—pays off, and Birdie's parents give her an organ at the book's end. Collectively, these Depression-era novels present young readers with lives not typically portrayed in children's literature of the period, yet their narrative structures and themes still uphold the middle class as ideal and accessible only to the worthy, hard-working poor.

This invites questions that literature for young people continues to struggle with today: Whose lives are reflected and identities nurtured in literature for children? How might literature more ethically represent the lives and language of young people in poverty and of the working class? What is the class position of a novel's imagined reader? Relatedly, what is at stake for the child reader of any class position when representations of young people in poverty are glossed or omitted in literature written explicitly for young people?

In the last three paragraphs of her 1939 acceptance speech for her Newbery Medal–winning *Thimble Summer* (the only 1930s medal winner to explicitly take up the Depression that young readers were living through), Elizabeth Enright paused in a four-sentence paragraph to acknowledge, "Of course in every childhood there is sorrow, too."[63] Yet she quickly tempered that truth with another claim, that "[f]ortunately" the "normal" and "loved" child "brought up safely" lives in a world that "is a secure, eternal place." Enright then closed with her only mention of the Depression shaping the lives of her young readers: "Let us all hope, even in such sick and troubled times as these, that someday it will be the privilege of every child to feel like this."[64] Reflected in Enright's speech and in the larger trends in children's literature of the Depression era is an expectation of middle-class childhood, a space where children are "loved" and kept safe, a "privilege" for some but certainly not accessible to all.

In fact, in the June 21 American Library Association press release for the Newbery Medal, *Thimble Summer* is described as "the story of Garnet Linden, a little girl who spends a happy summer on a Wisconsin farm."[65] *Thimble Summer* maintains a distance between the idylls of childhood and the inconvenience of poverty. In the first chapter, Garnet demonstrates her understanding that her family's stability is directly linked to whether or not it rains. "If the rain didn't come soon," she notes, "there would be no corn to harvest, and they would have to cut the oats for hay."[66] This worry runs parallel to her awareness of her father's mail, envelopes "thin and businesslike with small printed names of companies in upper left-hand corners" (*TS*, 6). Garnet knows that these bills meant "her father would sit late in the kitchen, worried and silent, doing sums on a piece of paper" (7). Though Garnet is aware of her family's precarious finances, thoughts such as these are always quickly followed by far less somber things, like her ability to "whistle between her teeth like a boy" and the "pleasant, far-off feeling" she gets from looking at the grazing sheep that adorn the calendar behind which she "hastily push[es] the bills" (4, 10). Garnet lives within Enright's ideal, the "privilege" of a sentimental childhood in which suffering can be hidden behind sylvan scenes for adults to find later. Enright's third-person limited narrator largely represents Garnet through language Caroline Hunt describes as "accurate but never childlike."[67] There are occasional moments that counter this reading, such as Garnet setting the table for breakfast ("Knife, fork, knife, fork, knife, fork, knife, fork but only a spoon for Donald" [9]), but largely her thoughts are polished into tidy grammatical sentences by the narrator before reaching their audience of child readers.

The rest of the novel's plot is propelled by two intertwined storylines grounded in economic precarity but not fully focused on it. First, the Lindens receive a government loan for a barn; and second, while making lime for the barn's concrete foundation, a poor orphan stumbles hungrily into their camp. A wild boy of the road, Eric Swanstrom is invited to leave behind hitchhiking and quickly earns a place in the Linden family. Enright includes for the reader details of Eric's life, as such uncertainty serves as a foil to the lives of Garnet and her brother, Jay. The night Eric arrives, for example, he is asked by adults to tell them about himself. He is reluctant to speak, and "[a] shadow seemed to pass over the boy's face" (*TS*, 44). It takes several pages before he tells them the story of his young life, which Garnet notes "was hard to imagine" (47). The reader learns that Eric's life is essentially a twentieth-century version of Alger's nineteenth-century Ragged Dick: His mother died when he was young, his immigrant father lost his arm in a tragic farm accident, the father and son had to move to the city (where his father, of course, soon thereafter died), and so Eric began hitchhiking. Now he works when he can but always leaves if the threat of being placed in an orphanage looms too near.

There is one moment near the end of the chapter, however, that Enright allows to be suggestive of Eric's suffering rather than illustrative: "'I had a bad time after [returning to Colorado],' said Eric, frowning again. 'I don't like to remember it or talk about it. But I got out all right; I always do!'" (*TS*, 50). Intratextually, Eric's self-censorship acknowledges his understanding of the difference between him and his audience. This is further evidenced by Garnet's response in the next paragraph: "You felt that anything was possible in this moment" (50). Enright glosses here the disconcerting disconnect between how the suffering of a child in poverty is read as inspirational to a child in a more stable class position—and, presumably, to a middle-class reader. At the end of this chapter, Enright again affirms the Linden children's privilege by Garnet's final reflection on Eric's life of suffering: "It made her feel safe and warm to know that she belonged to [her family] and they to her" (53).

Enright quickly deemphasizes Eric's status as orphan and previous life in poverty by the good deeds that ingratiate him into the Linden family. In the next chapter, the reader is told that "there was nothing that Eric couldn't do" (*TS*, 54). Yet it is not until the end of the novel that he is mentioned beyond a quick note about work ethic or tasks completed. In the penultimate chapter, which marks the nearing end of summer, Mrs. Linden wonders how they "ever got along without Eric" (121), and the narrator tells the reader that Garnet now considers him a "part of the family now, a brother" (127). For Enright, it seems, the most egregious and dangerous kind of poverty comes when the child is without the safety and nurturance of a family structure.

The novel's final chapter oddly conflates the motif of the title (which alludes to a solid silver thimble Garnet finds early in the summer and promptly declares to be magic) and Eric's integration into the Linden family. Jay asks Eric what he will "do when [he] grow[s] up" (*TS*, 132). Like a ruralized Horatio Alger protagonist, Eric answers quickly, "I have it all planned. I'm going to work hard for your father as long as he'll let me, and save every penny I make. Someday maybe I'll get a farm of my own. In this valley I'd like it to be; near your father's and about the same size and style as his" (133). Jay, the rightful heir of such a paternal legacy, does not understand Eric's desire to farm, for it is "no way to see the world" (133). For the first time in nearly one hundred pages Enright grants Eric the privilege of speaking at length. "I've seen plenty of the world," he begins, "[and] I like this better" (133). To Jay's counterargument—the ever-present nuisance of uncertainty in farming life—Eric responds almost without reservation: "You've never had trouble; you're darn lucky and you remember I said it. [. . .] You don't know what trouble is, Jay" (133–34). Meghan Sweeney reads Eric's language here as a "small but stern reminder that Depression continues."[68] Might we also read this tense moment as Enright's inability—or at least unwillingness—to nuance a narrative of childhood grounded in the realism of the Depression? It is as though definitive moments in Eric's life, such as the aforementioned traumatic event in

Colorado and his ongoing search for food, shelter, and safety, are unsayable in this story of a thimble summer.

This reading is furthered by the novel's denouement. Instead of an argument between the children, Enright crafts a happier resolution. Jay admits that perhaps after "see[ing] the world" he will return to farm, and Garnet proffers the narrative of her silver thimble, the source of "all nice things" that summer, to Eric (*TS*, 134). Neither Linden child dwells on Eric's life of "trouble"; instead, they both respond within the context of their privilege: Jay "reflectively" considers his luck, and Garnet attributes Eric's presence to a small cylindrical piece of perforated metal (134). Thus, the truths of Eric's poverty remain guarded and are kept from children with thimble summers, those listening to Eric within the chapter and likely those reading the chapter, too. "I'm much obliged to [the thimble] for bringing me here," Eric says to close their conversation, acquiescing to the Linden children's inability to understand his suffering. The quick shift from his aggressive use of the pronoun "you" in his earlier rebuttal to the formalized diction of his final sentence indicates Eric's understanding of what is expected of his language as an outsider. He ends the novel continuing to occupy its margins, working and earning his keep in order to prove himself worthy. (After all, if Alger's sentimental formula holds, Eric will not only "[buy] land next to [theirs]" but also marry Garnet.)

Enright's 1968 essay, "Realism in Children's Literature," justifies her gloss of Eric's poverty. In the lives of fictional children, she writes, living "is apt to be kinder than the real thing; also neater, more just, and more exciting." Furthermore, realism for children ends "at the high point," for "[i]t is our privilege to leave them in their happiness forever." Enright's recurring motif of privilege in her analyses of the craft and social function of children's literature serves as a sharp contrast to her otherwise keen observations about crafting language for children within the same essay: "[A] child begins to perceive life through details[, for he] is too young for generalities," and the believability of such language is "not [. . .] overlaid with the dust of repetition," for it comes from one who "treat[s] language as though it were his own, a perpetually new and valued means of conveying to others his reaction and experience."[69] Ironically, Enright did not choose to allow Eric to speak freely. Despite its commitment to a realist aesthetic, Enright's novel omits the material realities of poverty and the linguistic variances of those outside the standard use by carefully managing the discomfort of her assumed middle-class reader to preserve thimble summers.

WHAT CHANGES WHEN THE TEXT IS WRITTEN FOR THE CHILD? THE *New Pioneer* framed the child as agentive and, though providing a heavy-handed script, positioned and made space for young people to write within and against it. The New Reading Materials Program was a revolutionary and flawed project. While it certainly broadened representations of race and class, it also harmfully reinforced cultural stereotypes of ethnic groups, often reducing complex cultures into a single representation or relying on racist caricatures for villains in adventure or mystery stories.[70] When we read these texts alongside commercial books for children in the Depression era, we see an attempt to widen class representation, but there is still a largely uniform adherence to middle-class norms and values despite the fact that the target readership for each type of book was different. If we read across these tightly controlled genres chronologically, from texts explicitly political to texts explicitly educational and commercial, we can find moments of anti-language or resistance surfaced by working-class children and children in poverty.

Epilogue

Rereading Depression-Era Children

Tending closely to the language describing, ascribed to, and used by young people in poverty in modernist and children's literature of the Depression era, *Reading the Classed Child* offers a model for rereading such language not as tangled errors, as is often the case, but as innovative discourse. The astonishingly complex voices that the child in poverty in these representations is pressed into, the choices made and claims asserted, which may seem bizarre and ill-fitting and outrageous, in fact work to reclaim power within these texts. These voices are an artistic and political triumph that functions as an ethical understanding and elicits a moral engagement in which we as readers learn to listen to a kind of self-presentation that works within and against cultural scripts, that asks us to respond and to comprehend.

Returning to the archival letters to Mrs. Roosevelt, which began this project, closes *Reading the Classed Child* with the reminder that the most subversive authority within the letters to Mrs. Roosevelt is the forthright way in which the defamiliarizing language of the child suggests solutions to an adult reader. The parallel deference and authority with which these children in poverty write makes plain their ability to both follow cultural scripts and attempt to rewrite them. These letters were largely secret, just like Vardaman's metaphors, Pearl's thoughts, Mazie's understandings; however, they were also carefully constructed for an audience, like Wright's recollections of his childhood, children's rhymes as cataloged by Ellison's field notes and *New Pioneer* child authors, Dimps's verbal sparring with the police, and even Enright's Eric Swanstrom. Within the texts that are the focus of *Reading the Classed Child,* we find a compelling counter-narrative about childhood in the Depression era. Not static and listless during the widespread suffering of the 1930s, young people were working, playing, talking, arguing, laughing, creating, watching, learning. This is not to suggest that children were not affected in profound ways by the brutal economic and cultural contexts in which they lived. Instead, this is to suggest that these texts, taken together, help us more ethically read and return to the language of the child in poverty.

The voice of the child in poverty has always been in our cultural record. *Reading the Classed Child* asks us to consider how it has always been easy to ignore this voice because the language used to represent it is so rich, so messy, so divided, so complex. But in that tangle of efforts to survive, we hear the voice, we comprehend its desire for agency, and we cede it its rights, all in an ethical responsiveness that is a novel synthesis that we are being instructed in hearing. In *Ethics in Light of Childhood*, John Wall contends that we must "not only be disrupted by the other but also to disrupt and recreate ourselves in the process."[1] Reading for anti-language in the cultural record—in texts fictional, epistolary, and performed—reveals purposeful patterns of resistance: over- and relexicalization, play within cultural scripts, the active choice of silence, dialectical semantics, and grammatical inversions. And it is in working through these patterns that the work becomes ours and we must consider our response.

B.J.R. wrote to "MRSROSEVELt" during February of her first year of school and at the age of six with a blend of upper- and lowercase letters (see figure 23).[2] One of the youngest letter writers in the archive, she was also one of the few children who were likely born after the Depression began. On accounting ledger paper preprinted for school expenses, the child often worked to space many of the letters in relationship with each differently sized cell, rarely choosing to offer space between words that corresponds with the applicable ledger cells or punctuation to separate thoughts into sentences. Her penultimate clause shares that her "dAddy HeLpedme towRItyou," which invites us as readers to consider in what way her father provided help. While such an answer is unknowable, the process through which the child and the parent negotiated the writing of the letter requires the child to be an active participant with choices to make: Who initiated its moment of exigency or its contents and structure? Who provided the paper? Was the letter composed within a parent's line of sight or while a parent's hands were busy with everyday tasks of home or work? Who was spelling the words, including "Sherley" or "writ"?

Many of the choices made by this child can help us see what she thought would matter most to her imagined reader. Before sharing her name with Mrs. Roosevelt, for example, she identifies her age, first year of attendance in school, and race. Next, the syntax of her request for a Shirley Temple doll leads with "IwiSHyouwoLD," which has the effect of softening her request to "pLEASESeND" the doll.[3] Her rationale for needing the doll uses the passive voice (her doll "GOtBROKe"), though she uses the active voice to promise that she'll "tAKeGOODCARe" of the replacement. The letter also closes with a row of six *x*'s, signifying the "LotSOFKisses" of her letter's valediction. The child's purposeful choices demonstrate the strength of young letter

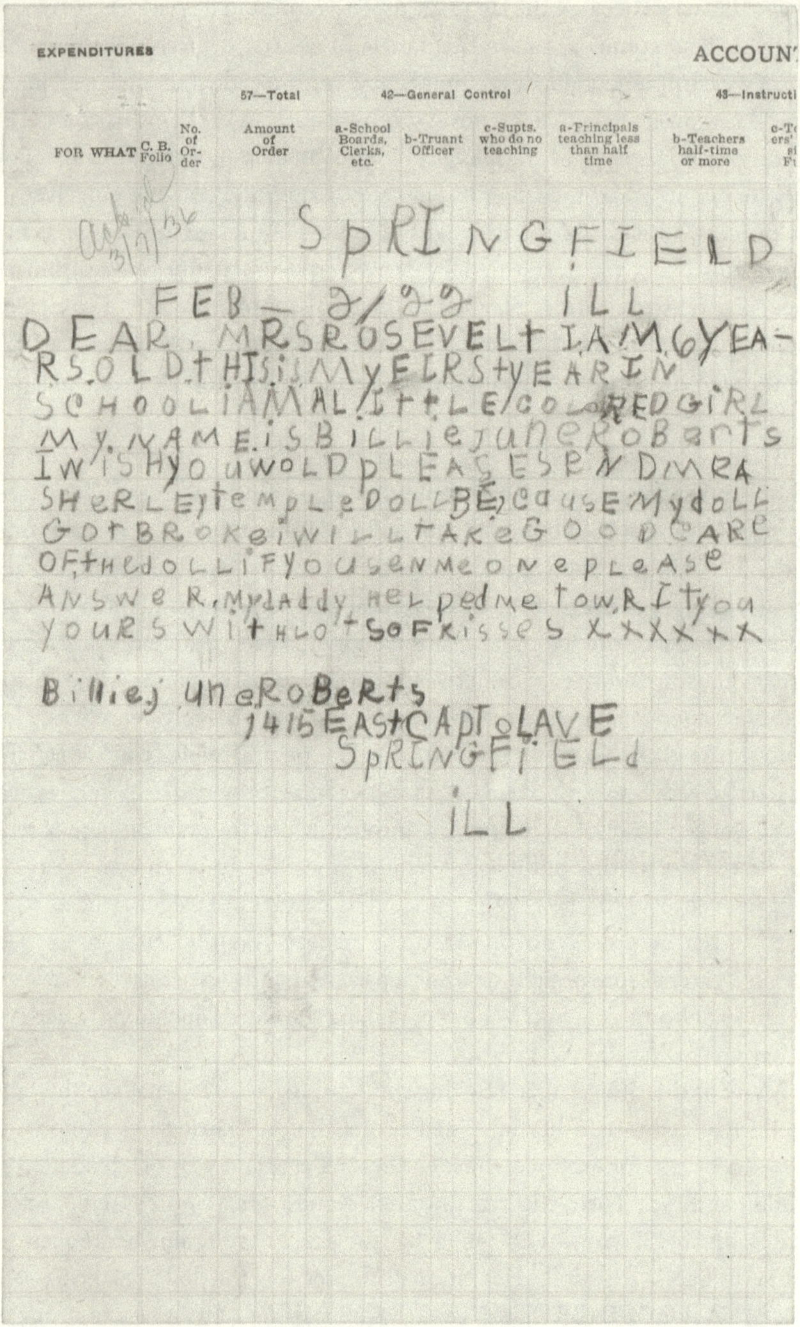

EXPENDITURES | ACCOUN

			57—Total	42—General Control			43—Instructi		
FOR WHAT	C. B. Folio	No. of Order	Amount of Order	a-School Boards, Clerks, etc.	b-Truant Officer	c-Supts. who do no teaching	a-Principals teaching less than half time	b-Teachers half-time or more	c-T ers'

ack 3/7/36

SPRINGFIELD

FEB — 2/22 ILL

DEAR. MRS ROOSEVELT I AM 6 YEA-
RS. OLD. THIS IS MY FIRST YEAR IN
SCHOOL I AM A LITTLE COLORED GIRL
MY NAME IS BILLIE JUNE ROBERTS
I WISH YOU WOLD PLEASE SEND ME A
SHERLEY TEMPLE DOLL BECAUSE MY DOLL
GOT BROKE I WILL TAKE GOOD CARE
OF THE DOLL IF YOU SEND ME ONE PLEASE
ANSWER. MY DADDY HELPED ME TO WRITE YOU
YOURS WITH LOTS OF KISSES XXXXXX

Billie June Roberts
1415 EAST CAPTOL AVE
SPRINGFIELD
ILL

FIGURE 23 B.J.R.'s 1936 letter to Eleanor Roosevelt, February 22, 1936. Box 1031, series 35:150.1, Anna Eleanor Roosevelt Papers, Part I, 1884–1964, Franklin Delano Roosevelt Archive, Franklin D. Roosevelt Presidential Library and Museum, Hyde Park, N.Y.

writers' belief not only that they would receive a response but also that they had the right to ask. That belief empowered these children to write because they knew that the letter would reach an audience with the power to respond. "iFYOUseNMeONepLeASeANSWer," B.J.R. wrote, in effect naming only one response that she would like to receive. Such letters are compelling examples of how young people in poverty intentionally created a public sphere in which the "norm society and the deviant group confront and negotiate."[4] The child, by choosing to write, is convinced of their right to speak, to articulate their position, and to negotiate through language something better.

There is one detail about B.J.R.'s letter that I would like to return to for the purpose of once more making plain the argument of this book. For the child to attempt to negotiate through language something better required B.J.R.'s father to engage in the process of writing—in some capacity—with his daughter. Rather than seeing her father's participation as diminishing the child's autonomy or claiming that his help in some way legitimized a letter written by a child, I would argue that her father models for us a crucial component of an ethic of relationality that preserves the child's agency: "MydAddy HeLpedme towRItyou." B.J.R.'s father did not dismiss her desire to write to the First Lady of the United States to ask for a doll; instead, he supported her efforts to do so by entering into the work alongside her.

WHAT IS OUR ROLE as a reader? The mixed patchwork of the language of the child in poverty—and *constructed for* the child in poverty—needs to be heard over and over and in subtly different ways, but always with the awareness that children know and speak within and through cultural scripts. The language of the child in poverty operates subversively by unsettling discursive systems and forcing us to negotiate a new discourse, one of which we are unsure. And in that space of uncertainty, a by-product of disruption, our response has the potential to be an ethical one, one predicated on listening first in order to learn from and then respond to that which we now see differently.

Notes

Prologue. Writing as the Classed Other

1. Szalay, *New Deal Modernism*, 63.

2. Freedman, *Children of the Great Depression*, x.

3. Thompson and Austin, "Introduction: The Children," xi, xx.

4. Similar to Robert Cohen's 2002 *Dear Mrs. Roosevelt: Letters from Children of the Great Depression*, the first scholarly publication to focus exclusively on children's letters to Mrs. Roosevelt, I've chosen to not use in my prose the full names of children whose letters I was privileged to read in the archive. Cohen writes the following about his editorial decision: "The privacy of the letter writers has been preserved by identifying them only with their initials and hometowns. I have, however, removed even the initials of those who specifically requested in their letters that Mrs. Roosevelt not make their correspondence public" (30).

5. Eleven-year-old child to Eleanor Roosevelt, March 12, 1935, box 1025, series 34:150.1, Anna Eleanor Roosevelt Papers, Part I, 1884–1964, Franklin Delano Roosevelt Archive, Franklin D. Roosevelt Presidential Library and Museum, Hyde Park, N.Y.

6. Cohen, *Dear Mrs. Roosevelt*, 16.

7. Injured child to Eleanor Roosevelt, November 28, 1941, box 1052, Roosevelt Papers.

8. Tired child to Eleanor Roosevelt, November 22, 1939, box 1044, Roosevelt Papers.

9. F.B. to Eleanor Roosevelt, May 1934, box 1013, Roosevelt Papers; C.D. to Eleanor Roosevelt, February 1934, box 1014, Roosevelt Papers.

10. Sánchez-Eppler, "In the Archives of Childhood," 226, 222, 220.

11. While the youngest letter writers often begin by identifying their age, older youths do not include their age until it seems most persuasive; in other cases, an approximate age can be inferred instead from details about school, family, or work. It is important to state that there is much work to do in this archive. How did young people, for example, work within and against cultural norms of race, gender, and region in their requests? What, if anything, within the contents of letters shifted the formulaic responses of Mrs. Roosevelt's secretaries?

12. Throughout *Reading the Classed Child* I primarily use the term "child" to describe young people in the Depression era. According to historian Kriste Lindenmeyer, policymakers in the 1930s used "children" to describe young people under the age of eighteen; "youth," then, spanned eighteen to twenty-five (*Greatest Generation Grows Up*, 6). The fictional and historical young people who are the focus of this study all fall under the age of eighteen. Additionally, this study primarily focuses on fictional and historical young people who are in poverty. There are some examples of the language of working-class children as well (see chapter 4). I'm not interested in developing a metric to differentiate between these polysemic class positions, which are defined differently across disciplines and texts, *though always by lack*. Instead, my interest is in a sustained exploration of the language of and constructed for young people positioned as the classed other in Depression-era literature and culture.

13. Fowler, *Literature as Social Discourse*, 147.

14. Halliday, "Anti-Languages," 576, 583.

15. Cohen, *Dear Mrs. Roosevelt*, 17.

16. Halliday, "Anti-Languages," 582.

17. Fowler, *Literature as Social Discourse*, 150.

18. T.L. to Eleanor Roosevelt, 1936, box 1030, Roosevelt Papers.

19. Cohen's introduction to the letters closes with a paragraph explicating his choice to "[resist] both the temptation to correct grammatical or spelling errors and the condescending use of [*sic*]" (*Dear Mrs. Roosevelt*, 31). The paragraph closes as follows: "The letters' authors were often aware that their limited education left them unable to write standard English, and many apologized for this in their correspondence. If an apology is necessary, however, it should be from the social and educational system of 1930s America, which left many youths too little schooled to spell or communicate well enough to work in white-collar jobs. In this sense too the errors in the letters—all of which are published verbatim—are themselves valuable as markers of class and social inequity in Depression America" (31). While I applaud Cohen's preservation of the spelling choices of young people, I counter the blanket assignment of blame to 1930s schools and teachers, as well as the classist assumption that "white-collar" employment is (or should be) the aim of public education. Most of all, however, the exigency of *Reading the Classed Child* is the need to build a case to counter the broad assumption that children in poverty and from the working class do not "communicate well."

20. Halliday, "Anti-Languages," 576, emphasis in original.

Introduction. Reading the Classed Other

1. For more on the literature of the Young Pioneers, see chapter 4.

2. Potamkin et al., *Pioneer Song Book*, 16, 18, 20, 31. See chapter 4 for an extended discussion of anti-language within texts of the Young Pioneer movement.

3. Ibid., 19.

4. Levander and Singley, introduction, 4.

5. Daniel Thomas Cook, *Commodification of Childhood*, 15.

6. Gillian Brown, *Consent of the Governed*, 16. Sánchez-Eppler importantly notes that the child, "inchoate," continued to be used as a metaphor when adults were denied personhood (*Dependent States*, xxiv), a truth in our contemporary culture as well.

7. Mintz, *Huck's Raft*, 76.

8. Hochman, *"Uncle Tom's Cabin,"* 123; Marten, introduction, 4.

9. Duane, *Suffering Childhood in Early America*, 17.

10. Sánchez-Eppler, *Dependent States*, 152.

11. Sánchez-Eppler, "Playing at Class," 40.

12. Bremner, *From the Depths*, 77.

13. Ibid.

14. Thernstrom, "Poverty in Historical Perspective," 179, 164.

15. Ibid.

16. Moeller, "Cultural Construction of Urban Poverty," 8; Bremner, *From the Depths*, 213. Reformers who refused to find nineteenth-century ideas of child labor as inevitable

attacked both short- and long-term consequences of child labor. Arguments were both economic (children in the labor market depressed the wages of adults [Bremner, *From the Depths*, 215]) and moral (children deprived of play "often reassert[ed] their right to it in manhood, as vagabonds, criminals, and prostitutes" [215]). These arguments returned in the 1930s.

17. Moeller, "Cultural Construction of Urban Poverty," 12.

18. Crain, *Reading Children*, 6.

19. Sánchez-Eppler, *Dependent States*, xviii; Zelizer, *Pricing the Priceless Child*, 57.

20. Mintz, *Huck's Raft*, 81; de Schweinitz, "'Waked Up to Feel,'" 15; Sánchez-Eppler, *Dependent States*, xviii.

21. Mintz, *Huck's Raft*, 93.

22. Ibid., 92.

23. Zelizer, *Pricing the Priceless Child*, 60.

24. Ibid., 209.

25. Bremner, *From the Depths*, 213–14.

26. Zelizer, *Pricing the Priceless Child*, 6, 62–63, 70, 72.

27. Lumpkin and Douglas, *Child Workers in America*, 218.

28. Zelizer, *Pricing the Priceless Child*, 97.

29. See Szto, "Documentary Photography."

30. Willmann, "Lewis Hine, Ellis Island, and Pragmatism," 224.

31. Lowry, "Lewis Hine's Family Romance," 186.

32. Ibid., 188, 190.

33. Stott, *Documentary Expression and Thirties America*, 5–7, 6, 8. Innately propagandistic and often focused on persons "simplified and ennobled," social documentary was largely the focus of the decade (57). Stott further delineates the definition by presenting human documentary as a representation of the natural experiences of the Everyman and social documentary as "show[ing] man at grips with conditions neither permanent nor necessary, conditions of a certain time or place" (20). Also crucial is the audience's engagement in the issue at hand if there is any hope of social change (28).

34. Rabinowitz, *They Must Be Represented*, 2.

35. Kazin, *On Native Grounds*, 493, 497.

36. Allred, *American Modernism and Depression Documentary*, 9, 11. Moving away from traditional understandings of documentary, Allred finds within the very flaws Kazin cataloged a new purpose for the truth that "form can no longer master content"; therefore, documentary's "frequency and extravagant violations of authenticity" purposefully and effectively "confront their readers with vulgar materials that disrupt overarching metanarratives, most prominently, those secular 'myths' of identity, nation, and a transcendent humanity" (14).

37. Ibid., 13.

38. Entin, *Sensational Modernism*, 1, 3, 20, 258.

39. Brooks Hefner's 2017 *Word on the Streets* is concerned with the ways modernist literature of the early twentieth century experimented with vernacular speech, though his argument is focused on the literary language of adults. I'll return to his argument in chapter 1.

40. Phillips, *Representations of Childhood in American Modernism*, 4, 6, 7.

41. Callahan et al., "Introduction: How American Literature," 383, 385, 386.

42. Wald, *Writing from the Left*, 7.

43. Mickenberg, *Learning from the Left*, 15, 53.

44. Rabinowitz, *They Must Be Represented*, 217.

45. Rabinowitz, "'Between the Outhouse,'" 32, 41, 44, 40, 39.

46. Levander and Singley, introduction, 11.

47. Gavin Jones, *American Hungers*, 4.

48. Chouliaraki and Fairclough, *Discourse in Late Modernity*, 48. To date, very few literary scholars have, to borrow Fairclough's terminology, recontextualized discourse analysis for literary studies ("Dialectal-Relational Approach," 165). Patrick Colm Hogan's 2013 *Narrative Discourse: Authors and Narrators in Literature, Film, and Art*, for example, blends cognitive science and linguistic discourse analysis to reexamine the constructions of author, narrator, and reader. On a smaller scale, Danielle Cowley's 2012 essay in the *Journal of Literary & Cultural Disability Studies* offers a rereading of a poem in which the poet's language choices offer a counternarrative to the standard cultural discourse of disability.

49. Beaugrande, "Discourse Analysis and Literary Theory," 436, 437.

50. Lang, *Syntax of Class*, 7, 6.

51. Foley, *Radical Representations*, x.

52. Wodak and Meyer, *Methods of Critical Discourse Analysis*, 6. The tools of discourse analysis help uncover and resist systems of inequality as represented in language. First, they help draw attention to the fact that many persons are involved in the creation of a text; therefore, texts "show traces of differing discourses and ideologies contending and struggling for dominance" (10). Second, parsing this struggle reveals patterns and parameters of domination as well as discursive resistance (9). Many times, such struggles circulate markedly around issues of class. Jaworski and Coupland, for example, argue that a person exhibits "discursive dispositions" that vary by class and invariably "reproduce class divisions" ("Editors' Introduction to Part Six," 475). The discourses that govern our lives and work "institutionalize and regulate ways of talking, thinking and acting" (Wodak and Meyer, *Methods of Critical Discourse Analysis*, 35). There are two ways to understand this institutionalization and regulation. The first is Norman Fairclough's discussion of the politics of representation within modernity, in which he asks a series of questions: "Whose representations are these, who gains what from them, what social relations do they draw people into, what are their ideological effects, and what alternative representations are there?" ("Global Capitalism and Critical Awareness," 150). The second is to realize how this language maintains its power not purely from top-down social constructions (which Fowler would call either "verbal violence—advertising, abuse, rant—[or] verbal intimacy—the solidarity of shared class languages" [*Literature as Social Discourse*, 85]) but rather from our willingness to use language to engage with one another and, most importantly, use that language as though it is mere information. Both demonstrate language as a complex system of asymmetrical relationships of power maintained largely without intentional efforts.

53. Fredric Jameson, *Political Unconscious*, 17.

54. Fowler, *Literature as Social Discourse*, 80.

55. Quoted in Chouliaraki and Fairclough, *Discourse in Late Modernity*, 49.

56. Fowler, *Literature as Social Discourse*, 94.

57. Lang, *Syntax of Class*, 7.

58. Quoted in Bannet, *Structuralism and the Logic of Dissent*, 182–83.

59. Fairclough, "Global Capitalism and Critical Awareness," 155; Machin and Mayr, *How to Do Critical Discourse Analysis*, 2.

60. Halliday, "Anti-Languages," 576, 583, emphasis original.

61. Fowler, *Literature as Social Discourse*, 142.

62. Fowler, *Linguistic Criticism*, 187, 189.

63. Fowler, *Literature as Social Discourse*, 150.

64. Carter and Nash as quoted in Fowler, *Linguistic Criticism*, 186.

65. Fowler, *Literature as Social Discourse*, 150, 146, 157.

66. Ibid., 158, 146.

67. Ibid., 146.

68. Alger, *Ragged Dick and Mark, the Match Boy* (hereafter cited in text as *RD*). Innately cyclical, a jeremiad traces its history to the Old Testament prophet Jeremiah, who called for the return of Israel to its covenant state with God. Bercovitch argues that the jeremiad "helped [America] sustain a national dream" that enabled generations to "justify their way of life" (*American Jeremiad*, xi, xiv). Beginning by noting the differences between the European jeremiad of lament and the early American jeremiad of "unshakeable optimism," he stresses the fact that Puritan jeremiads affirmed their mission by both arguing that theirs was a "culture on an errand" and "evok[ing] the mythic past not merely to elicit imitation but above all to demand progress" (7, 23, 24). This created a culture of anxiety that "fed on the distance between promise and fact," a culture determined to "impose metaphor upon reality" (23, 62). During the war for independence, patriots drew on the same tropes and schemes of the Puritan jeremiads, permanently linking religion and national myth "in a single synthetic ideal," a civil religion (132, 176). This ideal "defines itself through antithesis," thus equating the idea of America to that which is right and good (178). Therein lies the jeremiad's most pervasive quality: Because "the very hope of improvement was the American way," critique of America was always "couched in terms that reaffirmed the basic tenets of the culture" (170, 184). In other words, to critique America implies an inherent belief in that which America claims to be.

69. Lang, *Syntax of Class*, 107.

70. Noteworthy is the center item in Dick's list of sins: "if I hadn't spent my money in goin' to the theatre, and treatin' boys to oyster-stews, and bettin' money on cards, and such like" (*RD*, 75). For Alger, caring for other boys is part of the economic frivolity that leaves him penniless. However, once on the path to becoming a self-made man, Dick exchanges instruction in his studies for lodging from a fellow orphan boy. This generosity is praised, perhaps because it is a savvy business deal on Dick's behalf, not charity heedlessly given when one's own needs are not assured.

71. Early in the novel in a rare somber moment, Dick confesses to Frank that "when I've seen boys with good homes, and fathers, and mothers, I've thought I'd like to have somebody to care for me" (*RD*, 99). Several moments in the novel provide Dick with a brief taste of what that would be like, yet it is not until the last chapter that Dick is granted a surrogate father figure. Because he saves a rich businessman's son from drowning, he is given a new suit of clothes and an invitation to work in the counting room of James Rockwell, the wealthy businessman. It is at this point that Dick, now Richard, gives up his shoe-shining business and the novel can properly end. Scholars have noted that Alger's novel challenges myths of class mobility, for work ethic alone is not enough for Dick to leave his status as

orphan. It is noteworthy that the beginning of the novel positions Ragged Dick as a very successful bootblack with "a frank, straight-forward manner" that enables him to earn enough money to partake of both food and entertainment; he earns more, moreover, than he could earn in an office clerk position, which would leave him "skin and bones" by the end of one year (73). Necessary is intervention from surrogate middle-class siblings and parents, and Dick is made worthy only by his willingness to leave behind his sinful ways.

72. Fowler, *Literature as Social Discourse*, 153.

73. Mintz, *Huck's Raft*, 5.

74. Fielder, *Love and Death*; Altschuler, "Motherless Child."

75. Twain, *Adventures of Huckleberry Finn*, 212 (hereafter cited in text as *HF*).

76. Fowler, *Literature as Social Discourse*, 147.

77. Halliday, "Anti-Languages," 582.

78. Fowler, *Literature as Social Discourse*, 149.

79. Ibid., 158.

80. Saunders, introduction, xx.

81. Gubar, "Hermeneutics of Recuperation," 293, 295.

82. Conrad, *Time for Childhoods*, 4, 9.

83. Many more recent monographs are also rooted in the study of nineteenth-century texts and contexts, including, for example, Laura Soderberg's 2021 *Vicious Infants* and Crystal Lynn Webster's 2021 *Beyond the Boundaries of Childhood*. Katharine Capshaw Smith's 2004 *Children's Literature of the Harlem Renaissance*, however, is one example of a twentieth-century project centering children in the study of American literature, as is Mickenberg's aforementioned 2006 cultural studies monograph *Learning from the Left*.

84. For a comprehensive entry point into the conversation of children's agency, see Flynn et al., "Forum: Divergent Perspectives."

85. Owen, *Queer History of Adolescence*, 136–37, emphasis original.

86. Wall, *Ethics in Light of Childhood*, 3.

87. Sánchez-Eppler, "Playing at Class," 40.

88. Hart and Boyden, "Childhood (Re)materialized," 83.

89. Wall, *Ethics in Light of Childhood*, 91.

90. Callahan et al., "Introduction: How American Literature," 389.

91. Mickenberg, *Learning from the Left*, 55.

92. Di Donato, *Christ in Concrete*, 82, 33, emphasis original.

93. Wirth-Nesher, introduction, 10.

94. Zugsmith, *Reckoning*, 18, 25, 30–32.

95. Entin, *Sensational Modernism*, 20, 258.

96. Newell, *Expanding Adaptation Networks*, 6.

97. Wall, "Childism," 68.

Chapter One. The Silences of Southern Poverty

1. Trachtenberg, *Incorporation of America*, vii.

2. Caldwell and Bourke-White, *You Have Seen Their Faces*, x.

3. Ibid., n.p.

4. Dow, *Narrating Class in American Fiction*, 193.

5. Allred, *American Modernism and Depression Documentary*, 95; Agee and Evans, *Let Us Now Praise Famous Men*, 9 (hereafter cited in text as *LUN*).

6. Rabinowitz, *They Must Be Represented*, 37.

7. Ibid., 48.

8. Allred, *American Modernism and Depression Documentary*, 10, 13, 11.

9. Fredric Jameson, *Political Unconscious*, 20; Allred, *American Modernism and Depression Documentary*, 17.

10. Allred, *American Modernism and Depression Documentary*, 14.

11. Cox and Gardner, "Editors' Introduction," 1.

12. Trachtenberg, *Incorporation of America*, 192, 184.

13. Allred, *American Modernism and Depression Documentary*, 15.

14. Benfey, *Double Life of Stephen Crane*, 59.

15. Sante, introduction, xv.

16. Irving, *Immigrant Mothers*, 76.

17. Riis, *How the Other Half Lives*, 137.

18. See, for example, *In the Home of an Italian Rag-picker, Jersey Street* (1889), in ibid., 43.

19. Watkins, "Same People, Same Time," 294; Bryson Shahn, *Ben Shahn*, 134.

20. Watkins, "Same People, Same Time," 297, 295, 300.

21. Coleman, "Rehabilitating the Region," 209.

22. Kao, "Ben Shahn and the Public Use," 39.

23. There are five photographs of this family in Shahn's series of 124 images, *Small Towns in Arkansas, Oct. 1935. Poverty-Stricken Families in the Ozark Mountains*, within the FSA Photograph Collection at the Library of Congress. Those not reproduced here include another of the mother and youngest child. We see no doll, nor are they looking at the camera; a line of clean laundry is visible in the background. Two photographs show four members of the family present. One is a blurred image in which the mother carries the youngest child in front of the cabin's doorway. The boy is at her left, hand in pocket, and the little girl is at her right, balancing on the threshold on one foot. The second doorway image seems to precede this one, as the two oldest children are in motion, exiting the cabin, and the mother and baby are both looking at the baby's hands. In no images do we see the implied head of household, "Destitute Sharecropper," named in the photo's captions.

24. Shahn, *Shape of Content*, 150–51.

25. Bailey, "Female Gothic Fiction," 270, 271.

26. Goodwin, *Modern American Grotesque*, 1.

27. Ibid., 1.

28. Denning, *Cultural Front*, 123.

29. Riis, *How the Other Half Lives*, 137.

30. Allred, *American Modernism and Depression Documentary*, 11.

31. Benfey, *Double Life of Stephen Crane*, 80–81.

32. Ibid., 83.

33. Crane, "An Ominous Baby," 167 (hereafter cited in text as "OB").

34. Bill Brown, "American Childhood," 443.

35. Crane, "A Dark Brown Dog," 180 (hereafter cited in text as "DBD").

36. The namelessness of both Tommie and the dark brown dog is perhaps another way Crane intended to imply impermanence. Tommie comes, after all, from "a dark region

where, from a careening building, a dozen gruesome doorways gave up loads of babies to the street and the gutter," and the few who survive continue to live in a building that "quivered and creaked from the weight of humanity stamping about in its bowels" ("DBD," 7). Both "An Ominous Baby" and "A Great Mistake" follow an inquisitive baby who first studies closely the object of his desire. When his desire for the object becomes too great to suppress, he acts with confidence. Through the unbroken confidence of Bowery children, perhaps Crane is suggesting that this way of seeing poverty is most helpful: All that is left is the reality of the situation, a world of action and reaction.

37. Crane, *Maggie*, 17.

38. Faulkner, *As I Lay Dying*, 66 (hereafter cited in text as *AILD*).

39. Allred, *American Modernism and Depression Documentary*, 16, 7.

40. Ibid., 7.

41. While her argument is not focused on Vardaman alone, Jolene Hubbs reads Faulkner's use of stream-of-consciousness narration in the novel broadly as a means to "[explore] poor white intellect, disputing the longstanding vilipending of poor white people as unintelligent" (*Class, Whiteness, and Southern Literature*, 46). Hubbs illustrates how in much literature of the Depression era authors position white people in poverty in the South as "bring[ing] into relief urbanites' modernity" (46).

42. Hale, "*As I Lay Dying*'s Heterogeneous Discourse," 12.

43. A striking example of this is in Vardaman's first section of narration, in which he describes the way the act of crying moves from a thing separate from him to something he possesses. After fleeing to the barn, for example, Vardaman goes into the stall of Jewel's horse: "Then I can cry then I vomit the crying" (*AILD*, 54). While he searches for a stick, "[t]he crying makes a lot of noise," but after using the stick against Peabody's horses, "[i]t does not make so much noise now" (54, 55). Once his act of violence against the horses is complete, the final shift occurs: "I can cry quiet now, feeling and hearing my tears" (56). Emotions foreign to the child are something expellable and out-of-body, while linguistically, a manageable emotion is relegated to something internal, possessable, and intensely personal.

44. Widiss, "Fit and Surfeit in *As I Lay Dying*," 104.

45. Ibid., 103; Boren, "The Southern Super Collider," 27.

46. Delville, "Alienating Language and Darl's Narrative Consciousness," 63; Mortimer, "Significant Absences," 232. Delville argues that the third narrative section "provides [Vardaman] with a verbal means of representing the mother's body he misses so tragically" ("Alienating Language and Darl's Narrative Consciousness," 63). Mortimer, however, argues that "his emotional task in the novel becomes the conceptual one of creating continuity by accepting the existence of the past. Until he does, his perceptions are fragmented, and verbs of simple prediction dominate his speech" ("Significant Absences," 233).

47. Mellette, *Peculiar Whiteness*, 120.

48. Faulkner speaking during a question-and-answer session during Frederick Gwynn's undergraduate class in contemporary American literature, John Coleman's undergraduate class in writing, and Gwynn's graduate class in American fiction at Rouss Hall, University of Virginia, May 2, 1958. See *Faulkner at Virginia*, University of Virginia, n.d., https://faulkner.lib.virginia.edu/display/wfaudio26_1.html.

49. As quoted in Zeitlin, "Seeing into the Heart," 104.

50. Willis, "Learning from the Banana," 590.

51. Hubbs, "William Faulkner's Rural Modernism," 465.

52. Willis, "Learning from the Banana," 590, 591.

53. Fowler, *Literature as Social Discourse*, 147.

54. Ibid., 151.

55. Atkinson, *Faulkner and the Great Depression*, 11.

56. Caldwell, *Tobacco Road*, 117 (hereafter cited in text as *TR*).

57. Gavin Jones presents Erskine Caldwell's 1932 *Tobacco Road* as an easily dismissible novel whose "characters are stunted and diseased spiritually, morally, and intellectually" and "engage in acts of almost unspeakable moral depravity, physical brutality, and financial irresponsibility" (*American Hungers*, 111). He positions *Tobacco Road* as the obverse of Faulkner's *As I Lay Dying*, a text he argues "illustrates the complexities of representing characters who are both poor and white" (110). Jones does, though, concede the novels' engagement of the poor Southern white motif as indicative of the "power of poverty to damage the poor" (110). This aligns in part with Jay Watson's reading of *Tobacco Road*, in which he traces the language of Caldwell's 1930s characters as a rhetoric of exhaustion, "incapable of complex, or even simultaneous thoughts" ("Rhetoric of Exhaustion," 218). Watson's argument, however, is based on the effects of poverty on Caldwell's depressed characters, not on their lack of capacity.

58. Denning, *Cultural Front*, 123.

59. Gavin Jones, *American Hungers*, 108, emphasis original.

60. Caldwell, "Rachel," 68 (hereafter cited in text as "R").

61. Sylvia Jenkins Cook, *Erskine Caldwell and the Fiction of Poverty*, 116.

62. Fearnow, *American Stage and the Great Depression*, 107; Mixon, *People's Writer*, 58.

63. Fearnow, *American Stage and the Great Depression*, 110; Mixon, *People's Writer*, 59.

64. Kirkland, *Tobacco Road*, 49, 167, 52–53.

65. Before Vardaman ever speaks (on page 38 in the first section Anse narrates), Faulkner is careful to establish his smallness. The Bundrens' neighbor Cora provides the novel's first mention (and omission) of Vardaman. The next mention of Vardaman, by Cora's husband, Tull, twice positions Vardaman as between childhood and manhood: "That boy comes up the hill. He is carrying a fish nigh long as he is. He slings it to the ground and grunts 'Hah' and spits over his shoulder like a man. Durn nigh long as he is," and when describing how the fish slips from Vardaman's hands in the yard, "Vardaman cusses it. He cusses it like a grown man, standing a-straddle of it" (*TR*, 30). Tull's measure of Vardaman's small stature—equal to the length of the carp—is aged by the small body's actions and language, both "like a grown man." How fitting, then, for Vardaman's first words of the novel to be the words one expects not of a child but of an adult. "[B]loody to his knees" from cleaning the fish, Vardaman sits on the steps and says, "I'm pure tired" (38). For the length of the novel, Faulkner reinforces Vardaman's smallness, abandoning these early comparisons to manhood and firmly characterizing him as a child. After Peabody, the family doctor, notices that Addie "watches the boy as he leaves the room," he describes Vardaman's awareness of his mother's illness by emphasizing his size (44). "The durn little tyke is sitting on the top step, looking smaller than ever in the sulphur-colored light," he says (45). A few pages later, Vardaman watches Addie die while standing behind Pa's leg, "peer[ing] with his round head and his eyes round and his mouth beginning to open" (47). He is, in fact, the last person Addie looks at before she dies, which causes "all color [to drain] from his face

into his mouth, as though he has by some means fleshed his own teeth in himself, sucking" (49). Infant once more, sans teeth, he flees. Later that night, he shows up at Tull and Cora's door, Tull "never notic[ing] how low down on the door the knocking was till I opened it and never seen nothing" (69).

66. Kirkland, *Tobacco Road*, 16, 57.

67. Ibid., 2, 57.

68. Samuels, *Culture of Sentiment*, 5.

69. Fearnow, *American Stage and the Great Depression*, 114.

70. Kirkland, *Tobacco Road*, 5, emphasis mine.

71. Fowler, *Literature as Social Discourse*, 146, 150.

72. Dhawan, "Hegemonic Listening and Subversive Silences," 58–59.

73. Fowler, *Literature as Social Discourse*, 146, 147, 150.

74. Ibid., 157, 158.

75. Comparing Faulkner's narrative style in *As I Lay Dying* to Caldwell's in *Tobacco Road*, Sylvia Jenkins Cook reads in Caldwell's language no chance for the Lesters "to redeem themselves through any secret and sensitive consciousness normally hidden from the world" (*From Tobacco Road to Route 66*, 67–68). "There are no interior monologues," she continues, "and external language is reduced to the most mechanical and formulaic utterances which scarcely constitute a means of communication" (68). By not discussing Pearl's silence (and erroneously simplifying the remaining Lesters' and Caldwell's narrative choices), Cook neglects to realize one way Caldwell's youngest character's language is subversive.

76. Sylvia Jenkins Cook, *Erskine Caldwell and the Fiction of Poverty*, 108, 109.

77. Palmer, "Bourgeois Blues," 121.

78. Scarry, "Poetry, Injury, and the Ethics of Reading," 42, 45, 46–47, 48.

Chapter Two. Discourses of Play and Control

1. Ellison, "What These Children Are Like," 68, 67, 69.

2. Ellison, "1963, 5 September," box 170, folder 2, Speeches, Lectures, and Interviews, Ralph Ellison Papers, Library of Congress, Washington, D.C.

3. Ellison, "What These Children Are Like," 74.

4. Fowler, *Literature as Social Discourse*, 146, emphasis original.

5. Gavin Jones, *American Hungers*, 109, 147.

6. Hefner, *Word on the Streets*, 10, 11–12.

7. Fowler, *Linguistic Criticism*, 233.

8. Wright, *Black Boy*, 4 (hereafter cited in text as *BB*).

9. More recent scholarship, such as Kinohi Nishikawa's "Richard Wright Between Two Fronts," traces the paratexts of *Black Boy* to argue how the book's journey to publication shaped its reception and lingering beliefs, even today, about Wright's radicalism or lack thereof. A main tenet of Nishikawa's argument is that to read Wright as either a "sellout or radical" is a narrow, reductive approach (181).

10. Mutnick, *No Race, No Country*, 81.

11. Smith as quoted in Gavin Jones, *American Hungers*, 143. Earlier nineteenth-century examples of careful control of language abound. Harriet E. Wilson's 1859 *Our Nig*, for example, maintains a rigid commitment to the polite and well-educated presentation of

language, both narration and speech, required of the antebellum sentimental genre. Nevertheless, its very existence, coupled with Wilson's elaborate inventiveness, is a subversive act whose demands on the genre reveal no tidy, satisfactory ending for the protagonist. Wilson's choice of a third-person limited narrator sympathetic to the protagonist's plight allows the reader access to the thoughts of Frado, or N——g, as she is derogatorily called by the Bellmont family, for whom she is an indentured servant. Karen Sánchez-Eppler's research demonstrates that there was a "preponderance of child readers" of this text from "white, middle-class, northeastern homes" (*Dependent States*, 41). Therefore, unlike *Uncle Tom's Cabin* (seven years *Our Nig*'s senior), which filters the caricatured slave life of Topsy through a white, middle-class narrator for white, Northern, middle-class readers (many of whom were children), Wilson's novel gives a Black woman access to a readership often carefully guarded behind the protective barriers of middle-class childhood. Across the novel, Frado's punishments are both cruel and symbolic of forced silence: Mrs. Bellmont again "plac[ed] the wedge of wood between [Frado's] teeth, [and] beat her cruelly with the raw-hide" (93). Frado's inability to speak freely is consistently displayed through the barriers placed in her mouth as she endures abusive and cruel punishments. The fact that Frado narrates this abuse within the act of writing to an audience of largely white, middle-class children, however, unsettles the inherent antebellum power structure by removing Frado's barrier to speech. In addition to the subversive act of writing, Frado's speech within the novel offers subtle examples of the anti-language of a child whose world is framed entirely by those who are white. For example, in chapter 4, after receiving a succession of beatings from Mrs. Bellmont, seven-year-old Frado runs away. She is brought home by the Bellmont sons. Once she is home and has been fed, James, the eldest of the brothers, tries to encourage Frado to be "good":

> "Who made me so?"
> "God;" answered James.
> "Did God make you?"
> "Yes."
> "Who made Aunt Abby?"
> "God."
> "Who made your mother?"
> "God."
> "Did the same God that made her make me?"
> "Yes."
> "Well, then, I don't like him."
> "Why not?"
> "Because he made her white, and me black. Why didn't he make us *both* white?" (50–51, emphasis original)

Using the very paradigm many Northerners were brandishing to speak publicly against the evils of slavery, Frado simplifies the ironies of Christianity by questioning the idea of a creator who arbitrarily assigns race knowing full well the ramifications that assignment includes. Furthermore, by demonstrating such a quick and complete assurance of her dislike, Frado's dialogue here represents an anti-language that relexicalizes the qualifiers "black" and "white" to assign to the first a second-class position of servitude and to the second the authority of command over such secondary persons. "White" is aligned less with God and more with privilege. Sánchez-Eppler argues that "Wilson figures childhood as labor and burden, but insists that these costs are compensated by play and even mischief" (*Dependent States*, 44). Such an argument does draw attention to Frado's pranks and intentional acts of subversion, yet I think Wilson's calculated risks of weaving into her sentimental plot bits of anti-language that the genre's polite discourse can never quite mask bear mention as well. (And, as Laura Soderberg notes, *Our Nig* is a semiautobiographical novel, as Wilson was "indentured as a child due to family poverty" [*Vicious Infants*, 23].)

12. Halliday, "Anti-Languages," 582.

13. Wright gives another example of this self-awareness in the boys' modifications of the hymns of church. "*Amazing grace, how sweet it sounds*" became "*A bulldog ran my grandma down*" as they "twisted [the Bible stories and hymns], secularized them to the level of our street life, [and] reject[ed] all meanings that did not fit into our environment" (*BB*, 82–83, emphasis original). Grace becomes another violent act, for it is something foreign that "did not fit" the paradigm of their street.

14. Fowler, *Literature as Social Discourse*, 155.

15. Mutnick, *No Race, No Country*, 68, 70, 69.

16. Cappetti, *Writing Chicago*, 202, 200. Cappetti quotes Michel Fabre to note that when Wright's family moved to Chicago, Mary Wirth was their case worker. Wirth's husband, Louis Wirth, was a sociologist who "repeatedly provided Wright with reading lists of sociological material at the graduate level" and introduced him to others in the Chicago school of sociology, including Robert Park and Robert Redfield, as well as St. Clair Drake and Horace Cayton, his later collaborators on *12 Million Black Voices* (185).

17. Bryant, *Byline, Richard Wright*, ix, 34, 58, 59.

18. Sharon Lynette Jones, "Black Excesses and Deprivations," 35.

19. Wright, "Blueprint for Negro Writing," 405, 407, 412, 406.

20. Ibid., 407, 408, 410, emphasis in the original.

21. Ellison, *Shadow and Act*, 7, 147.

22. Hirsch, "Federal Writers' Project," 361. The largest emphasis of scholarly attention in literary studies on the FWP has been to trace the influence of the project on major literary figures who were employed by it, such as Zora Neale Hurston, Richard Wright, Meridel Le Sueur, Nelson Algren, and Ralph Ellison.

23. Butts, *Dark Mirror*, 144; Rutkowski, *Literary Legacies of the Federal Writers' Project*, 34.

24. Botkin, "WPA and Folklore Research," 263. This shift—recording and studying folklore as performance—gained traction in folklore studies in the 1960s (Hirsch, "Federal Writers' Project," 372).

25. Botkin, *Treasury of American Folklore*, xxi; Botkin, "We Call It 'Living Lore,'" 190; Hirsch, "Federal Writers' Project," 366.

26. Boettiger, *Children's Play Indoors and Out*, 13.

27. Schwartzman, *Transformations*, 133.

28. Henricks, "Play Studies," 119.

29. Henricks, *Play and the Human Condition*, 209, 76.

30. While children's rhymes are now intentionally separated as a distinct category within the Folklore Project files at the Library of Congress, the rhymes collected were recorded by a wide variety of field-workers who also recorded other folklore later filed across

a host of categories. Each state's files are categorized primarily by the function of the folklore (e.g., "ghost stories," "dreams," and "local lore" are common across each state's slightly different files), though many states separated out the folklore of specific groups of people. "Children's lore," "Negro lore," and "Indian lore" are the most common categories, though "pioneer lore" is occasionally found as a category in the files from Midwestern and Western states.

31. Opie and Opie, *Lore and Language of Schoolchildren*, xxiv.

32. Ibid., xxiv.

33. Ibid., 4, 8, 2, 18.

34. Conrad, *Time for Childhoods*, 10; Gubar, "Hermeneutics of Recuperation," 304.

35. Bernstein, *Racial Innocence*, 29.

36. Sánchez-Eppler, "Geographies of Play," 41.

37. Capshaw Smith, *Children's Literature of the Harlem Renaissance*, 124.

38. Rutkowski, *Literary Legacies of the Federal Writers' Project*, 53. I first learned of Ellison's work collecting rhymes from Rutkowski's *Literary Legacies*, which prompted me to undertake the archival work detailed here.

39. Ibid., 50.

40. Halliday, "Anti-Languages," 576.

41. Fowler, *Literature as Social Discourse*, 152.

42. Halliday, "Anti-Languages," 582.

43. Opie and Opie, *Lore and Language of Schoolchildren*, 320.

44. Ibid., 306.

45. Henricks, *Play and the Human Condition*, 2, 205, 210, 209, 164, emphasis original.

46. Miscellaneous, box A647, Children's Lore, Folklore Project, New York City, Works Progress Administration, Federal Writers' Project, Library of Congress, Washington, D.C. (hereafter FPLC).

47. Negro Lore: Frank Byrd, Ralph Ellison, box A648, FPLC.

48. One more folder also contains children's rhymes, most of them from 1939: Ellison Records, WPA, box A1086, folder 8, FPLC. This set of thirty-six pages, some of which appear to be final drafts of the rhymes largely unorganized in A648, is labeled "Copy 2" in the top left-hand corner. A648 rhymes often have pen and pencil edits, which the copies at the beginning of A1086 typically do not. Lastly, some of the rhymes on pages filed in A1086 are numbered and labeled according to purpose (e.g., "taunt" or "ball bouncing"), suggesting a final draft Ellison might have submitted. Ellison's rich ethnographic notes are absent from these supposed final drafts, suggesting that what was required of the assignment was only the text of the rhyme, the geographic location of its recitation, and its purpose. The first drafts of Ellison's FWP field notes often included rhymes from his own childhood, labeled as "R.W.E. Oklahoma City, 1925"; these are carefully paired with rhymes from Harlem children. It is as though Ellison was reminded of the language of his own youth.

49. Negro Lore, box A648, FPLC.

50. Hurvitz, "Jews and Jewishness in the Street Rhymes," 142–43.

51. When used exclusively by Jewish children in 1925, the rhyme was shortened: "Red, white and blue / The color of the Jew." Here Hurvitz reads the evocation of the American flag by Jewish children was "an effort on their part to identify with a major symbol of American life" (ibid., 142).

52. Gardner, "Some Counting-Out Rhymes in Michigan," 534.

53. Negro Lore, box A648, FPLC.

54. Mangione, *Dream and the Deal*, 252. While it was a common hope that FWP writers would find opportunities for publication of literary works influenced by their time on the project, only *American Stuff: An Anthology of Prose & Verse by Members of the Federal Writers' Project* (Viking Press, 1937) was published by the project. However, many other existing outlets, such as the magazine *Poetry*, published issues devoted to literature by FWP workers. The *New Masses*, May 10, 1938, issue referenced here is another example.

55. Rolland, "Street Songs of Children," 109. In the rhyme Rolland records, the threat is that the policeman "will squeeze me like a lemon / Achalachke zol em nehmen." Abrahams offers a history of the "Macy's" rhyme as recorded in popular and scholarly publications (*Jump Rope Rhymes*, 97).

56. Rosner, *Playing with History*, 4.

57. Halliday, "Anti-Languages," 571.

58. Negro Lore, box A648, FPLC.

59. Ellison, "Hidden Name and Complex Fate," 161, 164.

60. Ellison, "Art of Fiction," 172.

61. Schor, "Ralph Ellison, Journeyman," 69, 64.

62. Foley, *Wrestling with the Left*, 116.

63. Rutkowski, *Literary Legacies*, 56, 55, 53.

64. Floreani, "Oklahoma City and 'the Territory,'" 17.

65. Ellison, "That I Had the Wings," 48 (hereafter cited in text as "TIH").

66. Ellison, *Three Days Before the Shooting*, 89. This question is originally asked with sarcasm by the white reporter McIntyre. I would argue, however, that this question guides much of the novel's remaining pieces and parts. Put in the mouth of any of the main characters and several of the memorable characters who dominate only a single scene (e.g., Miss Maud in book 2), the answer to this question becomes a map of sorts that the reader uses to follow Ellison's oft-trod paths through the iterations of the novel's different drafts and revisions. Strewn upon these paths are often children's rhymes (a commonplace, as I've shown, in his earliest short stories, too).

67. Butts, *Dark Mirror*, 165.

Chapter Three. The "Damaged" Child's Polyvalent Language

1. Gold, "Notes of the Month," 5, emphasis original.

2. Foley, *Radical Representations*, 55. See Constance Coiner's chapter "The Thirties' Literary Left" in *Better Red* and Michael Denning's chapter "'The Literary Class War': Rethinking Proletarian Literature" in *The Cultural Front* for discussions of defining proletarian literature in the Depression era.

3. Gold, "Notes of the Month," 5.

4. Denning, *Cultural Front*, 233.

5. Gold, *Jews Without Money*, 19, emphasis original.

6. In his chapter "'The Tenement Thinking': Ghetto Pastorals," Denning notes the powerful influence that the success of Gold's novel had on other contemporary proletarian writers' choice to write about "ghetto life" and childhood (*Cultural Front*, 233–34).

7. Ibid., 260.
8. Gordon, "Dorothea Lange's Oregon Photography," 573.
9. Entin, *Sensational Modernism*, 51.
10. Stein as quoted in ibid., 280.
11. Gordon, "Dorothea Lange's Oregon Photography," 574, 581.
12. Entin, *Sensational Modernism*, 51, 46.
13. Gordon, "Dorothea Lange's Oregon Photography," 51.
14. Mickenberg, "Pedagogy of the Popular Front," 228, 234.
15. Gold, "Proletarian Child," 678.
16. Mickenberg, "Pedagogy of the Popular Front," 233.
17. "Art Issue," 27.
18. Entin, *Sensational Modernism*, 51; Gavin Jones, *American Hungers*, 3.
19. "Art Issue," 17.
20. Allred, *American Modernism and Depression Documentary*, 13.
21. Lumpkin, *To Make My Bread*, 29. In some ways, this emphasis presents these female writers as the proletarian ideal, the "heroic housewife" whose "party duty" was to be wife and mother (Hapke, *Daughters of the Great Depression*, 77). In many early 1930s proletarian works there is a fraught tension between motherhood and organizing. This tension is often housed, of course, in children for whom a sentimental childhood is inaccessible. Genevieve Taggard's 1936 poem "Feeding the Children," for example, chronicles such tension in four short stanzas. With lines that sharply alternate between sarcasm ("Women are conservative. That is / They want life to go on . . ." [1–2]) and actuality ("I must feed my children" [4]), the documentary-style poem is largely constructed of mothers' dialogue identifiable by its right feeling, not signifying punctuation (which also allows the dialogue to be representative of all, not just the experiences of one). The swift conversion of the mothers to the Left is prompted by the horrendous living conditions depicted in stanza 3, as well as the realization that "[o]ut in the street they demonstrate [the mother's] question" (11). The final stanza of the poem is a cacophonous chorus that shifts the poem's refrain from a statement of critique to a claim of political action:

> We must feed the children. Have you joined the Union?
> We must feed the children. March today.
> We must feed the children. How shall we feed the children?
> We must feed the children. Vote the strike! (13–16)

No longer "I must," the responsibility of sustaining the children rests on the collective by the end of the poem. Taggard proposes that political food will sustain where physical food falls short. Regardless of the ability of the women to nurture or their courage to picket in male spaces, by the end, Taggard's poem has made it clear that there is still not enough meat or milk for the children who are hungry now. There is no room for hope, a hope that moves individuals into groups but does not provide.

22. Foley, *Radical Representations*, 327.
23. Lumpkin, *To Make My Bread*, 29 (hereafter cited in text as *TMMB*).
24. Though child labor was not federally outlawed until 1938, Lumpkin's 1932 novel comments on the increasing national conversation about its abolition taking place early in the thirties. On the one hand, the novel shows the literal damage mill work does to the bodies

of mill children; on the other, it anticipates the "misguided paternalism" of the New Deal that failed to "address the systemic roots of poverty" (Webb, "'Ain't Worth a Damn for Nothing,'" 109, 115). Mothers at work in the mills leave behind children who must care for children and in turn have little time for luxuries such as education. Soon, these children become mill workers and mothers themselves. It is only as adults, however, that John and Bonnie achieve "revolutionary class consciousness." John becomes integral to the mill strike that is the novel's climax, and Bonnie realizes that, to the company, she is less than a machine, for she "don't get paid for wear and tear on [her]self" (*TMMB*, 319). Yet Bonnie's participation in the union's efforts results in her murder, and just as the children's fairy tale to which the title of the novel alludes, the novel argues that capitalism consumes: Her children are taken into state custody, an act that "couldn't be helped" (383). Lumpkin's allusion to "Jack and the Beanstalk" prompts the reader to look for an evil giant who eats humans. This is easily achieved, for Lumpkin describes the mill workers' faces as "hav[ing] no flesh, [. . .] made of bone with skin stretched tightly over it" (270). The same allusion, however, requires a child whose wit and pluck slay the giant. The final chapter of the novel seems to want to suggest hope; its last words are, after all, "This is just the beginning" (384). This sentence illustrates Foley's definition of the proletarian bildungsroman tidily: "Positioned to identify with the protagonist's 'conversion,' readers presumably carry the text's implied lessons over into their own lives" (*Radical Representations*, 327). Where, though, is Lumpkin's Jack? We can read Lumpkin's Jack as necessarily grown up: Bonnie's brother John, who symbolically stands up at the end of the novel. Or, perhaps, the novel suggests that within the world of the mills, Jack cannot escape the giant.

25. Zugsmith, "Room in This World," 48 (hereafter cited in text as "RTW").

26. Zandy, introduction, 5.

27. Cantwell, "Little Magazines," 295; Coiner, *Better Red*, 145, 174.

28. Denning, *Cultural Front*, 249. Most Olsen scholarship stakes a claim about the relevance of the novel's publication history. Corinna Lee notes the multiple functions of Olsen's framing of her "*twice* unfinished" novel both as biography and, more importantly, as an argument for "revalu[ing] the aesthetic and political significance of creative interruption" ("Documents of Proletarian Fiction," 115, emphasis original). Though Linda Ray Pratt's 2004 introduction to *Yonnondio* finds power in the constructed text, she argues that we "gain little from pursuing" its makings and archival scraps (vi). Panthea Reid's pointed biography of Olsen reprints Olsen's 1935 plan for the "1930s Proletarian Novel" to Donald Klopfer at Random House (*Tillie Olsen*, app. C, 347–49). This narrative arc contrasts, understandably, with the "unpublished material" in the 1989 Delta edition of *Yonnondio*, which extends the novel with seventeen pages of "fragments" of the unfinished chapters of the project.

29. Lerner, "The Iron Throat," 3 (hereafter cited in text as "IT"). The opening paragraph of "The Iron Throat" twice names "Marie" as the child at the center of the story. By the second page, however, the child is called Mazie, and "Marie" refers to Marie Kvaternick, a neighbor whose thirteen-year-old son begins work in the mines that day. I would argue that page 1 is a one-letter typo, as the entirety of the story consistently names the child Mazie.

30. Olsen, *Yonnondio*, 1 (hereafter cited in text as *Y*).

31. Calhoun, "Child Mind as a Social Product," 81.

32. Lee, "Documents of Proletarian Fiction," 126. Lee's essay, which is focused on the full novel, argues that reading *Yonnondio* as a failed proletarian bildungsroman (in which

characters achieve class consciousness, which leads to revolutionary action) opens possibilities for seeing the text as commentary on the "unresolved political consciousness of [the 1930s]" (125). Her discussion of Mazie's monologue is grounded in chapter 1.

33. Olsen's revisions to "The Iron Throat" in chapter 1 of *Yonnondio* are minimal: Grammar and punctuation are slightly more conventional, mostly through the use of dashes and commas (though many of the errors in "The Iron Throat" [e.g., missing quotation marks at the front end of clearly framed dialogue] suggest typos), a few sentences are shortened (to reduce redundancy, it seems) or their order inverted, and Jim calls Mazie "Bigeyes" twice. Olsen softens dialect twice through standardized spelling as well: "Gawd" becomes "God" (4, 3) and "sez" becomes "says" (9). Lastly, Olsen entirely omits two examples of racist language when Jim describes Mazie's intelligence—"Smart rascal. Guess she gets it from Anna's k——ke blood" (9)—and when the omniscient narrator describes the thirteen-year-old Kvaternick son underground in the rain-saturated mine—"water dripping through a n——rhead" (6).

34. Steadman, "Critique of Proletarian Literature," 150.

35. Cantwell, "The Little Magazines," 297.

36. Here I'm following the method Barbara Foley articulates in *Wrestling with the Left*, in which she reads Ellison's *Invisible Man* in this way: "I depart from the circular practice of reading *Invisible Man* through the palimpsest supplied by Ellison's writings after 1952 and, more generally, by the Cold War narrative that bindingly shapes most discussion of American writers—especially African American writers—and the left. Drawing upon an examination of the multiple drafts, outlines, and notes for the novel, as well as Ellison's early journalism and fiction, I read forward to *Invisible Man*" (6).

37. Elizabeth Jameson, "Written, They Reappear," 142.

38. Hapke, *Daughters of the Great Depression*, 81, 85.

39. Rabinowitz, *Labor and Desire*, 130.

40. Tillie Olsen, journal page, "Yonnondio, makings," collection M667, series 1, box 15, folder 28, Tillie Olsen Papers, Special Collections and University Archives, Stanford University.

41. Denning, *Cultural Front*, 249.

42. Robé, "Saint Mazie," 167–68.

43. Mara Faulkner, *Protest and Possibility*, 43, 42.

44. Fowler, *Literature as Social Discourse*, 152.

45. Mara Faulkner, *Protest and Possibility*, 43, 42.

46. Orr, "'People Who Might Have Been You,'" 205.

47. Olsen, "Vision of Fear and Hope," 138.

48. Rabinowitz, *Labor and Desire*, 132.

49. Fowler, *Literature as Social Discourse*, 85.

50. Coiner, *Better Red*, 191, 194.

51. Ibid., 239.

52. Halliday, "Anti-Languages," 582.

53. Pancake, "Story Time," 297, 304–5.

54. Tillie Olsen, "There were shadows," "Yonnondio, makings," collection M667, series 1, box 4, folder 5, Olsen Papers.

55. Tillie Olsen, "Towards noon," "Yonnondio, makings," collection M667, series 1, box 4, folder 5, Olsen Papers. A revised version of Mazie's question does appear within the last half

of one sentence in chapter 5: "[N]o fun to see the young'uns pulps with charity starches drowse and chant the lesson after the teacher: we-are-the-richest-country-in-the-worr-uld" (*Y*, 64).

56. The idea of "text" within the novel has been marginally discussed, such as Denning's brief mention of the role the texts of magazines and film play in Jinella's and Mazie's imaginings at the dump tent (*Cultural Front*, 141) or Elizabeth Jameson's reader-response discussion of pedagogy and the novel, which catalogs the recurring motif of "the power of texts to take you '*places your body aint ever been*'" ("Written, They Reappear," 143, emphasis original). Both of these discussions, however, note but do not unpack the role of the child in these respective scenes, as well as Olsen's curious use of the word "text" in a novel committed to "*Lament for the* [working class] . . . a song, a poem of / itself—*the word itself a dirge* . . ." (Whitman as quoted in *Y*, viii, emphasis original). Chapters 7 and 8 serve as the turning point of the novel: Mazie's discovery of her own text.

57. Olsen, *Yonnondio*, 1989 ed., 144, 146; Tillie Olsen, "Yonnondio, makings," collection M667, series 1, box 4, Olsen Papers.

58. Fowler, *Literature as Social Discourse*, 147.

59. Rabinowitz, *Labor and Desire*, 132.

60. Tillie Olsen, "Early Correspondence, 1930–1939," collection M667, series 3, box 19, Olsen Papers. Filed in Olsen's papers are many typed or handwritten pages that detail developmental milestones of children, research that Olsen seems to have gathered from multiple sources but that is not always attributed. One typed page from the 1930s begins with the first sentences from Robert MacDougall's "The Child's Speech: Words and Meaning," published in the *Journal of Educational Psychology* in 1913: "The beginning of speech is the most momentous event in the history of the child. Its understanding is a key to the whole storehouse of knowledge, and upon its use all human fellowship depends" (29). The rest of the typed page notes John Dewey's theories of the influence of language on others, notes how responses are "in relation to environment," lists "McCarthy's classifications of speech, a modification of [Jean] Piaget's," and ends with retyped notes about what factors influence children's verbal responses.

61. Rabinowitz, "'Between the Outhouse,'" 41, 44.

62. Butler, "Ordinary, Incredulous," 34.

63. Ibid., 35.

64. Ibid., 35.

Chapter Four. Reading (in) Class

1. *New Pioneer* 2, no. 11 (March 1933), box 35, Radical Pamphlets, Center for Southwest Research, University of New Mexico (hereafter CSR).

2. Campion, *Who Are the Young Pioneers?*, n.p.

3. Mickenberg, *Learning from the Left*, 53.

4. Also of note is the recurrence of the Great Depression as a setting in children's historical fiction focused on recounting experiences of poverty and written long after the 1930s. The Newbery medal list alone yields *Out of the Dust* (1998), *Bud, Not Buddy* (2000), *Roll of Thunder, Hear My Cry* (1977), and *A Year Down Yonder* (2001). There is more work to be done on the problem of poverty in children's literature, especially the oft-lingering

nineteenth-century American habit of valuing only the poor deemed worthy by their pluck and obedience. There is also a trend within children's literature to invite the reader to see economic struggle as a site in which the suffering of those in poverty is secondary to the moral instruction the child reader has to absorb, such as the redemptive qualities fostered by living a life of poverty or being a sympathetic witness to those who are poor.

5. Returning to the March 1933 back cover of *New Pioneer* demonstrates how layered representations of this resistance often were. One could argue that Mary is largely illustrated as middle class, with her tidy haircut and matching sweater and skirt. She does, after all, readily make change when charging her principal the cost of the already-burned *New Pioneer* issue. Prohaska's more subtle class markers, though, are contained to the very next panel, in which we see Mary talking with three male friends as they walk after school through the deep Montana snow: Not all wear coats, a knee patch is visible, none wear winter hats, and hands are either tucked tightly into pockets to stay warm or drawn without mittens. Lastly, it is not Mary—the only child not illustrated walking in lock step—who articulates the plan to sell "subs[criptions]" tomorrow but one of the male comrades with whom she walks.

6. Mickenberg, *Learning from the Left*, 53. See all of chapter 2 for further discussion of what different groups under the broad umbrella of the early twentieth-century Left (prior to the Popular Front) believed to be true regarding children of various class positions and how those beliefs informed their political philosophies and the texts that they produced and/or promoted for young people. Paul Mishler's chapters 2 and 3 also detail the differences between the socialist models that "saw their task as educating children for political participation in the future" and Communist models that sought to "organize children for political activity" in the present (*Raising Reds*, 42, 41).

7. Mickenberg, *Learning from the Left*, 52, 55; Mishler, *Raising Reds*, 25, 42–43; Hodgson, *Young Reds in the Big Apple*, 33. One of Mickenberg's central claims is the radical commitments to racial equality of the Left (*Learning from the Left*, 73).

8. *New Pioneer* was preceded by *Young Pioneer*, which was denied the use of second-class mail by the U.S. Post Office in January 1931. For more on the Young Pioneer protests in response to this, see Hodgson, *Young Reds in the Big Apple*, 116–17, as well as the chapter's broader focus on the "strong periodical culture" in the organization. For a comprehensive overview of the *New Pioneer* magazine and its impact on the careers of many children's authors and illustrators, see Mickenberg, *Learning from the Left*, 67–79.

9. Hodgson, "From the Bronx to Stalingrad," 69; Hodgson, *Young Reds in the Big Apple*, 2–3.

10. Mickenberg, *Learning from the Left*, 56; Mishler, *Raising Reds*, 44, 42; Hodgson, *Young Reds in the Big Apple*, 3. The fifth item in the 1932 "Rules and Regulations of the Young Pioneers of America" states that "[a] Pioneer organizes the children around him. He takes part in the life and interest of these children and draws them into the Young Pioneers. He is the model for all workers' and farmers' children" (Hodgson, *Young Reds in the Big Apple*, 165).

11. Hodgson, *Young Reds in the Big Apple*, 5.

12. Campion, *Who Are the Young Pioneers?*, 21. Campion also edited the 1935 *New Pioneer Storybook*, which includes articles reprinted from issues of the *New Pioneer* magazine. (No authors are listed in the *Storybook*, though the magazine does list the adult authors of the stories.) Max Bedacht's one-page introduction spends four paragraphs offering evidence of

why children's stories from mainstream culture and school are capitalist fairy tales and lies. The last three short paragraphs from the *Storybook* offer something different: "Reading these stories will help you understand the life about you. As you learn to *understand* life, you will learn to shape your own lives. [. . .] You will not only be part of history, but you will become makers of history" (6).

13. Mishler, in fact, argues that the early thirties mark the "high point in the development of the Young Pioneer movement" because of the exigency of the suffering of the Depression (*Raising Reds*, 60). Multiple scholars note the emergence of the Popular Front and the shift in focus of the organization and its publications "as Communists looked beyond their traditional working-class constituency and sought recruits from the middle class" (60; see also Mickenberg, *Learning from the Left*, 71). While the Young Pioneers of America dissolved in 1934, the *Young Pioneer* magazine was published until 1939 (Mishler, *Raising Reds*, 51; Hodgson, *Young Reds in the Big Apple*, 117).

14. The first issue's list of contributing editors includes, in order of appearance, Mike Gold, Grace Lumpkin, and John Dos Passos, all well-known proletarian writers.

15. *New Pioneer* 1, no. 1 (May 1931): 2, box 35, Radical Pamphlets, CSR.

16. *New Pioneer* 1, no. 2 (June 1931): 21, 20, 6, box 35, Radical Pamphlets, CSR.

17. *New Pioneer* 3, no. 11 (March 1934): 261, box 35, Radical Pamphlets, CSR.

18. *New Pioneer* 1, no. 8 (December 1931): 21, and *New Pioneer* 1, no. 7 (November 1931): 18, box 35, Radical Pamphlets, CSR.

19. Maynes, "Age as a Category of Historical Analysis," 116, 119.

20. *New Pioneer* 1, no. 9 (January 1932): 18, box 35, Radical Pamphlets, CSR.

21. *New Pioneer* 1, no. 7 (November 1931): 18, and *New Pioneer* 1, no. 8 (December 1931): 21, box 35, Radical Pamphlets, CSR.

22. *New Pioneer* 2, no. 7 (November 1932): 19, box 35, Radical Pamphlets, CSR.

23. Elliott, *Theorizing Adaptation*, 198; Newell, *Expanding Adaptation Networks*, 8.

24. *New Pioneer* 2, no. 2 (June 1932): 19, box 35, Radical Pamphlets, CSR.

25. Hitchcock and Gann, *Music in the United States*, 20. "My Country 'Tis of Thee" is itself an adaptation.

26. See part 3 of Hodgson's *Young Reds in the Big Apple* for multiple examples of the poetry and adaptations to popular song lyrics and rhymes that children submitted across the 1920s and 1930s to other children's leftist magazines, such as *Young Comrade* (111).

27. McMahon and Sutton-Smith, "Past in the Present," 302, 304, 305.

28. Fowler, *Literature as Social Discourse*, 150.

29. *New Pioneer* 2, no. 6 (October 1932): 17, box 35, Radical Pamphlets, CSR.

30. *New Pioneer* 1, no. 3 (July 1931): 16, box 35, Radical Pamphlets, CSR.

31. *New Pioneer* 1, no. 9 (January 1932): 8, box 35, Radical Pamphlets, CSR.

32. Opie and Opie, *Oxford Dictionary of Nursery Rhymes*, 227.

33. Eysteinsson as quoted in Allred, *American Modernism and Depression Documentary*, 16.

34. *New Pioneer* 3, no. 11 (March 1934): 243–44, and *New Pioneer* 2, no. 10 (February 1933): 4, box 35, Radical Pamphlets, CSR.

35. Grieve, "Visual Production of Citizenship," 26–27.

36. Ibid., 27.

37. Mickenberg, *Learning from the Left*, 27.

38. As quoted in Findlay, *WPA Children's Books*, 14–15.

39. Van Hook, *Taro Taki*, 11.

40. Ibid., 6.

41. Sinks, *Riquitin and the Old Men*, 2, 3–4, 12, 23, 25.

42. Children's books focused on class or representations of class positions below the middle-class norm are atypical even today. Recent articles by Vikki Terrile and Adam Szetela take up this topic in contemporary picture books.

43. As noted, economic hardship is commonplace across the readers, especially as the genesis of the story and the severity of the hardship range in predictable patterns that are aligned with the class position of the protagonists. *Behind the Fireplace*, for example, follows the Evans family as they move out of their New York apartment to a quieter neighborhood on Long Island because a house payment is more manageable than their previous rent. In this particular reader, the four Evans siblings find antiques and gold coins when exploring their new home that are valuable enough for their family to return to their apartment in the city (though the narrator frames the children's pleas to stay with the new friends they've found as noble). Such an improbable climax isn't the norm, however.

44. Sinks, *Bull Who Would Not Fight*, 2, 4, 5, 9, 11.

45. Ibid., 33, 15, 32, 16.

46. Peck, *Tommy and Tugboat George*, 27.

47. See note 43, chapter 4, for a description of *Behind the Fireplace*.

48. Peck, *Tommy and Tugboat George*, 12. Many stories follow the Ragged Dick model, in which the absent father dies working. John E. McHugh's *The Little Engineer*, for example, follows Jimmy and his mother and his younger invalid sister, who live by the railroad tracks. Jimmy "tried to take his father's place in the family" after he died when his train went into the water because of a washed-out bridge (2). After school (purposefully mentioned for the reader, one assumes), Jimmy picks up coal alongside the tracks to keep their home warm and the stove fueled (for which he has permission, as "all the railroad men knew" his father), while his sister, Mary, who cannot attend school, sews small things and "helps her mother a great deal by selling them" (6, 3). Mary dreams of the country, though Jimmy had "no time for dreams" (4). The family's move to the country at the end of the reader comes after Mary sees through her window a man hurt on the tracks, and Jimmy saves the man from an oncoming train. The man is Mr. Gordon, the president of the railroad, and as a reward he gives the family a small farm he owns in the country and the promise for Jimmy of his own engine after he takes care of his mother and sister and "grow[s] to be a man" (21). In general, the adult male laborers in these readers love their work and take pride in doing it well: "Everyone who loves his work is happy in doing it," Jimmy's mother says of railroad engineers, never expressing anger at the labor that killed her children's father (13).

49. Eberle, *Oh, but a Gander Can't Talk, Book II*, 41.

50. Dunn, *Bobby and Bones*, 22.

51. Boulton, *Verses of All Sizes and Shapes*, 22. Grieve also notes that the stories uphold traditional gender roles and largely exclude characters presented as female, especially as protagonists.

52. Ibid., lines 1–4.

53. Barnet, "Two Giants," in *Read and Laugh Stories, Book One*, 26; Barnet, "Detective Dan," in *Read and Laugh Stories, Book Three*, 3.

54. "Dimps," in *Read and Laugh Stories, Book Three*, 17 (hereafter cited in text as "D").

55. Halliday, "Anti-Languages," 570.

56. Keating, *Mr. Chu*, 1 (hereafter cited in text as *MC*).

57. Keating expanded *Mr. Chu*, and it was republished in 1965 by Macmillan with wholly new illustrations from Bryson. While the premise of the story is largely the same, new material was added in the middle of the text to give a young reader insight into a typical Chinese New Year's Day celebration in America. One could argue that this addition makes the focus of the book more an exploration of Chinese culture in New York City and less the story of the relationship between Mr. Chu and Johnny. Bryson's illustrations, however, continue to offer visual emphasis on Johnny's vulnerability and poverty, which are more visible in both his clothes and a brief new scene that shows Johnny walking through "wind howl[ing] like an angry tiger" before he is invited to live with Mr. Chu (17). The revised text ends with Bryson's illustration of Mr. Chu and Johnny walking together, arm in arm.

58. "My Old Kentucky Home" was frequently played on radio stations across the nation in the 1930s and 1940s (Bingham, *My Old Kentucky Home*, 143).

59. Mickenberg, *Learning from the Left*, 89, 90, 104.

60. Estes, *The Hundred Dresses*, 10–12, 56, 63, 29.

61. Gates, *Blue Willow*, 92.

62. Lenski, *Strawberry Girl*, xi–xii. In the second paragraph of *Strawberry Girl*'s foreword, Lenski frames the cultural weight of the word "Cracker" by stating the following:

> After the Seminole War, 1835–1842, Anglo-Saxons from the Carolinas, Georgia and West Florida drifted south and took up land in the lake region of Florida. Then began a bitter struggle with the environment. Their descendants, in the second and third generation, were, in 1900 and the following decade, just prior to the coming of the automobile, living in frontier community, with all of its crudities, brutalities and cruelties. The "Crackers" lived a primitive life, an endless battle went on—a conflict with nature, with wild life, and with their fellow men. Their life was replete with drama, and being people of character and dignity, they lived it, and still live it, with vigor. (x)

Lenski goes on to celebrate "Crackers'" vitality in body ("unusual beauty of physical feature") and language ("have preserved a flavorsome speech"). While honoring Lenski's stated intent—to write a book that prompts the reader "to know and understand people different from ourselves" so the reader can "admire and love them" (xi)—her attribution of "Cracker" as a name deriving from "the cowmen [who] crack[ed] their long, rawhide whips" (93) does not account for a broader historical usage of the term. "Cracker" appeared as early as the 1760s (Isenberg, *White Trash*, 109) as a clear marker of class, a visual and rhetorical "symbol of poverty" that denoted "landless migrants" (107) as those "prone to lying and vulgarity" who were "indolent and immoral" (110). (See Isenberg's *White Trash* for a more detailed cultural history of the evolution of terms denoting white people in poverty in America.) Stetson Kennedy's 1942 *Palmetto Country*, a volume in the American Folkways series that Lenski cites as a book she consulted in the drafting of *Strawberry Girl* (xiii), relies on the term often, noting its use in the early nineteenth century to represent "poor white folk of Florida, Georgia, and Alabama (Kennedy, *Palmetto Country*, 59). While Kennedy notes that the "most popular" story of the origin of the term "Cracker" is from "their skill at cracking the whips used to drive their cattle" (59), *Palmetto Country* is peppered with the term as a placeholder not for cattlemen but for people who "were the Okies of their day (as they have been ever since)" (61).

63. Two years earlier, the 1937 Newbery winner, Ruth Sawyer's *Roller Skates*, was set in the 1890s. Remarkable in its depiction of a plucky central female character, the novel follows Lucinda as she explores her city, including rides with a jolly Irish cab driver and her new friend Tony's family, who emigrated from Italy. While there are many moments (gently evocative of Jacob Riis's 1890 *How the Other Half Lives*) in which class differences are made visible by Lucinda's adventures with the other half, such forays are almost exclusively contained to a chapter and swept within its margins as Lucinda reflects in her diary and moves to what is next. While Lucinda learns of the privileges of her own class position—"What she did not know was that you paid doctors to come and see you" (146)—she also earns money from walking the neighbor's dog and teaching another neighbor English. She does not question her opportunity to do so when less well-positioned others in her circle of acquaintances and friends cannot.

64. Enright, "Newbery Medal Acceptance Speech," 140.

65. Elizabeth Enright and Thomas Handforth, 1939, 2442010a, box 1, folder 1, Newbery-Caldecott Press File, American Library Association Archive, University of Illinois, https://digital.library.illinois.edu/items/c3d14d20-effb-013a-c636-02d0d7bfd6e4-5.

66. Enright, *Thimble Summer*, 4 (hereafter cited in text as *TS*).

67. Hunt, "Elizabeth Enright and the Family Story," 24.

68. Sweeney, "'Like a Vanishing World,'" 155.

69. Enright, "Realism in Children's Literature," 21, 22.

70. Schools within the district of the city of New York represented the racial and ethnic composition of the neighborhoods they served, yet when taken as a whole, the readers neglect to represent Black people and their neighborhoods and experiences. Grieve offers a reading of *The Crow and the Doves* that surfaces the ways authors and artists committed to a more progressive agenda for the books yet still invited nuanced conversations about race ("Visual Production of Citizenship," 26, 32).

Epilogue. Rereading Depression-Era Children

1. Wall, *Ethics in Light of Childhood*, 91.

2. B.J.R. to Eleanor Roosevelt, February 22, 1936, box 1031, Roosevelt Papers.

3. None question the ubiquity of Shirley Temple in the 1930s. The doll that was her namesake and made in her media likeness was first produced in 1934, and it quickly became the most popular doll in America even at a price point of three dollars. Robin Bernstein uses Temple as part of her analytical frame, noting that Temple's performance of white girlhood was part of a long line of "white angel-child[ren]" who operated publicly as the antithesis of blackness (*Racial Innocence*, 65). Most helpful in reading B.J.R.'s request for a Shirley Temple doll, however, is Bernstein's recasting of dolls "not as objects or texts that contain racial meanings but instead as things that script a repertoire of behaviors" (19). B.J.R.'s request for a Shirley Temple doll, then, must certainly be considered as representative of cultural discourses that cement white girlhood with scripts of racial innocence. To be clear, we do not know anything about B.J.R.'s broken doll. (Was it homemade or

store-bought? Raced Black or white?) Yet to Bernstein's point, if dolls are scriptive things and "[c]hildren do not passively receive culture," what script(s) was the child going to enact or revise? As a child actor, Temple was presented to the audience at the very center of films, a child whom adults stooped low to listen to. She also frequently performed characters in economic precarity or poverty. In what way might these media representations of class have informed the scripts B.J.R. was going to enact and/or revise? (For a reading of Temple focused on gender, see Pamela Robertson Wojcik's chapter 2, "Shirley Temple as Streetwalker," in *Fantasies of Neglect.*)

4. Fowler, *Literature as Social Discourse*, 150.

Bibliography

Abrahams, Roger D., ed. *Jump Rope Rhymes: A Dictionary*. Austin: University of Texas Press, 1969.

Agee, James, and Walker Evans. *Let Us Now Praise Famous Men*. 1941. Reprint, Boston: Houghton Mifflin, 2001.

Alger, Horatio. *Ragged Dick and Mark, the Match Boy*. 1867. Reprint, New York: Macmillan, 1962.

Allred, Jeff. *American Modernism and Depression Documentary*. Oxford: Oxford University Press, 2010.

Altschuler, Mark. "Motherless Child: Huck Finn and a Theory of Moral Development." *American Literary Realism, 1870–1910* 22, no. 1 (Fall 1989): 31–42.

Atkinson, Ted. *Faulkner and the Great Depression: Aesthetics, Ideology, and Cultural Politics*. Athens: University of Georgia Press, 2006.

"Art Issue." *New Masses*, October 1, 1935. https://www.marxists.org/history/usa/pubs/new-masses/1935/v17n01-oct-01-1935-NM.pdf.

Bailey, Peggy Dunn. "Female Gothic Fiction, Grotesque Realities, and *Bastard Out of Carolina*: Dorothy Allison Revises the Southern Gothic." *Mississippi Quarterly* 63, no. 1–2 (Winter–Spring 2010): 269–90.

Bannet, Eve Taver. *Structuralism and the Logic of Dissent: Barthes, Derrida, Foucault, Lacan*. Urbana: University of Illinois Press, 1989.

Barnet, George. *Poems*. New York: Works Progress Administration, New Reading Materials Program, 1938. University Archives, Rare Book and Manuscript Library, Columbia University.

———. *Read and Laugh Stories, Book One*. New York: Works Progress Administration, New Reading Materials Program, 1938[?]. University Archives, Rare Book and Manuscript Library, Columbia University.

———. *Read and Laugh Stories, Book Three*. New York: Works Progress Administration, New Reading Materials Program, 1938[?]. University Archives, Rare Book and Manuscript Library, Columbia University.

Beaugrande, Robert de. "Discourse Analysis and Literary Theory: Closing the Gap." *Journal of Advanced Composition* 13, no. 2 (Fall 1993): 423–48.

Benfey, Christopher. *The Double Life of Stephen Crane*. New York: Alfred A. Knopf, 1992.

Bercovitch, Sacvan. *The American Jeremiad*. Madison: University of Wisconsin Press, 1978.

Bernstein, Robin. *Racial Innocence: Performing American Childhood from Slavery to Civil Rights*. New York: New York University Press, 2011.

Bingham, Ann. *My Old Kentucky Home: The Astonishing Life and Reckoning of an Iconic American Song*. Lexington: University Press of Kentucky, 2024.

Boettiger, Elizabeth F. *Children's Play Indoors and Out*. New York: E. P. Dutton, 1938.

Boren, Mark Edelman. "The Southern Super Collider: William Faulkner Smashes Language into Reality in *As I Lay Dying*." *Southern Quarterly* 40, no. 4 (Summer 2002): 21–38.

Botkin, B. A. *A Treasury of American Folklore*. New York: Crown Publishers, 1944.

———. "We Call It 'Living Lore.'" *New York Folklore Quarterly* 14 (Autumn 1958): 189–201.

———. "WPA and Folklore Research: 'Bread and Song' (1939)." In *The Conservation of Culture: Folklorists and the Public Sector*, edited by Burt Feintuch, 259–63. Lexington: University Press of Kentucky, 1988.

Boulton, Cecil. *Verses of All Sizes and Shapes*. New York: Works Progress Administration, New Reading Materials Program, 1938. University Archives, Book and Manuscript Library, Columbia University.

Bremner, Robert H. *From the Depths: The Discovery of Poverty in the United States*. New York: New York University Press, 1956.

Brown, Bill. "American Childhood and Stephen Crane's Toys." *American Literary History* 7, no. 3 (Autumn 1995): 443–76.

Brown, Gillian. *The Consent of the Governed: The Lockean Legacy in Early American Culture*. Cambridge, Mass.: Harvard University Press, 2001.

Bryant, Earle V. *Byline, Richard Wright: Articles from the "Daily Worker" and "New Masses."* Columbia: University of Missouri Press, 2015.

Bryson Shahn, Bernarda. *Ben Shahn*. New York: Harry N. Abrams Publishers, 1972.

Butler, Judith. "Ordinary, Incredulous." In *The Humanities and Public Life*, edited by Peter Brooks, 15–37. New York: Fordham University Press, 2014.

Butts, J. J. *Dark Mirror: African Americans and the Federal Writers' Project*. Columbus: Ohio State University Press, 2021.

Caldwell, Erskine. Interview by Jac Tharpe. *Southern Quarterly*, Fall 1981, 64–74. Reprinted in *Conversations with Erskine Caldwell*, edited by Edwin T. Arnold, 138–47. Jackson: University Press of Mississippi, 1988.

———. "Rachel." In *We Are the Living*, 59–72. New York: Viking Press, 1933.

———. *Tobacco Road*. 1932. Reprint, Athens: University of Georgia Press, 1995.

Caldwell, Erskine, and Margaret Bourke-White. *You Have Seen Their Faces*. 1937. Reprint, Athens: University of Georgia Press, 1995.

Calhoun, Arthur Wallace. "The Child Mind as a Social Product." In *The New Generation: The Intimate Problems of Modern Parents and Children*, edited by V. F. Calverton and Samuel D. Schmalhausen, 74–87. New York: Macaulay Company, 1930.

Callahan, Clare, Joseph Entin, Irvin Hunt, and Kinohi Nishikawa. "Introduction: How American Literature Understands Poverty." *American Literature* 94, no. 3 (September 2022): 383–97.

Campion, Martha, ed. *New Pioneer Story Book*. New York: New Pioneer Publishing, 1935.

———. *Who Are the Young Pioneers?* New York: New Pioneer Publishing, 1934. Digital Public Library of America, http://historicpittsburgh.org/islandora/object/pitt%3A31735059397780.

Cantwell, Robert. "The Little Magazines." *New Republic*, July 25, 1934, 295–97.

Cappetti, Carla. *Writing Chicago: Modernism, Ethnography, and the Novel*. New York: Columbia University Press, 1993.

Capshaw Smith, Katharine. *Children's Literature of the Harlem Renaissance*. Bloomington: Indiana University Press, 2004.

Chesterman, Linda. *Music for the Nursery School: A Collection of Old and New Marches, Rhymes, Games, etc.* 1935. Reprint, London: Harrap, 1972.

Chouliaraki, Lilie, and Norman Fairclough. *Discourse in Late Modernity: Rethinking Critical Discourse Analysis*. Edinburgh: Edinburgh University Press, 1999.

Cohen, Robert. *Dear Mrs. Roosevelt: Letters from Children of the Great Depression*. Chapel Hill: University of North Carolina Press, 2002.

Coiner, Constance. *Better Red: The Writing and Resistance of Tillie Olsen and Meridel Le Sueur*. Oxford: Oxford University Press, 1995.

Coleman, Amanda. "Rehabilitating the Region: The New Deal, Gender, and the Remaking of the Rural South." *Southeastern Geographer* 50, no. 2 (Summer 2010): 200–217.

Conrad, Rachel. *Time for Childhoods: Young Poets and Questions of Agency*. Amherst: University of Massachusetts Press, 2020.

Cook, Daniel Thomas. *The Commodification of Childhood: The Children's Clothing Industry and the Rise of the Child Consumer*. Durham, N.C.: Duke University Press, 2004.

Cook, Sylvia Jenkins. *Erskine Caldwell and the Fiction of Poverty: The Flesh and the Spirit*. Baton Rouge: Louisiana State University Press, 1991.

———. *From Tobacco Road to Route 66: The Southern Poor White in Fiction*. Chapel Hill: University of North Carolina Press, 1976.

Cowley, Danielle. "Life Writing, Resistance, and the Politics of Representation: A Critical Discourse Analysis of Eli Clare's 'Learning to Speak.'" *Journal of Literary & Cultural Disability Studies* 6, no. 1 (2012): 85–95.

Cox, Karen L., and Sarah E. Gardner. "Editors' Introduction." In *Reassessing the 1930s South*, edited by Karen L. Cox and Sarah E. Gardner, 1–9. Baton Rouge: Louisiana State University Press, 2018.

Crain, Patricia. *Reading Children: Literacy, Property, and Dilemmas of Childhood in Nineteenth-Century America*. Philadelphia: University of Pennsylvania Press, 2016.

Crane, Stephen. "A Dark Brown Dog." In *Maggie: A Girl of the Streets and Other Tales of New York*, 175–82. 1893. Reprint, New York: Penguin, 2000.

———. "A Great Mistake." In *Maggie: A Girl of the Streets and Other Tales of New York*, 171–74. 1893. Reprint, New York: Penguin, 2000.

———. *Maggie: A Girl of the Streets and Other Tales of New York*. 1893. Reprint, New York: Penguin, 2000.

———. "An Ominous Baby." In *Maggie: A Girl of the Streets and Other Tales of New York*, 167–70. 1893. Reprint, New York: Penguin, 2000.

Delville, Michel. "Alienating Language and Darl's Narrative Consciousness in Faulkner's *As I Lay Dying*." *Southern Literary Journal* 27, no. 1 (Fall 1994): 61–72.

Denning, Michael. *The Cultural Front: The Laboring of American Culture in the Twentieth Century*. London: Verso, 1997.

de Schweinitz, Rebecca. "'Waked Up to Feel': Defining Childhood, Debating Slavery in Antebellum America." In *Children and Youth During the Civil War*, edited by James Marten, 13–28. New York: New York University Press, 2012.

Dhawan, Nikita. "Hegemonic Listening and Subversive Silences: Ethical-Political Imperatives." *Critical Studies* 36, no. 1 (2012): 47–60.

Di Donato, Pietro. *Christ in Concrete.* 1939. Reprint, New York: Signet, 1993.

Dow, William. *Narrating Class in American Fiction.* New York: Palgrave Macmillan, 2009.

Duane, Anna Mae. *Suffering Childhood in Early America: Violence, Race, and the Making of the Child Victim.* Athens: University of Georgia Press, 2010.

Dunn, Osler. *Bobby and Bones.* New York: Works Progress Administration, New Reading Materials Program, 1938. University Archives, Book and Manuscript Library, Columbia University.

Eberle, Irmengarde. *Oh, but a Gander Can't Talk, Book II.* New York: Works Progress Administration, New Reading Materials Program, 1938. University Archives, Book and Manuscript Library, Columbia University.

Elliott, Kamilla. *Theorizing Adaptation.* New York: Oxford University Press, 2020.

Ellison, Ralph. "The Art of Fiction: An Interview." In *Shadow and Act,* 167–83. New York: Vintage International, 1995.

———. "Hidden Name and Complex Fate: A Writer's Experience in the United States." In *Shadow and Act,* 144–66. New York: Vintage International, 1995.

———. *Shadow and Act.* New York: Vintage International, 1995.

———. "That I Had the Wings." In *Flying Home,* 45–62. New York: Vintage International, 1996.

———. *Three Days Before the Shooting . . . : The Unfinished Second Novel.* Edited by John F. Callahan and Adam Bradley. New York: Modern Library, 2011.

———. "What These Children Are Like." In *Going to the Territory,* 64–75. New York: Random House, 1986.

Enright, Elizabeth. "Newbery Medal Acceptance Speech, June 20, 1939." In *Thimble Summer,* 137–40. 1938. Reprint, New York: Square Fish, 2008.

———. "Realism in Children's Literature." *The Writer,* April 1968, 19–22.

———. *Then There Were Five.* New York: Farrar and Rinehart, 1944.

———. *Thimble Summer.* 1938. Reprint, New York: Square Fish, 2008.

Entin, Joseph B. *Sensational Modernism: Experimental Fiction and Photography in Thirties America.* Chapel Hill: University of North Carolina Press, 2007.

Estes, Eleanor. *The Hundred Dresses.* New York: Harcourt, Brace and World, 1944.

Eysteinsson, Ástráður. *The Concept of Modernism.* Ithaca, N.Y.: Cornell University Press, 1990.

Fairclough, Norman. "A Dialectical-Relational Approach to Critical Discourse Analysis in Social Research." In *Methods of Critical Discourse Analysis,* edited by Ruth Wodak and Michael Meyer, 162–86. Los Angeles: Sage, 2009.

———. "Global Capitalism and Critical Awareness of Language." In *The Discourse Reader,* edited by Adam Jaworski and Nikolas Coupland, 146–57. 2nd ed. New York: Routledge, 2006.

Faulkner, Mara. *Protest and Possibility in the Writing of Tillie Olsen.* Charlottesville: University of Virginia Press, 1993.

Faulkner, William. *As I Lay Dying.* 1930. Reprint, New York: Vintage International, 1990.

Fearnow, Mark. *The American Stage and the Great Depression.* Cambridge: Cambridge University Press, 1997.

Fielder, Leslie A. *Love and Death in the American Novel*. 1960. Reprint, Normal, Ill.: Dalkey Archive Press, 1997.

Findlay, James A. *WPA Children's Books by the Pennsylvania Writers' Project, the New York City New Reading Materials Program, and the Milwaukee Handicraft Project*. Fort Lauderdale, Fla.: Bienes Museum of the Modern Book, 2008.

Floreani, Tracy. "Oklahoma City and 'the Territory.'" In *Ralph Ellison in Context*, edited by Paul Devlin, 15–24. Cambridge: Cambridge University Press, 2021.

Flynn, Richard, Perry Nodelman, Sara L. Schwebel, and Marah Gubar. "Forum: Divergent Perspectives on Children's Agency." *Jeunesse: Young People, Texts, and Cultures* 8, no. 1 (Summer 2016): 248–310.

Foley, Barbara. *Radical Representations: Politics and Form in U.S. Proletarian Fiction, 1929–1941*. Durham, N.C.: Duke University Press, 1993.

———. *Wrestling with the Left: The Making of Ralph Ellison's "Invisible Man."* Durham, N.C.: Duke University Press, 2010.

Fowler, Roger. *Linguistic Criticism*. 1986. 2nd ed. New York: Oxford University Press, 1990.

———. *Literature as Social Discourse*. London: Batsford, 1981.

Freedman, Russell. *Children of the Great Depression*. New York: HarperCollins, 2010.

Gardner, Emelyn E. "Some Counting-Out Rhymes in Michigan." *Journal of American Folklore* 31, no. 122 (October–December 1918): 521–36.

Gates, Dorris. *Blue Willow*. 1940. Reprint, Viking Press, 1963.

Gates, Henry Louis, and Richard J. Ellis. Introduction to *Our Nig; or, Sketches from the Life of a Free Black*, xii–lxviii. New York: Random House, 2002.

Gold, Michael. *Jews Without Money*. 1930. Reprint, Garden City, N.Y.: Sun Dial Press, 1946.

———. "Notes of the Month." *New Masses* 6, no. 4 (1930): 3–5. https://msuweb.montclair.edu/~furrg/nm/goldnotes0930.pdf.

———. "The Proletarian Child." In *The New Generation: The Intimate Problems of Modern Parents and Children*, edited by V. F. Calverton and Samuel D. Schmalhausen, 673–79. New York: Macaulay Company, 1930.

Goodwin, James. *Modern American Grotesque: Literature and Photography*. Columbus: Ohio State University Press, 2009.

Gordon, Linda. "Dorothea Lange's Oregon Photography: Assumptions Challenged." *Oregon Historical Quarterly* 110, no. 4 (Winter 2009): 570–97.

Grieve, Victoria. "The Visual Production of Citizenship: Children's Literature of the Works Progress Administration, 1937–1942." *Children's Literature Association Quarterly* 38, no. 1 (Spring 2013): 26–47.

Gubar, Marah. "The Hermeneutics of Recuperation: What a Kinship-Model Approach to Children's Agency Could Do for Children's Literature and Childhood Studies." *Jeunesse: Young People, Texts, Cultures* 8, no. 1 (Summer 2016): 291–310.

Guerre, Alan. *Behind the Fireplace*. New York: Works Progress Administration, New Reading Materials Program, 1938. University Archives, Book and Manuscript Library, Columbia University.

Hale, Dorothy J. "*As I Lay Dying*'s Heterogeneous Discourse." *NOVEL: A Forum on Fiction* 23, no. 1 (Fall 1989): 5–23.

Halliday, M. A. K. "Anti-Languages." *American Anthropologist* 78 (1976): 570–84.

Hapke, Laura. *Daughters of the Great Depression: Women, Work, and Fiction in the American 1930s*. Athens: University of Georgia Press, 1995.

Hart, Jason, and Jo Boyden. "Childhood (Re)materialized: Bringing Political Economy into the Field." In *Reimagining Childhood Studies*, edited by Spyros Spyrou, Rachel Rosen, and Daniel Thomas Cook, 75–89. London: Bloomsbury Academic, 2019.

Hefner, Brooks E. *The Word on the Streets: The American Language of Vernacular Modernism*. Charlottesville: University of Virginia Press, 2017.

Henricks, Thomas S. *Play and the Human Condition*. Urbana: University of Illinois Press, 2015.

———. "Play Studies: A Brief History." *American Journal of Play* 12, no. 2 (Winter 2020): 117–55.

Hirsch, Jerrold. "Federal Writers' Project." In *American Literature in Transition, 1930–1940*, edited by Ichiro Takayoshi, 361–81. Cambridge: Cambridge University Press, 2018.

Hitchcock, H. Wiley, and Kyle Gann. *Music in the United States: A Historical Introduction*. 4th ed. Upper Saddle River, N.J.: Prentice Hall, 2000.

Hochman, Barbara. *"Uncle Tom's Cabin" and the Reading Revolution: Race, Literacy, Childhood, and Fiction, 1851–1911*. Amherst: University of Massachusetts Press, 2011.

Hodgson, Jack. "From the Bronx to Stalingrad: Harry Eisman and the Young Pioneers of America in New York City." *New York History* 103, no. 1 (Summer 2022): 68–84.

———. *Young Reds in the Big Apple: The New York Young Pioneers of America, 1923–1934*. New York: Fordham University Press, 2025.

Hogan, Patrick Colm. *Narrative Discourse: Authors and Narrators in Literature, Film, and Art*. Columbus: Ohio State University Press, 2013.

Hubbs, Jolene. *Class, Whiteness, and Southern Literature*. Cambridge: Cambridge University Press, 2023.

———. "William Faulkner's Rural Modernism." *Mississippi Quarterly* 61, no. 3 (2008): 461–75.

Hunt, Caroline. "Elizabeth Enright and the Family Story." *Lion and the Unicorn* 14, no. 2 (1990): 16–29.

Hurvitz, Nathan. "Jews and Jewishness in the Street Rhymes of American Children." *Jewish Social Studies* 16, no. 2 (April 1954): 135–50.

Irving, Katrina. *Immigrant Mothers: Narrative of Race and Maternity, 1890–1925*. Urbana: University of Illinois Press, 2000.

Isenberg, Nancy. *White Trash: The 400-Year Untold History of Class in America*. New York: Viking, 2016.

Jameson, Elizabeth. "Written, They Reappear: Rereading *Yonnondio*." *Frontiers: A Journal of Women Studies* 18, no. 3 (1997): 141–45.

Jameson, Fredric. *The Political Unconscious: Narrative as a Socially Symbolic Act*. Ithaca, N.Y.: Cornell University Press, 1981.

Jaworski, Adam, and Nikolas Coupland. "Editors' Introduction to Part Six." In *The Discourse Reader*, edited by Adam Jaworski and Nikolas Coupland, 473–79. London: Routledge, 2006.

Jones, Gavin. *American Hungers: The Problem of Poverty in U.S. Literature, 1840–1945*. Princeton, N.J.: Princeton University Press, 2008.

Jones, Sharon Lynette. "Black Excesses and Deprivations in Literature and Photography of the 1930s." In *African American Literature in Transition, 1930–1940*, edited by Eve Dunbar and Ayesha K. Hardison, 33–58. London: Cambridge University Press, 2022.

Kao, Deborah Martin. "Ben Shahn and the Public Use of Art." In *Ben Shahn's New York: The Photography of Modern Times*, edited by Deborah Martin Kao, Laura Katzman, and Jenna Webster, 39–73. New Haven, Conn.: Yale University Press, 2000.

Kazin, Alfred. *On Native Grounds: An Interpretation of Modern American Prose Literature*. New York: Harcourt, Brace & World, 1942.

Keating, Norma. *Mr. Chu*. Illustrated by Bernarda Bryson. New York: Works Progress Administration, New Reading Materials Program, 1938. University Archives, Rare Book and Manuscript Library, Columbia University.

———. *Mr. Chu*. Illustrated by Bernarda Bryson. New York: Macmillan, 1965.

Kennedy, Stetson. *Palmetto Country*. New York: Duell, Sloan & Pearce, 1942.

Kirkland, Jack. *Tobacco Road: A Play in Three Acts*. 1934. Reprint, New York: Samuel French, 1961.

Lang, Amy Schrager. *The Syntax of Class: Writing Inequality in Nineteenth-Century America*. Princeton, N.J.: Princeton University Press, 2003.

Lee, Corinna K. "Documents of Proletarian Fiction: Tillie Olsen's *Yonnondio: From the Thirties*." *Journal of Modern Literature* 36, no. 4 (Summer 2013): 113–32.

Lenski, Lois. *Strawberry Girl*. Philadelphia: J. B. Lippincott, 1945.

Lerner, Tillie. "The Iron Throat." In *Partisan Review: A Bi-Monthly of Revolutionary Literature Published by the John Reed Club of New York* 1, no. 2 (April/May 1934): 3–9.

Levander, Caroline F., and Carol J. Singley. Introduction to *The American Child: A Cultural Studies Reader*, edited by Caroline F. Levander and Carol J. Singley, 3–12. New Brunswick, N.J.: Rutgers University Press, 2003.

Lindenmeyer, Kriste. *The Greatest Generation Grows Up: American Childhood in the 1930s*. Chicago: Ivan R. Dee, 2005.

Lowry, Richard S. "Lewis Hine's Family Romance." In *The American Child: A Cultural Studies Reader*, edited by Caroline F. Levander and Carol J. Singley, 184–207. New Brunswick, N.J.: Rutgers University Press, 2003.

Lumpkin, Grace. *To Make My Bread*. 1932. Reprint, Lanham, Md.: Rowman & Littlefield, 2014.

Lumpkin, Katharine DuPre, and Dorothy Wolff Douglas. *Child Workers in America*. New York: Robert M. McBride & Company, 1937.

Machin, David, and Andrea Mayr. *How to Do Critical Discourse Analysis: A Multimodal Introduction*. Los Angeles: Sage, 2012.

Mangione, Jerre. *The Dream and the Deal: The Federal Writers' Project, 1935–1943*. Syracuse, N.Y.: Syracuse University Press, 1996.

Marten, James. Introduction to *Children and Youth During the Civil War*, edited by James Marten, 1–9. New York: New York University Press, 2012.

Maynes, Mary Jo. "Age as a Category of Historical Analysis: History, Agency, and Narratives of Childhood." *Journal of the History of Childhood and Youth* 1, no. 1 (Winter 2008): 114–24.

McHugh, John E. *The Little Engineer*. New York: Works Progress Administration, New Reading Materials Program, 1936. University Archives, Book and Manuscript Library, Columbia University.

McMahon, Felicia R., and Brian Sutton-Smith. "The Past in the Present: Theoretical Directions for Children's Folklore." In *Children's Folklore: A Source Book*, edited by Brian Sutton-Smith, Jay Mechling, Thomas W. Johnson, and Felicia R. McMahon, 293–308. Logan: Utah State University Press, 1999.

Mellette, Justin. *Peculiar Whiteness: Racial Anxiety and Poor Whites in Southern Literature, 1900–1965*. Jackson: University Press of Mississippi, 2021.

Mickenberg, Julia. *Learning from the Left: Children's Literature, the Cold War, and Radical Politics in the United States*. Oxford: Oxford University Press, 2006.

———. "The Pedagogy of the Popular Front: 'Progressive Parenting' for a New Generation, 1935–1945." In *American Child: A Cultural Studies Reader*, edited by Caroline Levander and Carol Singley, 226–45. New Brunswick, N.J.: Rutgers University Press, 2003.

Mintz, Steven. *Huck's Raft: A History of American Childhood*. Cambridge, Mass.: Harvard University Press, 2004.

Mishler, Paul C. *Raising Reds: The Young Pioneers, Radical Summer Camps, and Communist Political Culture in the United States*. New York: Columbia University Press, 1999.

Mixon, Wayne. *The People's Writer: Erskine Caldwell and the South*. Charlottesville: University Press of Virginia, 1995.

Moeller, Susan D. "The Cultural Construction of Urban Poverty: Images of Poverty in New York City, 1890–1917." *Journal of American Culture* 18, no. 4 (Winter 1995): 1–16.

Mortimer, Gail L. "Significant Absences: Faulkner's Rhetoric of Loss." *NOVEL: A Forum on Fiction* 14, no. 3 (Spring 1981): 232–50.

Murphy, Andrew R. "Longing, Nostalgia, and Golden Age Politics: The American Jeremiad and the Power of the Past." *Perspectives on Politics* 7, no. 1 (March 2009): 125–41.

Mutnick, Deborah. *No Race, No Country: The Politics and Poetics of Richard Wright*. Chapel Hill: University of North Carolina Press, 2025.

Newell, Kate. *Expanding Adaptation Networks: From Illustration to Novelization*. London: Palgrave Macmillan, 2017.

Nishikawa, Kinohi. "Richard Wright Between Two Fronts: *Black Boy* in the Black Metropolis." In *Against a Sharp White Background: Infrastructures of African American Print*, edited by Brigitte Fielder and Jonathan Senchyne, 179–98. Madison: University of Wisconsin Press, 2019.

Olsen, Tillie. "A Vision of Fear and Hope." In *Tell Me a Riddle, Requa I, and Other Works*, 133–38. Lincoln: University of Nebraska Press, 2013.

———. *Yonnondio: From the Thirties*. New York: Delta, 1974.

———. *Yonnondio: From the Thirties*. 1974. Reprint, New York: Delta, 1989.

Opie, Iona, and Peter Opie. *The Lore and Language of Schoolchildren*. 1959. Rev. ed. New York: New York Review Books, 2001.

Opie, Iona, and Peter Opie, eds. *The Oxford Dictionary of Nursery Rhymes*. Oxford: Oxford University Press, 1977.

Orr, Lisa. "'People Who Might Have Been You': Agency and the Damaged Self in Tillie Olsen's *Yonnondio*." In *What We Hold in Common: An Introduction to Working-Class

Studies, edited by Janet Zandy, 199–206. New York: Feminist Press and City University of New York, 2001.

Owen, Gabrielle. *A Queer History of Adolescence: Developmental Pasts, Relational Futures.* Athens: University of Georgia Press, 2020.

Palmer, Louis. "Bourgeois Blues: Class, Whiteness, and Southern Gothic in Early Faulkner and Caldwell." *Faulkner Journal* 22, no. 1/2 (Fall 2006/Spring 2007): 120–39.

Pancake, Ann. "Story Time: Working-Class Women's Interventions in Literary Temporal Conventions." *Narrative* 6, no. 3 (1998): 292–306.

Peck, Anne Merriman. *Tommy and Tugboat George.* New York: Works Progress Administration, New Reading Materials Program, 1938. University Archives, Book and Manuscript Library, Columbia University.

Phillips, Mason. *Representations of Childhood in American Modernism.* New York: Palgrave, 2016.

Potamkin, Harry Alan, Gertrude Rady, and Mary Morrow. *Pioneer Song Book.* New York: New Pioneer Publishing, 1935. Radical Pamphlet Collection, box 36, folder 5, Library of Congress, Washington, D.C.

Pratt, Linda Ray. Introduction to *Yonnondio: From the Thirties*, by Tillie Olsen, v–xvi. Lincoln: University of Nebraska Press, 2004.

Rabinowitz, Paula. "'Between the Outhouse and the Garbage Dump': Locating Collapse in Depression Literature." *American Literary History* 23, no. 1 (Spring 2011): 32–55.

———. *Labor and Desire: Women's Revolutionary Fiction in Depression America.* Chapel Hill: University of North Carolina Press, 1991.

———. *They Must Be Represented: The Politics of Documentary.* London: Verso, 1994.

Reid, Panthea. *Tillie Olsen: One Woman, Many Riddles.* New Brunswick, N.J.: Rutgers University Press, 2010.

Riis, Jacob A. *How the Other Half Lives: Studies Among the Tenements of New York.* 1890. Reprint, New York: Penguin, 1997.

Robé, Chris. "Saint Mazie: A Socialist-Feminist Understanding of Film in Tillie Olsen's 'Yonnondio: From the Thirties.'" *Frontiers: A Journal of Women Studies* 25, no. 3 (2004): 162–77.

Rolland, Fred. "Street Songs of Children." *New Masses*, April 10, 1938. https://www.marxists.org/history/usa/pubs/new-masses/Lit-Sups-1-7-1937-1938-New-Masses.pdf.

Rosner, Molly. *Playing with History: American Identities and Children's Consumer Culture.* New Brunswick, N.J.: Rutgers University Press, 2021.

Roth, Henry. *Call It Sleep.* 1934. Reprint, New York: Picador, 1991.

Rutkowski, Sara. *Literary Legacies of the Federal Writers' Project: Voices of the Depression in the American Postwar Era.* London: Palgrave Macmillan, 2017.

Samuels, Shirley. *The Culture of Sentiment: Race, Gender, and Sentimentality in Nineteenth-Century America.* New York: Oxford University Press, 1992.

Sánchez-Eppler, Karen. *Dependent States: The Child's Part in Nineteenth-Century American Culture.* Chicago: University of Chicago Press, 2005.

———. "Geographies of Play: Scales of Imagination in the Study of Child-Made Things." In *Reimagining Childhood Studies*, edited by Spyros Spyrou, Rachel Rosen, and Daniel Thomas Cook, 41–56. London: Bloomsbury Academic, 2019.

———. "In the Archives of Childhood." In *The Children's Table: Childhood Studies and the Humanities*, edited by Anna Mae Duane, 213–37. Athens: University of Georgia Press, 2013.

———. "Playing at Class." In *The American Child: A Cultural Studies Reader*, edited by Caroline F. Levander and Carol J. Singley, 40–62. New Brunswick, N.J.: Rutgers University Press, 2003.

Sante, Luc. Introduction to *How the Other Half Lives: Studies Among the Tenements of New York*, ix–xxii. New York: Penguin, 1997.

Saunders, George. Introduction to *Adventures of Huckleberry Finn*, ix–xxv. New York: Modern Library, 2001.

Sawyer, Ruth. *Roller Skates*. 1936. Reprint, New York: Puffin Books, 1964.

Scarry, Elaine. "Poetry, Injury, and the Ethics of Reading." In *The Humanities and Public Life*, edited by Peter Brooks, 41–48. New York: Fordham University Press, 2014.

Schor, Edith. "Ralph Ellison, Journeyman: Three Early Stories." *MELUS* 15, no. 2 (Summer 1988): 57–69.

Schwartzman, Helen B. *Transformations: The Anthropology of Children's Play*. New York: Plenum, 1978.

Shahn, Ben. *The Shape of Content*. New York: Vintage Books, 1957.

Sinks, Alfred. *The Bull Who Would Not Fight*. New York: Works Progress Administration, New Reading Materials Program, 1938. University Archives, Book and Manuscript Library, Columbia University.

———. *Riquitin and the Old Men*. New York: Works Progress Administration, New Reading Materials Program, 1938[?]. University Archives, Rare Book and Manuscript Library, Columbia University.

Soderberg, Laura. *Vicious Infants: Dangerous Childhoods in Antebellum U.S. Literature*. Amherst: University of Massachusetts Press, 2021.

Steadman, R. W. "A Critique of Proletarian Literature." *North American Review* 247, no. 1 (Spring 1939): 142–52.

Steedman, Carolyn. *Strange Dislocations: Childhood and the Idea of Human Interiority*. Cambridge, Mass.: Harvard University Press, 1995.

Stott, William. *Documentary Expression and Thirties America*. Chicago: University of Chicago Press, 1986.

Sweeney, Meghan. "'Like a Vanishing World': The Role of the County Fair in Three Depression-Era Children's Books." *Children's Literature Association Quarterly* 32, no. 2 (Summer 2007): 142–62.

Szalay, Michael. *New Deal Modernism: American Literature and the Invention of the Welfare State*. Durham, N.C.: Duke University Press, 2000.

Szetela, Adam. "Small Acts of Kindness in an Unequal World: Picture Books During and After the Great Recession." *Children's Literature Association Quarterly* 48, no. 4 (Winter 2023): 395–411.

Szto, Peter. "Documentary Photography in American Social Welfare History: 1897–1943." *Journal of Sociology and Social Welfare* 35, no. 2 (June 2008): 91–110.

Taggard, Genevieve. "Feeding the Children." In *Calling Western Union*, 54–55. New York: Harper & Brothers Publishers, 1936.

Terrile, Vikki C. "Scenes from the Class Struggle in Picture Books: Depictions of Housing and Home in Books for Young Children." *Children's Literature in Education* 53, no. 4 (December 2022): 526–46.

Thernstrom, Stephan. "Poverty in Historical Perspective." In *On Understanding Poverty: Perspectives from the Social Sciences*, edited by Daniel P. Moynihan, 160–86. New York: Basic Books, 1969.

Thompson, Kathleen, and Hilary Mac Austin. "Introduction: The Children." In *Children of the Depression*, edited by Kathleen Thompson and Hilary Mac Austin, xi–xx. Bloomington: Indiana University Press, 2001.

Tompkins, Jane. *Sensational Designs: The Cultural Work of American Fiction, 1790–1860*. New York: Oxford University Press, 1985.

Trachtenberg, Alan. *The Incorporation of America: Culture and Society in the Gilded Age*. New York: Hill and Wang, 1982.

Twain, Mark. *The Adventures of Huckleberry Finn*. 1885. Reprint, Oxford: Oxford University Press, 1996.

Van Hook, Lane. *Taro Taki*. New York: Works Progress Administration, New Reading Materials Program, 1936. University Archives, Book and Manuscript Library, Columbia University.

Wald, Alan. *Writing from the Left: New Essays on Radical Culture and Politics*. London: Verso, 1994.

Wall, John. "Childism: The Challenge of Childhood to Ethics and the Humanities." In *The Children's Table: Childhood Studies and the Humanities*, edited by Anna Mae Duane, 68–84. Athens: University of Georgia Press, 2013.

———. *Ethics in Light of Childhood*. Washington, D.C.: Georgetown University Press, 2010.

Watkins, Patsy G. "Same People, Same Time, Same Place: Contrasting Images of Destitute Ozark Mountaineers During the Great Depression." *Arkansas Historical Quarterly* 70, no. 3 (September 2011): 288–315.

Watson, Jay. "The Rhetoric of Exhaustion and the Exhaustion of Rhetoric: Erskine Caldwell in the Thirties." *Mississippi Quarterly* 46, no. 2 (Spring 1993): 215–29.

Webb, Clive. "'Ain't Worth a Damn for Nothing': The New Deal and Child Labor in Southern Textiles." In *Reading Southern Poverty Between the Wars, 1918–1939*, edited by Richard Godden and Martin Crawford, 108–24. Athens: University of Georgia Press, 2006.

Webster, Crystal Lynn. *Beyond the Boundaries of Childhood: African American Children in the Antebellum North*. Chapel Hill: University of North Carolina Press, 2021.

Widiss, Benjamin. "Fit and Surfeit in *As I Lay Dying*." *NOVEL: A Forum on Fiction* 41, no. 1 (Fall 2007): 99–120.

Willis, Susan. "Learning from the Banana." *American Quarterly* 39, no. 4 (Winter 1987): 586–600.

Willison, Thomas S. "Revolutionary Art Today." In "Art Issue." Special issue, *New Masses*, October 1, 1935. https://www.marxists.org/history/usa/pubs/new-masses/1935/v17n01-oct-01-1935-NM.pdf.

Willmann, Sampsell. "Lewis Hine, Ellis Island, and Pragmatism: Photographs as Lived Experience." *Journal of the Gilded Age and Progressive Era* 7, no. 2 (April 2008): 221–52.

Wilson, Harriet E. *Our Nig; or, Sketches from the Life of a Free Black, in a Two-Story White House, North. Showing That Slavery's Shadows Fall Even There.* 1859. Reprint, New York: Vintage, 2011.

Wirth-Nesher, Hana. Introduction to *New Essays on Call It Sleep*, edited by Hana Wirth-Nesher, 1–15. Cambridge: Cambridge University Press, 1996.

Wodak, Ruth, and Michael Meyer, eds. *Methods of Critical Discourse Analysis*. 2nd ed. Los Angeles: Sage, 2009.

Wojcik, Pamela Robertson. *Fantasies of Neglect: Imagining the Urban Child in American Film and Fiction*. New Brunswick, N.J.: Rutgers University Press, 2016.

Wright, Richard. *Black Boy (American Hunger): A Record of Childhood and Youth*. 1944. Reprint, New York: Harper Perennial Modern Classics, 2005.

———. "Blueprint for Negro Writing." *Race & Class* 21, no. 4 (April 1980): 403–19.

Zandy, Janet. Introduction to *Liberating Memory: Our Work and Our Working-Class Consciousness*, edited by Janet Zandy, 1–15. New Brunswick, N.J.: Rutgers University Press, 1995.

Zeitlin, Michael. "'Seeing into the Heart': Teaching the Vardaman Narratives of *As I Lay Dying*." In *Approaches to Teaching Faulkner's "As I Lay Dying,"* edited by Patrick O'Donnell and Lynda Zwinger, 100–112. New York: Modern Language Association of America, 2011.

Zelizer, Viviana A. *Pricing the Priceless Child: The Changing Social Value of Children*. New York: Basic Books, 1985.

Zugsmith, Leane. *The Reckoning*. New York: Harrison Smith & Robert Haas, 1934.

———. "Room in the World" (1938). In *Writing Red: An Anthology of American Women Writers, 1930–1940*, edited by Charlotte Nekola and Paula Rabinowitz, 46–51. New York: Feminist Press, 1987.

Index

Locators in italics indicate a figure.

www.ingramcontent.com/pod-product-compliance
Lightning Source LLC
LaVergne TN
LVHW080736301026
851245LV00053B/335
* 9 7 8 0 8 2 0 3 7 5 6 1 8 *